Unless Recalled Earlier

DATE DUE

DEMCO, INC. 38-2931

wild cow-
boys

robert jackall

wild
cow-
boys

urban
marauders & the forces
of order

harvard university press
cambridge, massachusetts
london, england
1997

Library of Congress Cataloging-in-Publication Data

Jackall, Robert.

  Wild cowboys : urban marauders & the forces of order / Robert
Jackall.

    p. cm.

  Includes bibliographical references and index.

  ISBN 0-674-95310-X (alk. paper)

  1. Wild Cowboys (Gang) 2. Gangs—New York (State)—New York.
3. Organized crime—New York (State)—New York. 4. Dominican
Americans—New York (State)—New York—Social conditions.
5. Dominican Americans—New York (State)—New York—Economic
conditions. I. Title.

HV6439.U7N449 1997

364.1′06′6097471—dc21   97-11739

For Janice and Yuriko

my two great loves

contents

maps

wild cow-
boys

Map 1. Police Precincts in New York City, Early 1990s

prologue

This book tells a saga of urban marauders and the forces of order in the world's greatest city during the last years of this millennium. It follows police detectives and prosecutors as they independently investigate separate incidents of street violence and murder, discover a pattern in the mayhem, and then come together to do justice.

The book proceeds through a broken narrative that mirrors how the case came at investigators. It chronicles, from the streets through the courtroom, the ways of knowing and acting among men and women charged with making sense of seeming senselessness, and bringing order to seeming chaos. It reconstructs their habits of mind as they work through mazes of lies, multiple identities, crooked stories, and blind alleys, searching for pathways to truth.

The book also tells a tale of our troubled society, where the institutional logics of law and bureaucracy, the mainstays of modern social order, often go awry.

a quad in
the
bronx

Police Officer Elizabeth Gesualdo the first officer

to reach Beekman Avenue at 2245 hours (10:45 PM) on December 16, 1991, found a chaotic scene. Two Emergency Medical Service vehicles were already parked at the end of Beekman where it empties into East 141st Street. Gesualdo, a five-year veteran of the New York City Police Department, double-parked her radio car just past Oak Terrace, a dead-end street that juts off Beekman, and, with her partner, PO Timothy Leary, began to walk cautiously toward East 141st Street.

The door of the double building at 328–340 Beekman was half open, propped against the body of a Hispanic man who lay in a spreading pool of his own blood, shot fourteen times in the back. Gesualdo saw multiple shell casings from automatic weapons strewn across the entrance to the building and out into the street. When the officers reached the small alley next to the Mi Ranchito Grocery at 320 Beekman, they found a Hispanic woman lying at its entrance dressed in a green hooded jacket, a black and white sweater, blue jeans, and blue cap, clasping in her left hand a single yellow-topped clear plastic vial of crack cocaine. She had two bullets in her neck. Gesualdo shone her flashlight into the garbage-filled alley, which was about fifteen feet long and the width of her arm-span. The beam revealed a young black man beneath a fire escape that he had apparently tried to climb. He was dressed in a black jacket with the Trump Plaza logo on its back; underneath he wore a dark sweatshirt with Penn State on its front. In the right rear pocket of his gray pants he carried a screwdriver, pliers,

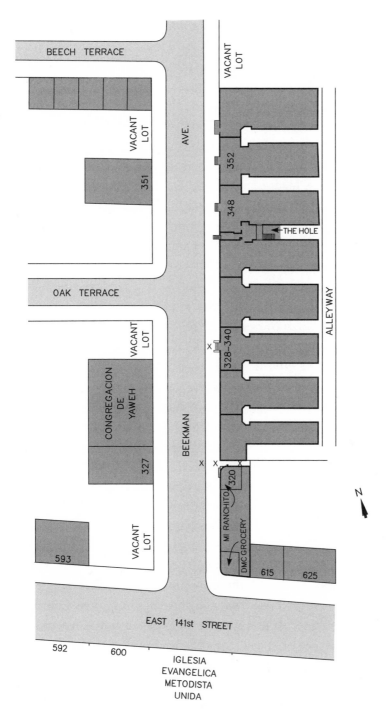

Map 2. Beekman Avenue, Bronx

and a two-pronged electrical plug, typical car-burglary tools. His left arm was emblazoned with two tattoos, one with the name Elisa and the other of a fish flopping on a hook. He had been shot six times in the back.

Gesualdo went directly to one of the EMS trucks and discovered technicians frantically trying to resuscitate a slightly built black teenager, whom they had found just outside the alley covered in his own blood, gut-shot several times and fading fast. A black man in his late twenties cradled the boy's head. Also in the EMS wagon was a middle-aged black woman shot in the back of her right shoulder, distraught but in stable condition. Other radio cars arrived and blocked the East 141st Street entrance to Beekman.

Gesualdo and Leary struggled to contain the noisy crowd of onlookers who flooded the street, even though the night was cold enough to freeze the ink in Gesualdo's pen. The officers returned to their radio car, retrieved a roll of inch-wide, unlettered red tape, and tried to establish a crime scene. They wanted to extend the tape from Oak Terrace all the way down to East 141st Street, cutting Beekman in half. But they ran out of tape and much of the crime scene remained unenclosed; later, Gesualdo found a bit of tape that she tied to Christmas decorations festooning the lobby of 328–340 Beekman to designate a crime scene there. As Gesualdo and Leary strung the tape in the street, they kicked shell casings toward themselves and away from the increasingly unruly crowd; many on the street were picking up the casings as souvenirs.

Some of the onlookers had drifted over from St. Ann's Avenue near St. Mary's Park, where a bit earlier two police radio cars rushing to the homicide scene before it was completely destroyed had crashed with each other while swerving to avoid a young man sprinting away from Beekman toward the park. Four police officers were injured. Extra speedy response to major crime scenes is a routine precaution in the Four-O precinct in the southernmost tip of the South Bronx in the

Map 3 .   40th Precinct, Bronx (see Map 4 for detail in center)

narcotics-saturated Mott Haven neighborhood, a precinct bounded by the Major Deegan Expressway on the west, the Bruckner Expressway on the east, and east to west by East 138th, East 149th, and parts of East 161st streets.

Hopping in and out of their radio car to keep warm, Gesualdo and Leary guarded the sprawling, makeshift crime scene until 0350 hours,[1] while detectives began to investigate the murders. Gesualdo and Leary then returned to the station house to voucher the ballistics evidence. The next day, Gesualdo went to the morgue and verified that the three bodies from the scene now in the hands of the Medical Examiner, corpses BX915323–5, were in fact those she had discovered on Beekman Avenue the night before. Two of the corpses now had names: Manuel Vera, who died trying to reach his home at 328–340 Beekman, and Cynthia Casado, a longtime crack addict.[2] No one knew or has ever discovered the identity of the young black man in the alley. The black boy in the ambulance turned out to be Anthony Green aka (also known as) Amp, a seventeen-year-old homeboy from the neighborhood. He died on the operating table at Lincoln Hospital. The man who had cradled him and accompanied him to the hospital was his brother Benjamin aka Chubby, a petty drug dealer who, with Amp, sometimes worked for Gerard Heard, the owner of the Yellow Top crack organization on Beekman Avenue. Yellow Top used to work out of 320 Beekman and had only recently expanded to the alley next to it. The surviving victim was Janice Bruington.

Detective Mark Tebbens of the Four-O precinct squad caught the case and arrived at the scene at 2255 hours with his partner, Pete Odiot. Tebbens is a working-class boy from the Bronx who won athletic scholarships for football and basket-

---

1. Police use military time, which proceeds on a 24-hour clock; midnight is 0000, spoken as "zero hundred hours."
2. All names referred to in this book are real, unless otherwise noted.

East 149th St.

BERGEN

East 148th St.

East 147th St.

East 146th St.

East 145th St.

East 144th St.

East 143th St.

East 142th St.

WILLIS

AVE.

BROOK

AVE.

St. ANN'S AVE.

CRIMMINS

AVE.

OAK TERRACE

BEECH TERRACE

BEKMAN

AVE.

St. MARY'S ST.

CYPRESS

AVE.

POWERS

AVE.

JACKSON

AVE.

E. 142

ST. MARY'S
PARK

N

East 141st

ST.

East 140th

ST.

East 139th

ST.

Map 4. The Mott Haven Neighborhood (detail of Map 3)

ball, first to New York's elite Dalton School and then to Northeastern University. He joined the NYPD in 1982. After a three-year tour in uniformed patrol in the Five-Two precinct in the Bronx, he worked in anticrime, a plainclothes unit deployed in dangerous areas to apprehend criminals in the act of committing crimes, and then in the Robbery Identification Program in the same precinct. In 1988 he was promoted to the Four-O precinct detective squad as a white-shield detective, the brief apprenticeship on the way to the coveted gold shield that distinguishes detectives from all other police officers. Tebbens carries his six-and-a-half-foot frame with middle-guard power and small-forward grace; his trademark battle cry "Zuuuu-luuuuuu" and his ear-shattering imitations of police sirens freeze street scenes and squad rooms alike.

After quickly surveying the crime scene, Tebbens went to Lincoln Hospital, where he interviewed Janice Bruington, a 43-year-old former heroin and crack addict who lived in a homeless shelter in Manhattan. Bruington said she had returned to the Beekman neighborhood, where she had lived most of her life, to visit her son and his girlfriend. She rode the #6 train from Manhattan to East 138th Street and Cypress Avenue, walked up Cypress, and over East 141st Street to Beekman. She came onto the block and saw three men get out of a white car. They began shooting toward the alley. She turned and ran but got shot in the back of her right shoulder. She crawled underneath an automobile to hide, witnessing part of the chaos from there. She was not about to tell Tebbens what she had seen in any detail, let alone name the shooters. Tebbens recognized the fear in her eyes. Tebbens also noticed Chubby Green at the hospital waiting for news about his brother. But Chubby made no statements to the police that night.

Immediately after the police reached the scene, a team of detectives began scouring the Beekman Avenue area, canvassing every apartment in every building to find witnesses to the slaughter. But no one wanted to be seen talking to the police, and no one admitted knowledge of the incident during the long days of canvassing that followed. Shortly after 0800 hours on December 17th, however, Tebbens got the first of two anonymous phone calls saying that Stanley Tukes aka Trigger, along with "the Dominicans," had done the shootings.

Later that afternoon, Jose Padilla aka Chi Chi came to see Tebbens. Chi Chi was a sometime Yellow Top pitcher—that is, street seller—who dreamed of the day when his big brother Eladio would get out of jail and take back Beekman Avenue from the Dominicans. On the night of December 16th, Chi Chi said, he had just walked out of 327 Beekman directly across the street from the alley when a white four-door car followed by a dark Delta 88 with tinted windows stopped in front of the alley. Stanley Tukes, whom Chi Chi had known for fifteen years and with whom he had gone to two public schools, got out of the white car from the rear seat on the driver's side while a Dominican man, about five feet, eight inches tall, medium to stocky build, got out of the passenger-side rear seat. Stanley was wearing a three-quarters-length leather coat. He asked Amp Green, who stood near the alley's entrance, to come over and talk. Amp hesitated but then strolled out into the street and spoke briefly with Stanley and the Dominican man for a minute. In the meantime, a black man dressed in a black hooded jacket got out of the front passenger seat of the white car and stared at the encounter. As Amp went back to the alley, Stanley and the male Dominican returned to the white car, reached into the rear seat, and came out with MAC-10 or MAC-11 guns blazing, cutting down everyone in the alley. Afterwards, they chased a man from the alley up the street, catching up with him at 328–340 Beekman. Padilla said that the pair jumped into the rear seat of the white car and sped down Beekman, turning left at East 141st Street and then disappearing from view. Tebbens asked Chi Chi to get a name on the Dominican man. Chi Chi seemed hesitant but agreed to do so.

In the afternoon of December 18th, James Singleton, who lives in the Mott Haven neighborhood off St. Ann's, spoke to Detective Tebbens. Singleton was suspected of being a thief, petty drug dealer, and robber who rode the trains carrying a sawed-off shotgun under a long leather jacket to assist him in plying his trade. He had been visiting a friend on Beekman in the building opposite the alley the night of December 16th, he said. As he leaned casually against his friend's building, suddenly two men, a black man and a Dominican, walked up to the alleyway, pulled out handguns, and began firing. The black man, the taller of the two, was dressed in a three-quarters-length coat; the Dominican man had on a long, dark-colored jacket. Singleton said he heard a woman scream before the pair turned around. He himself fled down Beekman to East 141st Street, hearing more shooting all the while, when a white car passed him, turned left on East 141st Street, went one block, and turned left again on Cypress Avenue.

Singleton recognized both men. The black man was Stanley Tukes; the Dominican was a well-known crack dealer in the area whose name he did not know. Singleton said that, more than a year before, he had "had a problem" with Stanley, which, Tebbens guessed, meant that Singleton had been stealing from Tukes. Singleton said that the Dominican man, along with a "fat kid," had held him down on the roof of 348 Beekman, while Stanley gouged his face with a nail, leaving a long, jagged scar. Then Stanley had put a gun to Singleton's head and threatened him.

Tebbens now had two identifications on Tukes, but he knew that district attorneys would find both witnesses extremely problematic. As it happened, Tebbens already knew Tukes well. Although Stanley's rap sheet listed only an arrest in May 1990 (for resisting arrest), he was the known culprit in three early-1991 complaints that were still unresolved. First, on New Year's Eve of 1990, Quentin Lee went to a party on the twelfth floor of a building on Cypress Avenue with his friend, Clifford Skinner. Lee and Skinner left the party to get some more beer, but when they got downstairs they decided to return and get their coats before heading into the cold. When the elevator arrived at the first floor, it held six people, three men and three women. Two of the men got off and left the building immediately. Skinner tried to get on but collided with a third man getting off, a person whom he knew as Stanley. Skinner said to Stanley: "You ain't gonna have such a happy New Year." Stanley responded: "You talkin' to me? You talkin' to me?" As the elevator began closing with Skinner and the women in it, Lee urged both Skinner and Stanley to forget about the dispute, since it was New Year's Eve. Stanley turned on him, saying: "Why the fuck you gettin' involved?" Since by that time the elevator was heading upstairs without him, Lee made for the stairs, when Stanley shot him five times in the buttocks, right arm, and back. According to later reports, Stanley had been rapping to one of the girls on the elevator, and when she put off his advances, he held a 9-millimeter pistol to her head. When the crowd in the elevator heard the shots, the woman said: "That stupid Stanley. Now he gonna shoot through the elevator door." The case went nowhere because no one, including the badly injured Lee, wanted to press charges.

Second, on January 18, 1991, Stanley approached Nathan Wilder at the corner of East 141st Street and Cypress. The two had a running dispute over a girl. Stanley stuck an automatic gun in Wilder's face and asked: "You still wanna get shot?" Wilder pushed the gun away and tried to run, but Tukes fired repeatedly, striking Wilder seven times in the head and back and leaving him completely blind. The police could find no other witnesses to corroborate Wilder's story, but the case was still active. And finally, on February 18, 1991, around mid-morning, Renee Brown aka Nee-Nee, who had been smoking marijuana at 354 Cypress despite being warned by Stanley not to do so lest she attract police, was standing on the first floor terrace of 370 Cypress Avenue. Stanley came up the stairs, grabbed her, and dropped her off the terrace to the ground one flight below. Brown broke her hip and left wrist in the fall but did not press charges against Tukes.

Tebbens spoke to Chi Chi Padilla again, and Padilla told him that Tukes's Dominican accomplice was called Platano (Pla'-tan-o) or Darkman, the latter because of his complexion. He drove a white BMW convertible with a blue rag top. Tebbens immediately recognized the name Platano because it had surfaced in an earlier investigation. Tebbens had assisted Detective Pete Odiot in investigating the murder of Rafael Ramirez aka Spec, who was shot to death in front of 419 East 157th Street on May 11, 1989. Spec had been dealing crack for a Dominican drug operation on Manor and Watson Avenues in the Four-Three precinct of the Bronx. Spec started freelancing, selling Jumps (a different brand of crack) for another operation on the side, ignoring warnings about the hazards of being a salesman for two bosses. Indeed, only a few days earlier, according to detectives' reports, Juan Astwood aka Johnny Handsome had put a gun to Spec's head, advising him to stop double-dealing. On May 11th at 2330 hours, Johnny Handsome, accompanied by a carful of comrades, drove up to Spec's spot, got out of the car, put his arm around Spec's shoulder, and asked him if he was still selling Jumps. At first Spec denied that he was. But suddenly he pulled back and said: "We all sellin' Jumps." Johnny Handsome yelled: "Watch the others, they all gonna go" and shot Spec twice, as his comrades opened up on Spec's co-workers, badly wounding several of them. An anonymous caller said that a Dominican man named Platano was one of the shooters.

After fruitless visits to RIP units' nickname files in the Three-Four, Four-O, Four-Two, Four-Four, and Four-Six precincts, Tebbens asked his own precinct's anticrime unit to detain Platano for questioning if any officers knew him. Months later, on October 7, 1989, PO Tim Burke saw and stopped the man he knew as Platano on a routine stop-and-frisk and brought him into the precinct, filing, as required, a UF-250 report, noting that Platano gave the name Wilfredo de los Angeles and had no criminal record. But Tebbens and Odiot were both off duty. Lieutenant Mike Bramble, the Four-O precinct detective squad commander, did not call them in. There was not much to go on at the time, and calling off-duty officers in on their regular days off produces substantial overtime costs. Squad commanders get judged as much by their administrative stringency as by their squads' clearance rates. Moreover, the police had no way of detaining Platano legally for more than a few hours. So the lieutenant ordered Platano released. No one thought to take his picture. Tebbens asked Burke to dig up the old UF-250 report, but it contained no further information.

On December 21, 1991, the Four-O precinct put out a city-wide radio transmission alerting all police that a dark-skinned Dominican called Platano, driving a white BMW convertible with a light blue rag top, was wanted for questioning in connection with the four-victim slaughter on Beekman that had already become known as The Quad. Later that same day, a detective from Brooklyn called the Four-O squad with some information. One of his confidential informants had heard of Platano. The informant knew "Mickey"—a manager for "Lenny"—and Platano at Red Top crack on Beekman Avenue. Mickey regularly brought his car to Romeo's Body Shop at 361 Metropolitan Avenue in Brooklyn, and, the informant thought, Platano probably did as well. The police quickly set up surveillance on the body shop and ran checks on every car that went in and out of the shop for days. But there was no sign of a white BMW with a blue top. So Tebbens directly confronted the owner of the body shop, who denied all knowledge of a Platano or, in fact, of any customer with such a car. The garage owner acknowledged that he had heard the same queries before, however. He showed Tebbens a business card from an FBI agent named Harold Bickmore, based in Newark, New Jersey, who was looking for Platano and the same car. Tebbens and his colleagues also pored over all stolen car reports trying, unsuccessfully, to locate information about the white BMW.

Although Tebbens had not been aware that Platano was part of Red Top, he had known about the crack operation at 348 Beekman for a long time. Beekman Avenue is a long-block street between East 141st Street and St. Mary's Park. The building at 348 Beekman has a regular front door complete with stoop that leads into the lobby, but also, to the right, a second front entrance directly off the street—a low, steel-door entry that leads down a set of metal stairs through a 30' X 30' tunnel-like basement passageway, into a dark courtyard. The courtyard empties into a tangle of alleyways between Beekman and Cypress Avenues. At each story above the courtyard, cat-walk-like balconies span the yard, joining the two sides of the building. The spot is called The Hole, and it is an ideal location for selling crack: it is not only private but secure. Sales are made off the street, away from routine police surveillance of drug locations. Since the buyers have to enter The Hole through the tunnel-like basement passageway, spot managers can screen potential robbers, the scourge of the crack trade, or, should robbers slip through, prevent their exit.

Red Top crack had begun using The Hole as its flagship sometime in 1988, just when Tebbens came to the Four-O precinct. That year, there had been a major fire at a long-time drug building, 603–605 Beech Terrace, a short-block street that runs perpendicular to Beekman. The city finished the demolition job. Suddenly The Hole opened up. Tebbens was sure that the operations on Beech Terrace and Beekman were connected, but it wasn't clear exactly how. Tebbens did know that Red Top had its own "kitchen" somewhere farther north in the Bronx, where kilogram bricks of cocaine were cooked, converted into crack, packed into small, clear-plastic vials or "bottles," and capped with a colored top, which simultaneously designated brand and organization. In a signature stroke, the Red Top crew taped the packed vials onto long strips of clear tape and rolled the strips into balls called bundles, with each bundle containing 100 vials. The individual vials were sold for $5 apiece on the street by pitchers, many of whom were themselves crack addicts.

At the street level, Red Top typified other drug operations throughout the city. Steerers—usually addicts or hangers-on—directed customers to sale locations for commissions. Pitchers, who did the hand-to-hand transactions, received $10 for every bundle they sold, payable in cash or trade. Lookouts kept their eyes peeled for the police, usually receiving $20 or $30 for an eight-hour turn, depending on their shift managers' largess. Salaried managers controlled and coordinated pitchers' and lookouts' work and the supply of crack on hand, and disciplined workers as needed. Enforcers, who are sometimes part-owners, kept everybody in line with requisite violence. And transporters ferried the drugs from scattered kitchens and stashes to the selling spots.

Since 1988, Tebbens had caught or knew about several cases in the Four-O and surrounding precincts involving the Beekman Avenue–area Red Top crew. On July 20, 1988, Jose Llaca aka Pasqualito killed Guy Gaines, a New York State Correction officer who was on Beech Terrace to buy bundles of crack for resale at $20 a vial in the Carolinas. Hearing a quarrel between Gaines and a Red Top manager, Pasqualito told Frankie Robles, then an eager fifteen-year-old errand boy, to get his gun from a house on Cypress Avenue. Pasqualito tracked Gaines down on Beekman Avenue, around the corner from Beech Terrace, and shot him, along with a local crackhead who was an unfortunate witness to the shooting. Gaines died immediately, but the crackhead survived and testified in the grand jury against Pasqualito, who was arrested for murder in early August 1988. He was acquitted at trial the following December and later bragged to his cronies how he had bought off the witness by plying him with crack. Subverting witnesses became one of Red Top's claims to fame.

Then on September 3, 1989, Tebbens had also caught the double homicide of Orlando Berrios aka Tito and Luis Rivera aka Chico, two heroin dealers from Marcy Place in the Four-Four precinct, an area that cops call The Devil's Triangle. At about 2200 hours, Chico, Tito, and two friends, Anthony Lopez and Rodney Baines aka G, had come to the vicinity of East 140th Street and St. Ann's in a livery cab driven by Clifford Halsey. Chico wanted to visit his girlfriend and baby. After ten minutes with his family, Chico returned to the car and told Halsey to drive to East 141st Street and Beekman so he could get some beer from the DMC Grocery on that corner. They were leaving the area when Chico spotted his friend Lamar Taylor aka L in the middle of East 141st Street. He told Halsey to stop the car so he could talk to L.

As Chico, Tito, Anthony, and Rodney stood outside the cab chatting to L, they were suddenly surrounded by eight men who had been eyeballing the meeting across the street in front of Iglesia Evangelica Metodista Unida. One of this crew yelled: "Kill them all!" and shot Tito in the stomach. Badly wounded, Tito ran eastbound on East 141st Street and north on Cypress Avenue, pursued by the original gunman along with another crew member. Another gunman shot Chico, who dove into the cab. The shooter continued to fire, wounding the driver Halsey and filling Chico with five bullets, even as Halsey sped west on East 141st toward Lincoln Hospital. Chico later died there. Anthony and Rodney fled on foot up Beekman Avenue toward St. Mary's Park, Rodney's lip creased by a bullet; they flagged down a police radio car in the park and brought the police back to the scene.

In the meantime, on Cypress Avenue, Tito made a frantic effort to escape his pursuers by diving through the open passenger window of a green car belonging to Jesus Maysonnet, a Cypress Avenue resident who had just dropped off his family after returning from a Labor Day picnic on Randall's Island. Tito grabbed the wheel as the startled Maysonnet scrambled out of his car, leaving the driver's door open. As Tito tried to drive off while still in the passenger's seat, he crashed Maysonnet's car into a van. Several gunmen surrounded the car and pumped ten shots into him, shooting the fingers of his right hand to bits in the process. As a finale, one gunman put one more bullet into Tito's chest, while invoking the name "Miguelito." Tito's beeper had begun to sound as the episode reached its climax. Someone tossed a quarter onto Tito's lap, saying: "Go make your phone call now, muthafucka."

Tebbens's investigation into the deaths of Chico and Tito, which came to be called The Double, led him to yet another murder. On May 31, 1989, detectives in Eastchester, New York, just north of the city, had found the body of Miguel Castillo aka Miguelito or Heater or Dice dumped in the grounds of a Leewood Country Club. Eastchester detectives discovered that Miguelito, a baseball player at Lehman College good enough to get a tryout with the Los Angeles Dodgers, had grown up in Washington Heights in upper Manhattan. In the course of their investigation into Castillo's death, they were told by Miguelito's Manhattan friends that he did business at Marcy Place in the Bronx and that police should look there for his killers.

As Tebbens probed The Double by focusing on the regular crowd on Beekman Avenue, he soon heard street rumors connecting his case to Miguelito's death, and he contacted the Eastchester detectives. They readily shared with him their investigative reports on Miguelito's circle of friends and their developing knowledge of the drug scene at Marcy Place, site of an especially strong market in heroin. Their information dovetailed with Tebbens's own knowledge. Along with Russell Harris aka Renny from the Bronx, the Washington Heights boys who surfaced as friends of Miguelito in the Eastchester investigation—Lenny Rodriguez, Danny Rincon aka Fat Danny, Victor Mercedes, David Polanco, and Manny Crespo—were all regulars on Beekman Avenue, and all members of the Red Top crew.

Tebbens had street information that Victor Mercedes, known to be one of the crew's most aggressive members, and Pasqualito had been involved in The Double. He worked on getting identifications from The Double's key witnesses. Anthony Lopez denied seeing the faces of the shooters but finally admitted that he had. Lopez, Rodney Baines, and Halsey picked a picture of Victor Mercedes out of a photo array, naming him as the gunman who began the shooting by assaulting Tito. Lopez and Baines also identified Pasqualito in a photo array as the gunman who shot Chico and Halsey. Following Bronx custom, no lineups were done. No other witnesses came forward, even though the streets had been crowded on the warm late-summer night of the shooting. Jesus Maysonnet had lived on the street for years and, police thought, obviously knew the shooters. But he said that he recognized nobody. Tebbens arrested Mercedes and Pasqualito on September 28, 1989; but with Lopez and Baines, both drug dealers, and Halsey, a cab driver who transports drug dealers, as the only witnesses, Bronx district attorneys were hesitant to try the case. Then even these witnesses disappeared. Mercedes and Pasqualito remained in jail almost two years, until August 1991, when the case was adjourned until the state could produce its witnesses. There had been at least one other shooter in The Double, but Tebbens could turn up no leads at all to his identity.

Clearly, however, the killings were gang-related, occurred on Red Top ground, and were connected to the death of Miguelito, a close friend of the Beekman Avenue crew. Tebbens suspected that Lenny Rodriguez, whom he knew to be Lenny Sepulveda from 171st Street and Audubon Avenue in Washington Heights, was the key boss of Red Top. But when Tebbens pressed his street sources for information about Lenny, no one would even speak about him, let alone implicate him in a crime. A bit later, Tebbens discovered that Lenny had a brother, Nelson, who worked with him. Tebbens knew that he could solve the riddle of The Double by unraveling the Red Top drug operation and its links to Miguelito's business on Marcy Place, which, Tebbens felt sure, was also drug-related.

But Tebbens had little time to focus on Red Top or indeed narcotics trafficking as such in any systematic way. Squad detectives catch the individual cases that come their way, and Tebbens's days were routinely filled with investigations of rooftop shootings into St. Mary's Park, domestic violence, street assaults, and other homicides. More importantly, Tebbens had no authorization to investigate narcotics organizations, normally the province of specialized borough units. The bureaucratization of the police department fragments hard-won knowledge of the streets' seeming chaos, not only among officers in different units but often among those in the same squad.

But in December 1991 The Quad blew the lid off Mott Haven. Its extraordinary public violence drew extensive media coverage, even in *The New York Times*, which routinely ignores uptown mayhem unless a story seems especially titillating to its readers. The publicity prompted borough commanders to assign a special task force to the case. Suddenly, surveillance vans and additional manpower, both scarce resources, became available. Because he caught The Quad, Tebbens was authorized to get to the bottom of the violence on Beekman and Cypress Avenues, respectively dubbed The Lion Pit and The Snake Pit. He was given the code name Spartacus to outfox drug dealers' routine monitoring of police radio transmissions.

Just after midnight on January 5, 1992, Tebbens did his first covert surveillance of The Hole at 348 Beekman. Cramming his huge frame into a dark van with opaquely tinted windows and a periscope disguised as an air vent, he and Detective Miguel Calderon took Chubby Green to Beekman to spot the Red Top players. Surveillance is normally boring, tedious work, punctuated by only brief glimpses of one's quarry. But in 1992, at any time of the day or night but especially after midnight, Beekman Avenue, along with other open-air drug markets of the South Bronx and northern Manhattan, had a Middle-Eastern-bazaar, street-theater air. Crack users formed long queues to buy vials from pitchers hawking their wares, watched closely by managers, in turn supervised by enforcers standing near sleek, polished cars with dark windows, guns bulging under leather jackets. Young children played in the streets, stopping to watch the procession of cocaine whores strutting the street hoping to turn a quick trick in exchange for crack, or staring at sudden face-slappings of willful women or the shuckin' and jivin' of homeboys. Indeed, the surveillance van immediately became a prop for the ongoing street drama, and Tebbens had to call for a radio car to cruise the block to prevent crackheads, who were swarming around the van, from breaking into it.

Once things settled down, Chubby, peering through the periscope, spotted a Hispanic man in a green hooded jacket whom he knew was a lookout for Red Top. But he could not identify the man. Shortly after 0100 hours, a black man, whom Chubby recognized as Linwood aka Cool Water, the twelve-to-eight night manager at The Hole, sauntered out of 348 Beekman to chat with some other unknown men on the street. Half an hour later, a black four-door Chevrolet Caprice arrived, driven by a tall, fair-skinned Hispanic male known to Chubby as Max. Max disappeared into The Hole. A stocky, medium-height, dark-skinned Dominican man emerged from the passenger side. Chubby identified him as Platano.

Tebbens immediately realized that he had seen Platano before. On December 5, 1991, he had been on Cypress Avenue at 140th Street interviewing a witness to the murder of Charles Walker, who had been shot to death while playing a bodega's slot machine. The assailant, later proved to be Cory Jackson, a local robber, had put the gun directly into Walker's face and then pulled the trigger. Suddenly, Tebbens saw a car, driven by a dark-skinned, stocky Dominican, speed past him up Cypress Avenue, followed by one of the Four-O precinct's anticrime cars. The fleeing car made a precipitous U-turn in front of 354 Cypress, losing the police car in the process, and raced back down the street toward the Bruckner Expressway. Tebbens jumped into his own car and followed the vehicle onto the expressway but lost it in the tangle of traffic on the Triborough Bridge.

Now that same Dominican identified by Chubby as Platano stood right in front of the surveillance van on Beekman, hands thrust nonchalantly in his pockets as he chatted with The Hole's lookouts. His hair was crew cut, and he was wearing a heavy black jacket, blue jeans, and black Timberland boots; Chubby thought that Platano looked bigger than usual and guessed that he was also wearing a bullet-proof vest under his jacket. As the detectives watched, Max returned and both men got into the Chevrolet Caprice and headed down Beek-man toward East 141st Street at about 0215 hours. Tebbens radioed his backup unit, a group of detectives in uniform in an unmarked car waiting on Cypress Avenue, and told them to apprehend and arrest Platano. Although the cops spotted the Caprice at the corner of East 141st and Cypress, Max and Platano also spotted them, turned the corner, sped to the Bruckner Expressway heading toward Washington Heights, and made a successful getaway.

Knowing that the wind was up on Beekman for the night, Tebbens drove the surveillance van over to the Three-Four precinct to look for the Caprice, driving up and down the crowded, winding streets of Washington Heights. What exactly were the connections between the Heights in Manhattan and Mott Haven in the Bronx? Who were these guys and how long was their reach? That night, Chubby Green gave Tebbens more information about the organization of Red Top. Its lookouts were posted on the rooftops all along Beekman Avenue, equipped with high-grade walkie-talkies; it controlled several stash apartments in the area, places with safes to hold drugs, money, and guns; and it had the strict hierarchy typical of the drug trade.

Chubby also told Tebbens what he knew about The Quad. A friend had tipped Chubby that Lenny Sepulveda, who was currently in prison, had ordered his brother Nelson to have Chubby and Amp Green and any Yellow Top customers in sight killed because Yellow Top was selling quality crack at $3 per vial, undercutting Red Top's price of $5 per vial. According to Chubby, Red Top's key enforcers were Stanley Tukes, Platano, Edd Sanchez aka OD, Linwood, Max, and three others he knew by the names of Chino, Mickey Tex, and Lace. Over the next several days Tebbens intensified his surveillance of The Hole and its neighboring area, looking in particular for the white BMW with the blue top and the dark Chevrolet Caprice.

On January 8th a street source told Tebbens that Fat Danny Rincon had been at the scene of The Quad. Tebbens knew Fat Danny, a young man built like an enormous egg with hamhock hands. Danny ran the main Orange Top crack operation at 600 East 141st Street, just down the block and around the corner from The Hole, with subsidiary spots at 592 East 141st Street and 613 and 597 East 138th Street. The East 138th Street spots, opened in mid-1989, were the first Orange Top operations. Initially, Fat Danny sold Red Top, so the relationship between the Red Top crew on Beekman and Fat Danny's current Orange Top operation was unclear. All that police knew for sure was that most of the key players in both Red Top and Orange Top were from the Three-Four precinct, knew one

another, and frequented the same unlicensed social club run
by Mireya Betancourt at 354 Cypress Avenue.

Tebbens had already caught some cases directly involving
Fat Danny. In July 1990, uniformed officers had radioed the
Four-O squad to come over to the 207th Street Bridge, where
they had just fished Eduardo Rivera of East 139th Street out of
the Harlem River. When Tebbens arrived at the scene, Rivera
was chatting amiably with officers about his recent swim. He
said that Fat Danny had thrown him off the bridge because of
a "business dispute." Tebbens guessed that Rivera was short
on a package of drugs or money that he was carrying for Fat
Danny. Rivera absolutely refused to press charges. Tebbens
gave Rivera his card, telling him to call in case he changed
his mind. Later that night, Tebbens received a call from the
anticrime cops in the Three-Four precinct. They had arrested
Rivera in the act of sticking up a bodega and discovered Tebbens's card in Rivera's pocket. Rivera claimed Tebbens as a
friend.

A few months later, on October 23, 1990, at 0115 hours on
East 141st Street near Cypress, someone shot Fat Danny seven
times, riddling his enormous body with bullets. When Tebbens
visited the hospital and asked Fat Danny for the shooter's
name, Fat Danny told Tebbens to perform an act both difficult and unnatural. Tebbens heard the street story that Andres
Carela aka Smiley and Fat Danny had gotten into an argument
because Smiley wanted to shoot out the street lights on Cypress for target practice. Fat Danny forbade it because it would
bring unwanted police attention. So Smiley "lit him up" instead. But Tebbens knew that there had to be more to the story.
Smiley hung out, it was said, at Manor and Watson in the
Bronx and was close to "Frankie," who was boss of operations
there. The fact that Smiley was on East 141st Street late at
night suggested some kind of relationship between Frankie and
Fat Danny, and perhaps between the operation on Manor and

Watson and the Orange Top operation. And if Orange Top, in turn, was also associated with Red Top, as suggested by the rumor that Fat Danny was at The Quad, what was the relationship between Frankie and Lenny Sepulveda, the boss of Red Top?

Fat Danny had an alibi for the time of The Quad. On January 10, 1992, uniformed cops in the Four-O precinct locked up Eddie OD Sanchez for shooting someone in the leg. When Detective Mike Lopuzzo queried Sanchez about December 16th, he said that he had been out that night with his good friend Fat Danny Rincon. OD said he and Fat Danny returned to East 141st Street and Beekman Avenue by taxi and saw the ambulances and police cars everywhere in the area. They did not, Sanchez said, go near the crime scene.

But that same January day another witness tied Stanley Tukes and Platano to The Quad. Martha Molina claimed that she had gone to the alley at 320 Beekman the night of December 16th to buy crack. She was there with a young black man called Rhasta, a Hispanic woman in a green coat whose name she didn't know, and Amp Green. She saw a white car pull up in front of the alley. Platano and Stanley exited the car, she said, and began shooting everyone in sight. Under fire, she managed to escape by slipping through a hole in the wire mesh fence that backed the alley. Although Tebbens was happy to have Molina's statement corroborating those of other witnesses, her testimony was as problematic as any that he already had. The young woman, the mother of two children who were scattered to the wind, was a prototypically gaunt, hollow-cheeked crack addict, nervous, jumpy, and erratic. When she used crack, her face twisted up, she couldn't sleep, and she imagined that bugs were crawling all over her. Her native intelligence had not improved from years of drug abuse; she had started using marijuana when she was eight and cocaine when she was thirteen years old. She had also gone into a mental hospital at the age of thirteen. Still, she readily picked

Stanley's picture out of a photo array assembled by Tebbens, saying that she had known Stanley for ten years.

In the course of questioning, Martha also told Tebbens about the murder of Oscar Alvarez. The police had discovered his body on May 12, 1991, on the rooftop of 592 East 141st Street, face-down in a puddle of blood, his cigarette lighter just inches from his hand. Alvarez died of multiple gunshot wounds in the chest and neck. Martha skipped a big party that night in George Santiago's apartment in the adjacent building at 600 East 141st and had been smoking crack upstairs with Oscar. Linwood Collins came up the stairwell. Martha had known Linwood for years; they had gone to Public School 65 together and both had lived at 666 Cypress; Linwood was close friends with her brother. She knew that Linwood was managing Orange Top at 600 East 141st Street; Oscar pitched for him, along with Oscar's best pal Shrimpo. Linwood was looking for Shrimpo, who owed him money. Oscar said he didn't know where to find him. Linwood turned to Martha and told her to "get the fuck off the roof." She went to the neighboring roof, and after a while she heard shots. Afterwards, Linwood came to her on the rooftop of 600 and told her: "Shhh . . . The reason I din't do nothin' to you is 'cause I know your brother."

The Quad was loosening tongues about many crimes. But Tebbens had to keep focused on the main task at hand. Later on January 10th, Tebbens brought Chi Chi Padilla back to the precinct, and he too picked Stanley's picture out of the photo array. He also told Tebbens that Stanley and Platano had taken him for a ride out to City Island, the Bronx's anomalous fishing village. Platano stuck a 9-millimeter pistol into Chi Chi's mouth and dry-fired it, warning him that if he spoke to police again, the gun would be loaded the next time around.

The police manhunt for Stanley and Platano intensified. Acting on a tip, the detectives finally caught up with Stanley and "took him down" at 2396 Morris Avenue on January 17, 1992, at 1300 hours. Apprehending suspects is an intrinsic part of investigation. It brings closure of a sort to the difficult work of identification. It encourages previously silent witnesses to come forward because they no longer fear for their safety. It provides police with the opportunity to get statements from suspects, whether formal or spontaneous; statements are often crucial pieces of evidence. Since Tebbens had obtained a warrant for Stanley's arrest, the police could not speak to him about the case. But Stanley made several spontaneous statements. As Detectives Tebbens, Hoering, Lopuzzo, and Addolorato burst into Apartment 5G, guns drawn, Stanley declared: "Go ahead and shoot me. Kill me." An hour later, he said: "The Dominicans did it." Shortly after that, he said: "Janice Bruington will tell you that I didn't shoot her. She won't testify against me." And, at 2000 hours, while in the bathroom, he said to Tebbens: "Howja know I was the guy?"

The very next day, Chubby Green came to see Tebbens with a new version of his brother's last moments. Green said that he rushed to Amp's side as he lay dying on the street and asked who had shot him. At first Amp said: "I feel like I'm gonna die, Chubby. If I die, I love you all." Chubby pressed his brother for the name of his assailant. And Amp said: "Stanley. Stanley shot me," a statement that he repeated in the ambulance en route to the hospital in the presence of Janice Bruington. When Tebbens asked Chubby why he hadn't mentioned this before, even during their long night of surveillance on January 5th, Chubby said that he had planned to kill Stanley himself but decided in the end that he didn't want his mother to lose another son to either death or prison. Chubby also confirmed that Stanley was the culprit in the violent incidents of early 1991 involving Quentin Lee, Nathan Wilder, and Renee Brown. Chubby said that Stanley always bragged that everyone was afraid to testify against him.

Only a few weeks later Stanley's lawyer, Howard Ripps, phoned Tebbens, telling him that Chubby Green had come to his office, where he recanted everything he had told the police about Stanley. Tebbens had heard a lot about Ripps. Ripps's office is located at 888 Grand Concourse at East 161st Street, just across the street from the Bronx Supreme Court, and up the hill from Yankee Stadium and its surrounding wilderness. Ripps and Michael Nedick occupy the same office building as the firm of Goldstein, Weinstein & Fuld, lawyers whose clientele includes many Dominican drug dealers; the names of both firms are on the facade. Ripps or Nedick regularly stands up for (appears for) Goldstein, Weinstein, or Fuld in cases throughout the city, and in multidefendant criminal gang cases Ripps or Nedick often represents lesser organizational figures, while Goldstein, Weinstein, or Fuld represents gang leaders. Ripps and Nedick are not officially affiliated with Goldstein, Weinstein & Fuld; but police and prosecutors see their relationship as symbiotic. By the time of Ripps's call notifying Tebbens of Chubby's recantation, however, there was plenty of other evidence to keep Stanley Tukes under lock and key.

Just a few days after Stanley's arrest, the investigation took an unexpected turn. James Singleton told Tebbens that he had remembered the name of the second shooter at The Quad, the man who accompanied Stanley. He said that it was Shorty—a well-known local crack dealer named Daniel Gonzalez, a diminutive, skinny man of sallow, fair complexion. Shorty had just gotten out of jail on December 15th for selling Red Top crack. Later, on January 28th, Singleton picked Shorty out of a photo array after a single glance. Singleton's identification caught Tebbens and his colleagues somewhat off guard because they had assumed, from the description Singleton had provided earlier, that he would name Platano as the second shooter. They suspected that Singleton was holding back because of his fear of Platano. In all likelihood, Singleton had seen more than two shooters. As it turned out, Singleton had cause to be worried about his safety. On February 7th Linwood Collins put a gun to his head, threatening to kill him if he testified against Stanley Tukes. Tebbens arrested Linwood for witness tampering on February 17th.

Shorty was, in any event, an entirely plausible participant in The Quad; he was a bad actor with a street reputation for abusiveness. On January 30th, the police found another eyewitness to The Quad, a local robber named Ramon Jimenez; he also picked Shorty out of the photo array. According to Jimenez, Shorty, "along with two or three other men," had shot Amp Green and the crowd in the alleyway. Since Jimenez always hung out on Beekman, the detectives knew that he too was holding back. But now the police had more than enough to lock up Shorty.

On January 30th Detectives Tebbens, Addolorato, and Calderon arrested Daniel Gonzalez aka Shorty on the street right in front of 320 Beekman. At 2030 hours, in a videotaped statement, Shorty said that he was employed by the grocery store at the corner of East 141st Street and Beekman, where he usually worked the four-to-midnight shift. He said that on the night of December 16th, however, he went home early, ate dinner, and watched a video; he was with his family when the four people were killed on Beekman Avenue. At 0500 hours the next morning, Shorty asked to speak to Mark Tebbens, saying that he had information that might help him solve the quadruple homicide. Shorty proceeded to lay out the entire structure of the Red Top crack organization, confirming in virtually every detail what Tebbens had already learned about Lenny and Nelson Sepulveda's operation on Beekman Avenue. Shorty admitted that he used to sell crack for Red Top but said he no longer did so because Lenny had refused to put up bail money after his last arrest. He added that Platano, who used to be a mechanic repairing cars on the street, regularly transported the crack from upper Manhattan to the Bronx, where it was kept in safes in different apartments. Other enforcers for the crew, namely Stanley Tukes and Platano's brother, whose name he did not know, usually accompanied Platano. Gonzalez said nothing about the Orange Top operation.

Tebbens tested Shorty's alibi. Later that day and the next, he interviewed Shorty's wife, her mother, and two other women who lived in the same apartment at 370 Cypress as Shorty and the boyfriend of one of the women. Tebbens got a mixed story. Three of the women said that Shorty never left the apartment the night of December 16th. But Shorty's wife, who had been visiting a friend at 340 Beekman, said that she saw Shorty on Beekman at 0015 hours from an upstairs window, where she watched the chaos on the streets below because police permitted no one to leave the building once they arrived on the scene. Moreover, the boyfriend said that Shorty was out of the apartment during the shooting, returned, and left again to find his wife. Everyone, including the owners of the DMC Grocery at East 141st Street and Beekman where Shorty claimed to work, said that Shorty never worked there but instead spent all of his time hanging out on that corner. Although Tebbens was sure that Shorty had been one of the shooters at The Quad, he also knew that Shorty was a bit player in the overall scheme of things.

There had been a lot of shooters at The Quad; street rumors also named a tall, skinny, light-skinned Hispanic man known only as the X-Man, because of his Malcolm X jacket, and a big, burly, dark-skinned Dominican man, about whom no one would speak. But despite confusing identifications typical of extremely violent crimes with multiple culprits, Tebbens knew that Platano had been there. Tebbens had become fascinated by Platano. As other detectives across the city reached out to him after the radio alert of December 21st, Tebbens discovered that Platano had a legendary street reputation as a methodical, thorough, and ruthless hit man. Like the name Lenny Sepulveda, the very mention of Platano's name stopped all street conversation. Moreover, Tebbens had once had Platano in his grasp, only to have him slip away to wreak more havoc on the streets, thanks to a lieutenant alert to administrative exigencies. Tebbens became determined to find, identify, and lock up once and for all the elusive Platano.

a death on the
the
highway

Detectives Jerry
Dimuro and Garry Dugan
were also
looking for Platano. Dimuro
worked in the detective squad in the Three-O precinct covering the west side of Manhattan from 133rd to 155th Streets.
He grew up in the south Bronx and joined the NYPD in 1983.
After a brief stint in the bag, that is, in uniform, he worked
undercover infiltrating the Bronx drug trade for more than five
years and was promoted to the squad in 1989. Dugan, a twenty-
three-year veteran of the force who spent his whole career in
the killing grounds of northern Manhattan, worked for the
Manhattan North Homicide Squad, a specialized unit that as-
sists precinct detectives in homicide investigations above 59th
Street. Dugan spent most of his time working on cases in his
old stomping grounds, the Three-Four precinct, where he had
spent several years as a uniformed cop and then as a detective
in the RIP squad.

At midnight on May 19, 1991, Dimuro had gone off duty
and was scheduled to resume work at 0800 hours. Because of
the turnaround, he slept at the station house instead of driving
home. When he awakened, the sergeant of the Nightwatch
Squad, a borough-wide unit that initiates or, as some detectives
say, destroys investigations between midnight and 0800 hours
when precinct squads are not on duty, told him: "You caught
a homicide and you got your hands full with this one."

Dimuro scarcely needed such counsel because the small
Three-O squad room was already packed. In addition to Garry
Dugan and other MNHS members and Dimuro's A-team part-
ners, there were Nightwatch investigators, visiting brass, and

several broadcast reporters clamoring for a statement. Twenty-year-old David Cargill of Tarrytown, New York, just returned from flight school at Embry-Riddle Aeronautical University in Daytona, Florida, had had his brains blown out at 0430 hours on the West Side Highway as he drove his candy-apple-red 1989 Nissan pickup truck home with two friends, Kevin Kryzeminski and John Riguzzi, former high school ice-hockey teammates.

Nightwatch detectives had already taken Kevin and John back to the scene of the crime and determined that the shooting had occurred on the highway around 145th Street, around lightposts 241B–244B, about one-half mile south of the exit ramp at 158th Street. By the time they got back to the Three-O squad, both Cargill's and Riguzzi's parents were present. Detective Maria Bertini consoled the Cargill family while Garry Dugan interviewed each of the boys separately. The initial interviews were difficult. Both boys were in total shock, petrified, and completely exhausted. They told the same story. They said they had gone to a Saturday night party near home and then traveled to Manhattan to look for "working girls." There was, they said, too much police activity near the Intrepid Museum where prostitutes congregate, so they headed home. On their way, the shooting happened on the West Side Highway.

Dugan found the story completely implausible. Something must have happened to provoke the catastrophe. Do people normally get shot on the West Side Highway at 4:30 in the morning? He confronted John's father with his son's story and asked him if he thought the story made sense. He asked Mr. Riguzzi to sit in on a subsequent interview with John, but the boy stuck to his original account. Dugan left Mr. Riguzzi with his son and talked to Kevin again. But Kevin became belligerent, insisting on the same version of events. The interview ended in acrimony. Dugan felt that both boys were holding back. He continued to work on Mr. Riguzzi, assuring him that his son was not in trouble and did not need a lawyer but did need to tell the police exactly what happened on the highway. Still, by late morning Dugan had made no headway at all, and the Riguzzis took both John and Kevin back to Tarrytown.

The boys returned to the Three-O squad early the next morning and gave more complete, and recorded, statements. John told Dimuro his story first. With David and Kevin, he said, he had gone to a party at Joe's[1] house in Elmsford, New York. The party had died down around 1:30 AM. The boys went to Lefty's, a local Tarrytown bar, because John had to see the owner about playing softball. David suggested that he "wanted a girl," so the boys decided to go to Manhattan. They drove around midtown, but there was so much police activity that they never approached any of the working girls. Around 4:30 AM, they decided to go home and headed north on the West Side Highway. David was driving, Kevin was in the passenger seat, and John was propped up on one of the speakers in the truck's jump seat. The music was very loud.

John noticed some bright lights behind them, turned around, and saw a car pulling to the truck's left. John looked directly at the car. He saw a Hispanic man sitting in the passenger seat with the window open. John did not make eye contact and then looked straight ahead. Suddenly the air was filled with the sound of exploding firecrackers, and shards of glass started flying in the truck's cab. John ducked down and then heard Kevin yelling incoherently at David. He saw David slumped over the wheel. Then Kevin somehow stopped the truck on the dividing space between the exit and the highway. John climbed out and, together with Kevin, dragged David, who was limp, out of the driver's seat, around the back of the truck, and into the passenger's side. With Kevin and David in the passenger seat, John drove the truck off the highway, running red lights

---

1. This is a pseudonym, as are the names of all civilians in this chapter except for the Cargill, Kryzeminski, and Riguzzi families.

to try to attract police attention, until they finally spotted an ambulance at 158th Street and Amsterdam Avenue that rushed David to Harlem Hospital.

But Kevin told a somewhat different story. He said that when they reached Lefty's, the bar was dead, so they decided to go into Manhattan. They stopped in Washington Heights near 158th and Amsterdam to buy cocaine. John handled the transaction, went with some street steerers, and came back to the truck with a $20 foil of coke. In a nearby park, Kevin and John snorted a few lines each. After checking out the working girls around 30th Street, they headed north on the West Side Highway. David was driving recklessly, speeding through yellow lights. At the 57th Street ramp to the highway, David ran the light though it was red and cut off a late model BMW, from around 1990, which got pinched against the wall. A second car, an old Monte Carlo, perhaps from 1982, maybe blue or white, possibly cream, was also cut off. The Monte Carlo went around the BMW and followed the boys onto the highway. David picked up speed on the highway, moving between the right and middle lanes. Kevin looked back and saw a dark-skinned Hispanic man in the Monte Carlo doing something with his hands. To Kevin it seemed that he was loading a gun. Suddenly, there were loud noises and bursts of light in the truck's cabin, and Kevin smelled something burning. Kevin looked past David and saw the Hispanic man with his arms out of the car's window firing a semiautomatic weapon, flashes blazing out of the gun's muzzle. Kevin stared into the shooter's face. He was dark, clean shaven, in his early twenties, with slim features. He wore a baseball cap turned backwards with gerry curls stuck out under it. Kevin saw that David was hurt and that the truck was starting to list into the left lane. He grabbed control of the steering wheel with one hand, pressing the brake pedal with the other until the truck stopped.

Dimuro and Dugan found neither story convincing. They had another detective reinterview John, who admitted buying the coke on Amsterdam and 158th Street. Although Dimuro and Dugan understood why John concealed that information, the deceit made the detectives, for whom mistrust is an occupational habit of mind, even more wary. They also learned that Kevin had a somewhat troubled past involving drugs. The homicide looked like a drug-related killing. Besides, how likely was it that Kevin would have had the presence of mind to maneuver the car to safety from high speed? Or that they would end up back at 158th Street and Amsterdam, where they admitted buying drugs earlier? Also, why did they drag David's body around the vehicle? Why not simply move him over to the passenger seat? The detectives felt that sheer happenstance or the boys' claims of acting in shock were just not good enough explanations. There had to be some reason for this murder. New York City hosts many horrors, but people do not normally get their brains blown out on the West Side Highway in the early morning for no reason at all, or for a minor traffic scrape.

In the meantime, a federal agent came forward. He said that, while off-duty, he had been at Club Savage downtown with a friend until 0400 hours the morning of May 19th. He began driving north on the West Side Highway toward the George Washington Bridge. He was in the middle lane when, somewhere after the 125th Street exit, a white BMW (300 series) tore past him on his left side going at least 100 miles per hour. Immediately afterwards, a red pickup truck passed him on his right, going just as fast. Both cars were veering in and out of traffic. The agent slowed his car. A short while later, he heard a noise, as if the cars had passed over a grating. Then the red truck lost control, lurching from the far right to the far left lane of the highway, then back again. The BMW accelerated and disappeared. The agent next saw the red pickup at the safety zone of an exit. The agent's friend only partly confirmed this story, saying that he became aware of the highway ruckus when the pickup truck passed him at high speed, chased, it seemed, by a "fancy, late model car."

In the next few days the detectives pursued all the investigative steps typical of every homicide investigation. They pulled in all available bureaucratic nets, that is, the formal administrative records that are the stuff of modern life, those that routinely note commercial transactions, property holdings, or violations of rules. Dugan got a list of all 1989–91 white BMWs and all 1981–83 blue or white Chevrolet Monte Carlos registered in New York City and began the tedious process of sorting through the lists of owners. Detectives also set up a hot line to take all tips about the murder, a procedure appropriate only for cases that are extensively covered by the mass media. They sent out an accident investigation team to see if there were skid marks at the 57th Street ramp that might indicate that some near collision had occurred, but the busy highway was literally covered with skid marks. They interviewed the New York City sanitation supervisor in the area to see if, by chance, any workers had been assigned to duty in the 57th Street area in the early morning of May 19th. They canvassed that area for several nights in a row, hoping to find some squeegee men—down-and-outers who panhandle by washing car windows at traffic lights—or perhaps even some pedestrians who regularly haunted the area, who might have witnessed the altercation that Kevin said happened at the ramp. They examined Cargill's pickup truck and found no damage whatsoever either to the truck's front fender or to its rear bumper. They submitted the single bullet recovered from David Cargill's body to the ballistics laboratory; at first glance, the bullet seemed to be 9-millimeter but might have been .38-caliber. The detectives also went to Tarrytown to interview the owner of Lefty's bar. He said that at 1:30 AM on May 19th the bar had been jammed with Marymount college girls, along with college boys from various area schools. He didn't understand why Kevin said that the place was dead. Nothing seemed to fit, and the detectives' suspicions about Kevin's and John's stories deepened.

Detective work requires an alertness to people's inveterate routines, particularly habits tied to occupations. Therefore, the following Saturday night, one week after the shooting, the detectives went to midtown and interviewed scores of prostitutes up and down the area. Some of the women "made" the detectives as cops even before they were approached and ran away. Others were willing to talk in the easy give-and-take that prostitutes often develop with police, knowing that information now means a break later. One helpful citizen, probably one of the prostitutes scared off her beat, placed a 911 call to the Midtown North precinct, telling the dispatcher that men impersonating detectives were hassling the girls on Eleventh Avenue; a radio car responded, and Detectives Dugan and Dimuro had to identify themselves to the cops. Finally, the detectives talked with one pross who described an incident involving a red pickup with out-of-state plates. She said that three white boys had gotten out of the truck and propositioned one of the girls on the street to go to a nearby hotel; but when the boys became abusive, her pimp intervened and scared them away. Suddenly, the detectives thought they had the real scenario: a pross's customers get out of hand, her pimp steps in, a fight ensues with her pimp's honor offended, the pimp gets his gun, follows the customers onto the highway, and blows one of them away.

But when the detectives returned to Tarrytown on May 25th to interview other youngsters who had been at Joe's beer party, they discovered that five other boys, in two cars, had also gone down to midtown after the party to hunt for working girls, leaving Tarrytown at 0045 hours and meeting at the Intrepid Museum. One of the boys, Sam Crane, told the detectives that he had taken one of the cars alone in order to score with a pross. He met a girl at 47th Street and 11th Avenue. The couple had just started oral sex when a police radio car passed by. The girl jumped out of Sam's car. He followed, insisting that she finish what she had started. When she told him that it was over, he demanded his money back, and she refused. Suddenly, the girl's pimp came on the scene, the argument became heated, and the pimp went to his own car trunk and pulled out an automatic handgun. Sam backed down and the boys ended their night on the town at an all-night hamburger joint on 145th Street. Interviews with the four boys who accompanied Sam to Manhattan confirmed his story.

On May 30th, off-duty PO Mark Traumer was riding his motorcycle up the West Side Highway when he spotted a handgun on the side of the highway one-half mile short of the 158th Street exit. He retrieved the 9-millimeter weapon and took it to his sergeant at the Two-Eight precinct. After the sergeant notified the Three-O squad, Detectives Dugan and Maria Bertini from Manhattan North Homicide arranged for the ballistics laboratory to examine the weapon. But the check revealed that the weapon had not fired the bullet recovered from Cargill's body. The detectives initiated a track on the weapon.

Dimuro and Dugan went back to Tarrytown the following day to continue their interviews. Joe said that nothing unusual had occurred at his party on May 18–19 and that David Cargill had not mentioned anything about going to Manhattan that night. In fact, Joe said, Cargill and he had gone to Manhattan earlier that very Saturday to get haircuts, and he found it curious that David returned to the city that night. Joe added that John was a very level-headed guy. But the detectives heard from Chris, another party guest, that Joe and John had gone to Manhattan in December 1990 to hunt for prostitutes and that John was so drunk that he passed out, something that happened regularly.

The confusion deepened on June 2nd when Peter Burns, another young man from Tarrytown, voluntarily showed up at the Three-O squad. Peter said that he had been talking to a friend on May 28th who said that his ex-girlfriend had told him that Cargill's killer was a "crazy Dominican drug dealer who owns 125th Street" in Harlem. Peter said that his friend's ex-girlfriend had heard the story from her girlfriend who, in turn, had heard it from yet another source. Peter refused to provide any names, and when Dimuro pressed him to do so, he abruptly left the station house. Dimuro immediately asked Manhattan North Narcotics for a list of all Dominican drug dealers arrested in the vicinity of 125th Street, but there were no readily apparent leads. On June 11th, however, Dimuro received a call from a police unit near Tarrytown telling him that yet another man had come in, saying he had information on the Cargill homicide. With three other detectives, and in the presence of the witness's family, Dimuro interviewed Tony Hill, who said that three weeks earlier his ex-girlfriend, Jane Smith, had related to him a conversation that she had with Susie Beste. Susie had told Jane that her (Susie's) boyfriend, Ramon, knew the man who had shot David. The shooter was a Dominican who sold drugs on 125th Street and drove a light-colored BMW. David was killed for cutting off the drug dealer's car on the West Side Highway. Moreover, according to Susie, Ramon said that Cargill had had an argument with the shooter when the traffic incident occurred.

With Tony's help, Dimuro and Dugan found Jane a week later. She confirmed the story and provided the detectives with Susie's address. Jane added that Ramon had attended Manhattan College but had been expelled for stealing. The detectives went that same day to Manhattan College and scoured the school's security records for expulsions for theft. But the school had expelled few students, and none named Ramon. The detectives were hesitant to approach Susie directly until they had more information about Ramon, fearing that he might get raised up, that is, so apprehensive that he would refuse to divulge what he knew. They deputized Jane to find out more about Ramon through Susie. A few weeks later, Jane called Dimuro, saying that she had learned that Ramon now worked at Memorial Hospital, but she still had no last name. The detectives went to the hospital and discovered that one Ramon Cordoba had been hired on July 8th. They interviewed him, but he said that not only did he have no information whatsoever about the Cargill murder but that he had never heard of Susie. Cordoba seemed to be truthful, and the detectives pursued the matter no further with him.

At this point, given the unreliability of Jane's information, Dimuro felt that he had to approach Susie directly, whatever the hazards. When he interviewed her, she said that she had met David Cargill through Tony, who used to date her best friend, Jane. Her own boyfriend's name was Ramon Cortes, not Cordoba. He was a student at LaGuardia Community College, not Manhattan College, and he worked at Lenox Hill Hospital, not Memorial. Moreover, Ramon had said that the killer was a big-time drug dealer from the 204–216 Street area of Washington Heights, not from 125th Street in Harlem. After doing a routine Bureau of Criminal Investigation check on Ramon, which not only showed him to have no criminal record but to be on the waiting list for the police department, the detectives finally met Ramon on September 28. By this time, the trace on the 9-millimeter found on the highway had revealed that a black man had purchased the weapon, along with a half-dozen other firearms, in a tiny Texas town. The purchaser had given a Florida address, though one far removed from Daytona, where David Cargill attended school. Still, was it possible that Cargill himself had been armed when he drove down to the city the fateful night of May 18–19 and had somehow provoked the shooting on the highway? Perhaps Ramon had the answers.

But Ramon bluntly stated that he had no specific information about the Cargill murder. He said that he had talked to Susie about the incident only in very general terms, saying that the shooter was probably a drug dealer with whom Cargill had probably had a traffic dispute, which might have led to the murder. The detectives knew that Ramon was lying, but they had no hold on him and no way of forcing him to yield what he knew. On November 20th, Susie called Dimuro to say that she was sure that Ramon had specific knowledge of the murder.

Such methodical slogging, fits and starts, hopeful hints and false leads, contradictory stories and fourth-hand hearsay, concealment of double lives, unlikely coincidences, misinformation, and outright lies, as well as tantalizing, shadowy glimpses of what actually happened, are all typical experiences of detective work. Throughout the ups and downs of the investigation, the detectives were also deeply involved with Cargill's parents: the mother, Anne Love, beside herself with grief over the death of her only son and becoming increasingly distraught as the case dragged on; the father, D. Innis Cargill, a tough Scotsman, clear-headed even in this worst of times, a man who came to America with $20 in his pocket and a St. Andrews Ph.D., made a successful corporate career in the pharmaceutical industry, and then, with his wife, built a thriving biochemistry business. The Cargills called Dimuro regularly to learn what progress he had made on the case and occasionally to pass on information that had come their way, such as the report that a bouncer at a local club had been abusive to both David and Kevin. Detective Maria Bertini became an emotional anchor for the Cargill family, consoling Mrs. Cargill at all hours, day and night.

The police hot line received scores of calls, most of them anonymous crank calls, or calls from lonely people who wanted to talk to an authority figure, or calls accusing someone of the crime in order to settle a score, naming, for instance, "Reuben" as the shooter, or placing "Daniel" in the back seat of the BMW. One evidently enraged woman even put the gun in her boyfriend's hands. And there was the call from the elderly insomniac who regularly walked his dog in the early morning hours near the West Side Highway. The old man said that a bunch of wild Dominicans used to ride up and down the highway testing their weapons in the wee morning hours before going to Twin Donuts at 218th Street and Broadway for breakfast.

The case looked unsolvable. After many fruitless sixteen-hour days "off the chart," Dimuro went back to the routine of catching the cases that pour into any busy squad, from petit larceny, domestic abuse, serious assault, to homicides. Moreover, Dugan, along with the rest of the Manhattan North Homicide Squad, was buried with work. He was still working many murders from 1990, which had produced a New York City record of 2,262 killings; 1991, which ended with 2,166 homicides, was not far behind. Indeed, in 1991 the Three-Four precinct won the citywide ghoul-pool for the highest number of murders (122)—an honor wrested from the long-time champ, the Seven-Five precinct in Brooklyn. Dugan squeezed out time for the Cargill homicide whenever he could.

Suddenly, on November 27, 1991, Detective Edwin Driscoll of the Joint Auto Larceny Task Force, which was a combined FBI and NYPD operation, contacted Dimuro to say that he was working with a confidential informant who was giving him bits and pieces of information on the Cargill murder. The informant, who frequented the area of 174th Street and Audubon, told Driscoll that Cargill was indeed shot because he had cut off the shooter in a traffic incident on the West Side Highway. The informant claimed that the shooter and his associates, all from Washington Heights, "kill for the fun of it" and had many bodies to their names in Manhattan alone.

On December 13th Detective Driscoll and FBI Special Agent Jamie Cedeno circulated an extensive memorandum to several police units, including the Three-Four precinct squad, with more details; and three days later both met with Dimuro at the Three-O squad to review the Cargill case. Driscoll's and Cedeno's confidential source had overheard a conversation at 174th and Audubon about the highway murder. According to the source, Raymond Polanco, a well-known gun dealer from Brooklyn, had just sold weapons to Lenny Sepulveda aka Lenny Rodriguez and Wilfredo [Last Name Unknown] aka Platano, when Cargill cut off their car on the highway. Lenny decided to test out one of his newly purchased weapons.

The informant described Platano as an extremely dangerous contract killer who drove a white BMW convertible with a light blue rag top and New Jersey license plates. The JALTF investigators also linked Platano to a homicide on March 3, 1991, in the Four-Six precinct. A drug dealer known as RT hired Platano to kill a rival dealer who frequented a take-out chicken shop near Jerome Avenue in the Bronx. Platano did not know the intended victim. So, in a ride-around, RT pointed his rival out in front of the shop. Platano circled the block, got out of the car, and opened up on the dealer. As it happened, the dealer was wearing a full suit of Kevlar body armor underneath his clothes. Platano's bullets knocked the dealer down uninjured but riddled the body of 13-year-old Leideza Rivera, who, holding her mother's hand, was exiting the chicken shop right behind him. According to the informant, the child's death bothered Platano. He spoke about it constantly for weeks afterwards, saying: "This ain't the way it 'spozed to be." Honor in the streets requires worthy opponents. Dugan knew about the girl's killing because one day, earlier in the fall of 1991, a terrified woman had called him saying that she feared for the safety of her daughter, who was sexually involved with a violent man named Lenny, who, with a hit man called Platano, had killed a little girl in the Bronx. When Dugan heard the name Lenny, he rushed to interview the woman. Dugan had been looking at West 171st Street, Lenny Sepulveda's home base, and at West 174th Street and Audubon, Lenny's main hangout, for a long time. But when he met with the woman, the Lenny at issue was Lenny Ovalles aka RT, not Lenny Sepulveda.

The JALTF memorandum of December 13th went on to say that Lenny Sepulveda owned a crack spot on East 141st Street and Cypress Avenue, one block from Beekman Avenue, in the Four-O precinct of the Bronx. Sepulveda had recently pleaded guilty in fall 1991 to a 1989 gun possession charge and was currently in prison. The JALTF memorandum had Sepulveda housed at Rikers Island, doing normal "city time" for gun possession. But Dimuro and Dugan discovered that he was actually upstate in Ogdensburg, a maximum security prison, an assignment normally reserved for the most dangerous felons.

Hoping to arrest Lenny Sepulveda for the Cargill murder while he was still under the law's thumb, Dimuro called for mug shots of him and Raymond Polanco in order to get a photo identification from David Cargill's companions on the night he was killed. Detectives Tommy McCabe and Maria Bertini showed the photos of Sepulveda and Polanco to both Kevin and John. Although both Sepulveda and Polanco looked familiar to Kevin, he said he couldn't be sure. John could make no identification at all. Dimuro still had only hearsay to link Sepulveda and Polanco to the Cargill killing and therefore no way to proceed against them legally. Moreover, none of the Manhattan detectives knew yet who Platano was or where to find him.

On December 16, 1991, The Quad ravaged Mott Haven. Both the police "Unusual" report and the extensive media coverage of the slaughter pinpointed the East 141st Street and Beekman Avenue area of Mott Haven described in the JALTF memorandum. The citywide radio alert of December 21st from the Four-O squad alerted all police to watch for a dark-skinned Dominican male known as Platano driving a white BMW, and directed all information to Detective Mark Tebbens.

Detectives know that the answers to the riddles they seek

to unravel are in the streets. Criminals, like everyone else, are creatures of habit, and drug dealers are particularly attached to their automobiles; big-time dealers always own more than one car, and sometimes as many as a dozen, all kept in tip-top condition. The search of New York City ownership records, as well as a look at New Jersey records after Driscoll's and Cedeno's December 13th memorandum, had yielded nothing. So Dimuro teamed up with Dugan for regular ride-arounds in Washington Heights looking for Platano's white BMW. The detectives queried attendants in garage after garage about the car, always receiving blank looks and denials of all knowledge. But on January 6, 1992, the detectives went to the next garage on their list, on 174th Street, asking their now-routine questions about the white BMW. They received the standard response and, as always, they demanded the garage's manifest, listing all the cars regularly parked there; the list included a white BMW.

They left the garage to make surveillance arrangements, and as they drove east on 174th Street only one block away from the garage, they saw, right around the corner facing them, a white BMW with a light blue convertible top. Two men sat in the car, one a dark-skinned stocky Dominican and the other an American black. Although the car had Massachusetts plates, it had to be what they were looking for.

The detectives knew that if it was Platano in the car, he was heavily armed. There was no time to call for backup. Dimuro and Dugan quickly circled the block to come up behind the BMW. But when they came around, they found that the two men had fled, leaving the car in the street. The detectives inspected the car, and then Dimuro placed a call to the Four-O precinct to reach Mark Tebbens, who happened to be out in the field. When Tebbens got back in touch, Dimuro asked him whether he had enough evidence to arrest Platano, should the latter return to his car. Tebbens told Dimuro to make the collar. So Dimuro and Dugan sat on the BMW for

several hours until early morning. But then their bosses refused to authorize further overtime, and they were ordered to
go off-duty and return to their commands. The next morning,
the car was gone, as they knew it would be. They ran the
Massachusetts plates and learned that the BMW was registered
to Felipe Capellan with an address in Haverhill, Massachusetts. Capellan had a prior criminal record in both New Jersey
and New York and had an address on 162nd Street in Washington Heights. But although Capellan had a pending case for
assaulting a police officer, he was nowhere to be found at
the time.

Months later, Dimuro caught up with him right before his
sentencing for the assault and interviewed him. Capellan acknowledged that he knew Platano, who, he said, worked for
Lenny. Lenny had wanted to buy Capellan's white BMW for
Platano. Capellan feared Platano, so he gave him the car for a
test ride. But Platano kept the car for a year. When he returned
it, he demanded another car from Capellan. When Capellan
refused, Platano put three bullet holes in the driver's side of
the BMW. So Capellan just gave him the vehicle outright.

On January 11th, Detective Bertini contacted Mark Tebbens, telling him that she and Detective McCabe, both of
MNHS, were also looking for Platano in connection with the
Cargill homicide. On January 14th Tebbens took a ride over
to the Three-Four squad, where he met with Detective Joel
Potter of the Manhattan North Homicide Squad and Three-
Four squad detectives Marta Rosario and Gil Ortiz. The trio
showed Tebbens the December 13th JALTF memorandum that
discussed Platano's role in the Cargill homicide, along with
other crimes. The following day, Tebbens met Jerry Dimuro
for the first time at the Three-O squad, and they talked about
their common search for Platano.

By this time, Dimuro had become worried that the case far
exceeded the resources available to a precinct squad detective.
David Cargill's death seemed connected to much bigger events,

involving large drug operations and homicides in two different jurisdictions, the Bronx and Manhattan. Despite enormous pressure from immediate colleagues to keep control of the Cargill investigation, Dimuro decided to reach out beyond his own circle to broader networks with more clout. Dimuro knew Joel Potter fairly well, both as Garry Dugan's colleague on the Manhattan North Homicide Squad and as one of the lead investigators of the Jamaican "posses." From 1985 to 1990, these raucous gangs totally controlled Edgecombe Avenue in Dimuro's own Three-O precinct, strolling the street with sub-machine guns at the ready, jointing (dismembering) rivals or informers with hand saws while their victims were still alive, and leaving the heads of their victims wrapped in black plastic garbage bags for local kids to use as soccer balls. In the Jamaican investigation, Potter had worked closely with Assistant District Attorney Walter Arsenault of the Homicide Investigation Unit of the New York District Attorney's Office. Arsenault's astonishingly detailed knowledge of Jamaican gang members, who are endlessly inventive in falsifying true identities and fabricating new ones to befuddle law enforcement, helped bring the Jamaican gangs down through both state and federal prosecution.

Arsenault became chief of HIU in 1990. His whip was Terry Quinn, a bulldog of a man who grew up in a cold-water Brooklyn flat. Quinn was a twenty-year veteran of the NYPD who retired as the detective sergeant for the Manhattan North Homicide Squad, where he had been one of Joel Potter's and Garry Dugan's bosses. Quinn had a reputation as a tireless investigator, a relentless if not artful interviewer, a leader of men, and, by his own admission, the person who had solved every major crime in Manhattan within recent memory. Also, Dimuro's new sergeant in the Three-O detective squad was Louie Bauza, formerly a detective in the Three-Four, where he worked closely during 1991 with one of HIU's lead prosecutors, Assistant District Attorney Fernando Camacho, in piecing together the case against the Gerry Curls gang headed by the five Martinez brothers, whose organization had terrorized West 157th Street for several years. At Bauza's urging, Dimuro met with Camacho; and at both Camacho's and Potter's urging, he talked to Terry Quinn on January 21st, laying out all the information that he, Dugan, and the JALTF had gathered about the Cargill murder, complete with scenarios and players. A few days later, Quinn interviewed one of his own confidential informants, a small-time drug dealer from Washington Heights, who, along with the usual melange of half-baked street gossip and rumors, confirmed that "Lenny's Boys" were major drug and gun players both in upper Manhattan and in the Bronx. Quinn saw a big case in the making, one with David Cargill, an innocent victim of gang violence, at its very center.

In the meantime, on January 24, 1992, Harold Bickmore, the FBI agent who had been looking for Platano and his car, contacted Dimuro with further information. A confidential informant had told him that a man called Platano regularly got a white BMW convertible with blue top serviced at a garage in Englewood, New Jersey. According to the informant, the car contained two *clavos,* secret traps for transporting guns and drugs located in back seats, in trunks, in doors, under dashboards, or over the fuel tank. Clavos are usually equipped with sliding panels on hydraulic piston-like frames, which are opened and closed while the motor is running by the improbable simultaneous use of a number of instruments, such as the left directional signal coupled with the windshield wiper, brake, and air conditioner. Moreover, Platano had bragged on several occasions that he had committed the West Side Highway murder. Indeed, the informant estimated that Platano had killed at least 14 people.

The break came a week later. FBI Agent Bickmore received further information from his confidential informant that Platano transported drugs for an operation in the Bronx. Late on January 29, 1992, the informant tipped Bickmore that Platano was on a mission that very night. With his informant's help, Bickmore picked up Platano driving the white BMW in the Bronx and tailed him to Bergen County in New Jersey. There, Platano dropped the car off to be serviced in Englewood, and then hopped into a gypsy cab. The agent followed the cab, while radioing Bergen County police that he was tailing a suspect who, he had reason to believe, had drugs on his person. New Jersey State Trooper Brian Long joined the tail, stopped the cab on Route 95 in Fort Lee, and found ten ounces of cocaine on Platano's person, several bags of marijuana, and a concealed 9-millimeter weapon. Trooper Long arrested Platano and took him to the Totowa Barracks; Bickmore called Dimuro with the news.

Dimuro and Dugan raced over to Bergen County early the next morning to talk to Platano before he got a lawyer. Although the man had given the name Paul Santiago when arrested, he had a piece of identification in his belongings with the name Wilfredo de los Angeles. He acknowledged that people called him Platano. He had no record of arrests and, according to Dugan, "behaved like a scared child" in custody. The detectives were, in fact, confronting Platano at an extremely vulnerable moment: he had no direct experience with the system, and as soon as he hit the pens other prisoners had begun sizing him up. For all he knew, he faced many years of imprisonment because of the drug arrest, and he had no idea how much detectives knew about his criminal activities.

When detectives confronted Platano with reports that placed him in a white BMW at the Cargill homicide, Platano gave and later signed the following statement, written out by Detective Dugan:

> This is in reference to last May of 1991. At that time, I
> was hanging around with Lenny Rodriguez and Raymond

Polanco. Raymond is from Brooklyn and he sells guns. Raymond had sold a box of guns to Lenny. The box was the size of a milk crate. One of the guns, and they were all Uzis, was not working properly. Raymond had altered them all to operate on a "fully automatic" position. Lenny paid a lot of money for the guns. Raymond took the bad Uzi back to work on it. Lenny runs a drug operation in the Bronx at Cypress and 141st Street. Lenny said that he was going to use the Uzis if there was a drug war. Lenny would pay Stanley Black to take care of any problems that would occur with the drug spot.

About one week after Raymond took the Uzi back to repair it, I went out with my girlfriend Maria Sanchez [a pseudonym]. It was on a Saturday night. I drove her in a white BMW, which belonged to my friend, Felipe Capellan. I'm watching the car for him while he's in jail. We went to the Limelight Club on 20th Street in Manhattan. We got there about 12:30 AM. About one half an hour later, Lenny arrived with Raymond and Frankie. I don't know Frankie's last name, but he owns the 20 de Mayo Restaurant on St. Nicholas Avenue between 173rd and 174th Streets. After they arrived, I stayed at the bar with Maria. The reason that we stayed at the bar was because we were having drinks that cost $7 each, and Lenny, Raymond, and Frankie were drinking champagne at $150 a bottle.

I'm not sure of the time, but about 3:30 AM, I left with Maria and walked one block, around the corner, to the parking lot, to get the BMW, a convertible with a light blue top. As we were pulling out of the parking lot, I saw Lenny, Frankie, and Raymond coming into the lot to get their car. The car that they were using is a 1987 Chevrolet Caprice, 4 door. It is two-tone in color, burgundy and maroon on the bottom. It is a "chop car." The car belonged to Raymond. He changed the ID number and had the engine souped up with a "nitro" button installed. This is a special tank installed in the trunk, which fuels the engine with a high power fuel, when the button is pushed.

As we left the parking lot, I drove to the West Side Highway and drove north. Then I continued north towards the ramp which leads up to the elevated highway at 57th Street. By the time I got to the ramp, Lenny, Raymond, and Frankie had already caught up to me. At the bottom of the ramp, as I proceeded to go up, a red pickup truck came out of 57th Street and made a wide turn into the ramp, and almost struck my BMW. The red pickup ended up in the right lane, and the maroon/burgundy Chevrolet was behind it with Lenny, Raymond, and Frankie in it. The pickup truck continued up the ramp in the right lane. It almost hit my BMW, but we never collided. As we got to the top of the ramp, the red pickup started to drive ahead of me. Then I looked into my rear view mirror, and saw the Chevrolet Caprice coming up in the right lane. Frankie was driving the car and Lenny was in the passenger side of the front seat. I continued driving in the far left lane, ahead of the red pickup and the Chevrolet Caprice. After about two exits, I saw Frankie move into the far right side and go around the pickup truck which was now in the middle lane. Frankie passed the truck and pulled into the middle lane, ahead of the truck. Frankie then slowed down with the pickup still behind it. Then Frankie moved into the far left lane, which allowed the pickup to pull up next to it. Then I heard a large amount of shots being fired quickly. I looked into my mirror and saw flashes coming out of the right window of the Chevrolet Caprice. The truck was still going forward, but then I lost sight of it. Then, I didn't see the Chevrolet any more. I think they got off at another exit.

I continued north on the West Side Highway up to the Dyckman Street exit. I drove to Broadway and continued north to the Twin Donut Shop at 218th Street and Broadway. Maria and I went in and got some cheeseburgers. Then I took her to my house where she stayed with me.

The next night (Sunday), I went down to the movie theater at 48th Street and Broadway. I think that Maria was with me. It was about 9:45 PM. The movie was to start at 10 PM, but I don't recall the name of the movie. I pulled up to the curb to look and see what time the movie started and I saw Raymond in front of the theater with two of his friends. One of them is Louie from Brooklyn and the other was a black guy. Raymond saw me first and he came over to the car. He said: "Yo, did you see what happened?" I said: "I heard something but . . ." He said: "Did you see what we did last night?" I said: "Yo, you people are crazy!" Raymond extended his hands out to his sides and smiled. Then he hissed with laughter. Then I went to park the car. Raymond left because he had already seen the movie.

The next Wednesday afternoon after that about 4:00 PM, I was up on 177th Street between Broadway and Wadsworth Avenue, with the white BMW. I was passing by. I saw Lenny in front of the lot. I stopped the car and shook hands with him. He was with two of his friends who play football in the park above Dyckman Street. I don't know their names. After his friends walked away, I said to Lenny: "What happened that day?" Lenny laughed and said: "I was testing that gun that jams!" After that, Lenny didn't talk about it anymore. After that, I heard other people saying that Raymond was bragging about the shooting of the pickup truck on the West Side Highway. I never spoke to Frankie about it.

The detectives knew Polanco as the major gun dealer from Brooklyn. "Frankie" had to be Franklin Cuevas aka Gus or Fat Frankie, who had been released from prison in November 1989 after serving nine years for burglary and assault. Cuevas, with his brother Miguel, owned the 20 de Mayo Restaurant at 173rd Street and St. Nicholas, a gathering place for drug dealers from Washington Heights. Dugan also knew that Cuevas had his own drug operation at Manor and Watson, the drug hub of the Bronx's Four-Three precinct.

According to Platano's account, David Cargill's death was just the result of a wildly improbable coincidence, a college boy's bad-luck blunder into a caravan of drug dealers feeling their oats after a night of drinking. But Platano's self-exculpation, along with the discrepancies between his story and Kevin Kryzeminski's version of events, made Dimuro and Dugan wary. From detectives' standpoint, criminals lie all the time, even to each other, but especially to the police. Even as they lie, however, criminals also give up part of the truth. The question is always: which part is which? Was Cargill already on the highway in his truck, or did he just enter the highway at 57th Street? Was the shooter's car a light-colored Monte Carlo or a maroon/burgundy Caprice? If the shooter was Lenny Sepulveda, who was actually in the car with him? If Platano turned out to be a participant in the shooting and not just an associate who happened to witness it, under New York State law his statement could not be used against Lenny Sepulveda without independent corroboration. Moreover, what should the detectives do about Raymond Polanco, who, in Platano's account, was the supplier of the murder weapon and occupant of the same car as the shooter, certainly making him an accomplice? Independent corroboration was also necessary in Polanco's case. Finally, why did the fearsome Platano give up Lenny so quickly, even though he knew, as he told the detectives, that Lenny would kill him if he ever discovered the betrayal?

As soon as they left Platano, Dimuro and Dugan went to the Bronx to see Platano's girlfriend, Maria Sanchez. The foyer of Maria's spacious apartment held a huge water tank filled with fish. An unidentified young woman sat on the floor of a barren living room. All the other rooms were also completely unfurnished, except for one bedroom that contained a large bed and accompanying side tables. Maria took the detectives into that room and sat on the bed. She was completely baffled when the detectives asked her if she had been with Platano near the West Side Highway on May 19th. Then, even as the detectives were talking with her, Platano called her several different times from jail, speaking in Spanish so excitedly that detectives could overhear the conversation. After the third call, Maria began pulling out and then shutting the deep drawer of one of the side tables, making sure that the detectives saw that it was jammed with cash, more money than Garry Dugan had ever seen in one place before. With each call, Maria changed her story until it was hopelessly confused, saying in the end that late one night she had been with Wilfredo on the West Side Highway when they heard shots in the distance. She also said she had never heard anyone call Wilfredo "Platano." As the conversation ended, Dugan noticed an addressed envelope on the bed; he sat down next to Maria and, before she realized what he was doing and removed it from view, he surreptitiously read the Manor Avenue address; the building's number, Dugan knew, was near Manor and Watson in the Bronx.

The detectives wanted to arrest Platano just to keep him off the streets, but they had nothing solid on which to hold him. His admission of knowledge of the Cargill homicide only made him a witness, not legally culpable. Moreover, Mark Tebbens, when informed that Platano was in custody, could not obtain an arrest warrant for his participation in The Quad from the Bronx district attorneys; prosecutors felt that the witnesses tying Platano to those murders were problematic at best. One of the hazards of detective work is knowing the ferocity of the Platanos of this world but being unable to prove it in court under the intricate legal rules of evidence. Platano quickly lawyered up, first with Elliot Fuld of Goldstein, Weinstein & Fuld, but then, after discharging Fuld, with a New Jersey lawyer, Robert Rosenberg. On February 4th Maria Sanchez and another young woman bailed Platano out of jail with $45,000 in cash; after leaving the court, the two girls went directly to the garage in Englewood that housed the white BMW, entered the car, got out, and then departed in a cab, leaving the BMW where it was. Platano did not go with the women but instead took a cab from the jail to an unknown location. A week later FBI Agent Bickmore's informant reported that Platano was on his way to Florida to ditch the white BMW. The informant also said that, because the NYPD had not arrested him while he was in the Bergen County jail, Platano felt confident that the police had no hard evidence linking him to any crimes.

Two days before Platano's release, Dugan and Dimuro drove eleven hours to Ogdensburg to talk with Lenny Sepulveda. Lenny told the detectives that he was represented by Barry Weinstein of Goldstein, Weinstein & Fuld. Initially, Lenny said to the detectives: "Is this about that Yeshiva shit?" Years before there had been a drive-by shooting at Yeshiva University in the Three-Four precinct that killed one rabbinical student and one security guard. Suspicion centered on a bunch of Dominican kids from the area of 135th–155th Streets who called themselves The Ballbusters. Although an entire task force was assembled to investigate the case, police had never cleared the shooting. After that single opening question, however, Lenny talked only about the irrationality of a New York City Dominican boy being sent to the freezing wilds of the Canadian border. It turned out that his sojourn in near-Arctic weather was due only to an overflow at Rikers Island.

fort
"yo no
sé!"

By early 1992, only a couple of months after The Quad in th

Bronx, it was becoming clear to detectives that a drug war had broken out on the streets of Manhattan's Three-Four precinct. As usual, most of the trouble centered in Washington Heights—the lower end of the precinct extending from 155th to 181st Street. Between 181st and 186th Streets, old Fort Washington, the last outpost to resist the British invasion of Manhattan Island during the American Revolution, once stood. After it fell on November 16, 1776, the British occupied Manhattan for seven years.

Washington Heights used to be an Irish-American enclave with some pockets of German Jews, though most of the latter lived in Inwood at the north end of the precinct. Since the 1960s Washington Heights has become home to waves of immigrants from the Dominican Republic. The surging sidewalk crowds, the clusters of men on street corners playing dominoes on makeshift tables, the blare of *merengue* music everywhere mingling with trumpetlike tunes from the horns of scores of gypsy cabs, the raft of *joyerías, bodegas, casas de cambio, envíos de valores,* the early-blooming, magenta or purple-lipsticked dusky girls in red shoes, with bracelet-sized gold earrings, speaking distinctively rough Spanish with raspy endings, or the boisterous hawkers on every main street, selling peeled oranges, or *helados,* or sticks of sugar cane, or sweaters, socks, compact discs in endless supply, and the markets redolent with the smells of mangoes and ripe plantains, garlicky yellow rice with *gandules verdes* cooking on open fires on sidewalks, all

Map 5. Washington Heights

This map covers only Washington Heights proper. In 1992 the
34th Precinct covered the entire sprawling river-to-river tip of
Manhattan from 155th Street to the Spuyten Duyvil, where the
Harlem River empties into the Hudson.

make one think that one has suddenly been transported to Santo Domingo.

Most Dominican immigrants fit the classic profile of hard-working, upwardly striving newcomers to America. Many Dominican immigrants arriving in the 1960s ended up in garment-industry sweatshops in Manhattan's fashion district or in cottage sewing industries in their own homes. Others opened the small businesses, restaurants, or social clubs that cram the narrow streets of Washington Heights. But some Dominicans make their living outside the law. No one, least of all the completely inundated Immigration and Naturalization Services, can provide accurate statistics for the total number of Dominicans in Washington Heights (estimates range from 250,000 to 700,000), let alone for the number of illegal aliens among them. Yet everyone who works in the community knows that the number of illegals is large. Precinct detectives regularly encounter the problem of illegals during their investigations of other matters.

Illegals generate illegality. The remarkable largess of the United States, the porousness of its social controls, and its unparalleled cultural license seem to many an invitation for exploitation. First, illegals need "legal" identities. Thus, Washington Heights hosts occupations, sometimes whole industries, that specialize in identity construction, so that illegal immigrants have the requisite documents to apply for legal benefits such as welfare, social security, medicare, and medicaid. Some travel agencies sell identity kits for about $400, complete with a bank letter verifying one's good credit standing, a social security card, IRS W-2 forms, and pay stubs from fictitious companies to demonstrate a record of employment. Phony green cards alone go for $400 apiece. Passports are the most prized identity-conferring document; in Washington Heights, blank Dominican passports usually sell at $3000 apiece. But one can also assume the identity of, say, a person who has died, or one who has gone to prison, or one who is leaving the country, by obtaining some legal identity document belonging to that person, such as a Human Resources Administration welfare benefits card, altering the photograph and other details as necessary, and then using the forged document to apply to other government bureaucracies, such as the Department of Motor Vehicles or the federal Social Security Administration, to validate one's assumed identity. Those who construct new identities usually retain the requisite documents to reassume their old identities as needed. Thus, depending on one's resourcefulness and propensity for deception, one can maintain any number of bureaucratically validated identities. The physical effects of homicide victims on the far side of the law in Washington Heights often include documents validating multiple identities.

Even rationalized systems for identifying and tracking persons, such as systematized fingerprinting, may unintentionally confer multiple identities. Fingerprint imaging systems, now in use for tracking criminals as well as welfare recipients, are only as good as the original fingerprints and the carefulness with which they were processed. Approximately one percent of all New York State identification numbers that state officials in Albany issue to arrested criminals on the basis of fingerprints are duplicates. Such mistakes are due, variously, to careless cops taking the original prints at station houses, or to clever criminals who know how to use Chapstick or Vaseline or simply a quick turn of the wrist to smudge their prints and make them unreadable, or to sleepy clerks in Albany who miss matches and issue a new number to a seasoned criminal under an alias. Such inadvertent conferral of multiple identities can be a bonanza, particularly for violent felons who, when arrested, get treated as if they are in the dock for a first offense.

In addition to requiring illegal documents, illegals enter or create illegal occupations in disproportionate numbers. These, in turn, require a network of illegal services. Thus car-theft rings need chop shops to dismantle cars and distribute the parts to stores all over the country, or shipping companies to crate and export intact luxury cars to the Caribbean or Latin America. Gun dealers and drug dealers need cars with *clavos.* The drug trade also needs laundries to wash dirty money, as well as a steady supply of still more illegals, young men from backwater towns-on-the-make willing to use extreme violence as a tool-in-trade in exchange for great rewards.

Washington Heights has long been the hub of the New York City cocaine trade, with Dominican dealers retailing coke imported wholesale by Cali-cartel Colombians based in Jackson Heights, Queens. In 1985 Washington Heights gave the world crack, a combination of cocaine, baking soda, and various additives, such as Bacardi rum, to provide flavor or extra kick, baked together into rocklike form and smoked in glass pipes. Its name derives from the crackling sound it makes when being smoked. Crack provides an instantaneous rush, followed by a thundering crash—a combination that is powerfully addictive. Of the several crack distribution rings flourishing in the Heights in the mid-1980s, police investigators and federal agents alike name Based Balls (called Baseballs on the street), a ring centered at 174th near Audubon, as singularly important. Official sources say the ring was run by two half-brothers, Santiago Luis Polanco-Rodriguez aka Yayo and Santiago Antonio Ysrael Polanco-Polanco aka Chi Chi, assisted by their enforcer Jose Roberto Mejia-Nunez aka Capo. Street legend has Yayo and Capo as the bosses, with Yayo as the actual inventor of crack. Whatever his pharmacological inventiveness, no one disputes Yayo's personal authority or the marketing ethos that, it seems, he set in motion. Long after Yayo fled to the Dominican Republic, he is still called the "King of Crack," and young men still talk about his visits to his spots in his gray hardtop-convertible Mercedes. Moreover, crack made in Washington Heights came to be sold not only throughout all of New York City but as far south as the Carolinas and as far north as Toronto.

On its surface, the drug underworld seems to be, and in fact often is, dark, forbidding, and entirely irrational and unknowable. But it actually consists of interconnected occupational communities governed by their own peculiar rules. It is this social reality that makes detective work possible. The most important rule in this world of action is that violence is the first resort to solve all problems. The drug trade breeds an extraordinary amount of violence and mayhem, and the most visible and verifiable index of drug-related violence is homicide counts. A systematic, detailed analysis of homicides and drug-related homicides in the 34th precinct for the seven-year period between 1987 and 1993 yields several patterns (see table).

The first and most obvious pattern is that 27.44 percent (104/379) of drug-related homicides in Washington Heights emerge directly and spontaneously out of robberies gone bad. Robbers go where the money is, and the drug trade in Washington Heights, as elsewhere, generates vast sums of cash. Apart from always brief periods of police crackdowns, much of Washington Heights, like many other neighborhoods throughout the city, was an open-air drug market from about 1985 through 1993, the result of several coinciding factors— the police department's restriction of narcotics arrests to specialized units because of fear of corruption; a growing street sophistication that exploited such bureaucratization; full prisons and revolving-door courtrooms; a political tolerance of flagrant disregard for the law in certain sections of the city that inevitably affected police policies; and, of course, the unquenchable demand for drugs.

Now much of the drug trade has moved indoors, but scores of steerers still stand on every block between 159th and 175th Streets, from Amsterdam to Broadway, directing buyers to drug-sale apartments in once-grand buildings. An average drug-

34th Precinct Homicides and Drug-Related Homicides, 1987–1993

Year	Homicides	Drug-related homicides	Percent of drug-related to total
1987	57	32	56%
1988	75	49	65%
1989	99	53	53%
1990	109	67	61%
1991	122	68	55%
1992	100	67	67%
1993	76	43	56%
Totals:	638	379	59%

sale apartment, selling either crack or powder cocaine, grosses between $15,000 and $25,000 per day. In addition to their sale apartments, big-time dealers retain two additional apartments in the same building, one a stash where they keep their drug supplies and cash receipts, and the other a safe house where they retreat when police raid the building. Safe houses are frequently the residences of elderly women who, in exchange for rent money, not only provide a ready refuge but also prepare food for the dealers and their regular customers. After a "weight" sale, stash apartments often have as much as $400,000 on hand, concealed in elaborately disguised floor compartments with trapdoors.

Such sums of money, along with caches of readily marketable narcotics and guns, make drug spots desirable targets for various kinds of robber crews. For instance, groups of young black men from northern New Jersey or Bridgeport, Connecticut, often related by blood or through sexual relationships with one another's sisters, regularly journey to Washington Heights to prey on Dominican drug dealers. Other crews, consisting usually of Dominican or Puerto Rican young men,

come together more haphazardly on local playgrounds in robber "shape-ups," where street reputations determine who gets
a piece of the action. Robber crews of both of these sorts
usually possess more physical brawn and courage than organizational sophistication. Their *modus operandi* consists essentially of scouting a sale apartment while making a preliminary
buy, returning under the pretense of making a larger score, and
then robbing the dealers for whatever is on hand, sometimes
torturing them to reveal the locations of their stash apartments. Detectives in the Three-Four precinct regularly see
badly injured or dead dealers with ears missing, torsos scarred
with cigarette burns or knife cuts, or genitals scorched by
curling irons. In summer 1992 one surviving drug dealer was
brought into the Three-Four station house with a metal drill
bit protruding from his skull.

Occasionally, robberies by such crews go badly and end in
wild melees, either because of the robbers' sheer ineptitude
and lack of planning or because the robbers are simply out-
gunned by always well-armed drug dealers. Bystanders or bit
players such as drivers sometimes get caught in the crossfire.
If the robbers are local, they fear the swift and final retaliation that later recognition by their victims will provoke, so
with some frequency they murder the dealers they rob. Once
robbed, dealers become overly cautious and, in anticipatory
retaliation, kill potential customers whom they merely suspect are about to rob them. In several cases, whole neighborhoods have joined dealers in chasing bungling robbers, killing
them in full public view right in the street.

When a robbery turns into a homicide, detectives may un-
cover its drug-relatedness in the course of the homicide investigation. In all likelihood, however, robberies that end in homicide represent only a small fraction of drug-related robberies.
A great many robberies in Washington Heights are drug-related, such as petty muggings of citizens wholly unconnected
to the drug trade in order to obtain money for drug use, but

there are no statistics kept on this issue. Certainly, neither drug dealers nor robbers report crimes committed against them in the course of robberies. Police receive reports of such incidents only when murder or debilitating assaults requiring involuntary hospitalization occur, and in the latter cases victims usually tell fantastic stories ("Walkin' down Broadway and a dude I never seen before comes up and shoots me in the stomach") to explain their injuries, blocking further investigation. Dealers and robbers alike also exhibit a fatalistic, almost insouciant indifference to physical injuries and, against all medical advice, often check out of the hospital even when they are gravely wounded.

A second major pattern one can discern is that 33.24 percent (126/379) of drug-related homicides in Washington Heights between 1987 and 1993 are cases of murder as a rational business tool. Some of these murders occur during robberies carried out by sophisticated robber crews that are wholly owned subsidiary operations, or collateral enterprises, of drug dealers. Wily dealers keep track of the movement of drugs in their geographical areas and bribe workers in rival operations to disclose stash locations. With the information, they send their robbery division to appropriate money, drugs, and guns and to dispatch not only their rivals but, almost always, their informants as well. Or dealers send their robbery division to take back drugs that they have just sold, a strategy that enables one to keep a retail business flourishing even when inventory is low. Or robber crews lie in wait for Colombian "mules" delivering drugs, rob and murder the couriers, and then hand over the drugs to their dealer-bosses, who claim to their Colombian suppliers that delivery was never made because of the regrettable lawlessness of the streets.

Because it simultaneously eliminates immediate encroachments and boosts one's reputation, murder as a rational business tool helps guarantee one's bailiwick against one's competitors. The competition for customers who flock to

Washington Heights from outside the area, as well as competition for local trade, is fierce. Prices for all drugs in the Heights are the lowest in the country. In general, the structure of the trade is highly decentralized, with territorial subdivisions on some blocks (for instance, in the low 160s near Broadway) demarcated building by building. While street steerers are expected to be, and in fact are, extremely aggressive in advertising their employers' wares, there is a general rule against poaching outside of one's recognized territory, which shifts depending upon others' perceptions of one's strength and ruthlessness. The ethos of the streets demands that extreme violence, or its attempts, not go unrequited, however, so territorial battles almost always become entangled with the ongoing struggles for honor at the core of street life. Murder demands retaliation, which in turn demands more murder.

But what is rational for one drug dealer operating in the highly decentralized crack trade in Washington Heights becomes wildly irrational for the community as a whole. Crossfire shootings of bystanders, while they only occasionally result in homicides, invariably provoke public outrage that permits and demands police crackdowns, however temporary. It is bad for the drug business itself when business strife and its accompanying claims of honor spill out onto public streets.

Drug dealers use violence in a rational way not just to maintain their territory against encroachers but also to settle internal organizational problems. One must always keep one's employees and one's debtors in line, punishing, sometimes severely, workers who skim drugs or money or who handle competitors' products on the side. The more crackheads one employs, the more tapping of vials (stealing the crack, replacing it with soap flakes or milk sugar, and selling these dummies) one must expect. But if one's customers complain or, worse, if one's workers begin to whisper that one is soft, catastrophe is just around the corner. One can lose one's business or become prey for robbers who smell an easy mark. The proper way of handling debtors who renege on high-interest loans, which afford one of many ways of laundering drug money, varies. Some debtors have valuable assets, like legitimate businesses bought with drug money, that one can simply appropriate without further complications. Sometimes one can persuade a debtor to find requisite funds by, say, killing his brother as a warning. But some bad debtors must themselves be eliminated, usually because debtors' own community connections make inaction against them appear as weakness or irresoluteness. Moreover, some bad debtors also pose another kind of threat. Debtors sometimes hire assassins to kill their creditors as a convenient way of reducing exorbitant interest rates and principals at once.

Much of this violence, whether external or internal to any particular drug organization, is carried out by semispecialized hit men or enforcers. Hit men are, of course, expected to be loyal to their bosses, but their bosses often loan them out to other dealers or give them permission to hire themselves out for the wet work, that is, the extreme violence of the drug trade.

A third pattern: 14.77 percent (56/379) of drug-related homicides in Washington Heights between 1987 and 1993 emerge from spontaneous emotional disputes among business associates. Some of these homicides are business-related, but the spontaneity of the violence distinguishes them from more calculated murders. For instance, on December 24, 1988, Cuba and Diego, both drug dealers, got into an argument. Cuba owed a third party, Burrito, money; Burrito owed Diego money. Diego felt that Cuba should just pay him (Diego) directly. Cuba disagreed, arguing that if he didn't pay Burrito directly the latter would still claim the debt. The argument escalated, with insults exchanged, and Diego ended up shooting Cuba.

The personal conflicts that mark all human relationships seem particularly exacerbated both within and between the informal crews of individuals who come together in the drug trade. The small disagreements, personal rivalries, competition with one's peers for prestige, for the realities and symbols of power, and for others' deference, fights over females' affections, assertions of masculinity, and quarrels about honor all regularly explode into violence in the drug world. The streets, nightspots, and social clubs that drug dealers haunt are arenas of action, not of words, social spaces with their own shifting hierarchies where appearance, style, mastery of urban cool, and perceived hardness bring one local fame and especially the envy of others, a key ingredient of prestige.

Across these three main categories of drug-related homicides, one discovers many skeins of interconnected murders involving the same people. One series of examples must suffice. On January 21, 1987, Curtis Cason aka Country was killed while trying to stick up a crack dealer, Billy Davis. Country's accomplice was said to be Larry Munroe aka Froggy, who escaped harm. On June 2, 1987, Froggy and someone named Green Eyes became the prime suspects in the robbery and murder of an unidentified drug dealer on West 164th Street. The same day, Froggy witnessed and gave a statement to police about the murder of Sylvester Townes, beaten to death by three men who came to rob a crack house that Froggy frequents. On September 3, 1987, Froggy, accompanied by John Boston, robbed and killed Arcadio Reyes on West 160th Street. On September 17th, Boston and Froggy attempted unsuccessfully to rob a drug spot on West 163rd Street; Boston, who used 16 aliases, and whose criminal record included 36 arrests for murder, robbery, and burglary, was killed and thrown out of a window. Froggy escaped harm. On April 11, 1990, Froggy, in the company of Tracy Lang, and two men named T and 26, robbed a drug apartment on West 161st Street, killing Ramon Rosa. The following day, Froggy, with the same crew, robbed another apartment on West 169th Street, killing Rafael Santos. Police apprehended both Froggy and Tracy and they confessed to the last two homicides. In brief, another rule in the world of drug-related murder is: today's witness is tomorrow's culprit is yet another tomorrow's victim or convict.

One can discern a couple of minor patterns in addition to the three major ones. Only 5.27 percent (20/379) of the drug-related homicides in Washington Heights between 1987 and 1993 are induced by drug consumption. Sometimes homicides induced by drug consumption are accidental, as when a young girl delivering hot food to a drug apartment is shot through the door by a dealer, who, crazed by his own product, mistakes her timid knock for the usual thunder of the police. But more typically, drug-induced homicides emerge out of personal disputes between addicts. So, in a classic case, a woman crack addict burns down the crack apartment that she frequents in order to avenge perceived maltreatment from some of her regular cronies. But they have already left, and she ends up killing two other addicts instead. Or Junebug and Nelson, both with their skulls blasted by free-basing cocaine, start arguing over a pipe that both claim as their own. Junebug, reaching for his satchel, tells Nelson to take the pipe if he is man enough. Nelson, thinking Junebug is reaching for a gun, pulls his own gun, saying: "You don't know who you fuckin' with." Junebug tries to leave the apartment; Nelson follows and shoots him three times, saying later that even if Junebug didn't die (which he did), at least he would be paralyzed for life.

Of course, drug dealers also use drugs, but typically only marijuana and powdered cocaine. Crack use is generally prohibited among serious players in the trade; crackheads, often called "meat" by dealers, are considered debased, weak, and even subhuman. Although any sort of drug use exacerbates the recklessness and aggression central to the ethos of violence that rules the drug underworld, drug use in and of itself does not cause these patterns of violence.

As a second minor pattern, 1.31 percent (5/379) of drug-related homicides were police killings of drug dealers ruled justifiable by grand juries.

Finally, the causes for 17.94 percent (68/379) of the homicides in Washington Heights during this period are simply
unknown, although it is clear in every case (whether because
of location of the murder, identity and criminal pedigree of
the victim, or physical evidence at the scene) that they are
drug-related. Several were probably robberies accompanied by
murder; many were execution-style murders (hands bound or
cuffed, two in the head), with the bodies dumped in remote
corners of the Three-Four precinct; some were in all likelihood
retaliations for real or rumored past offenses. In some cases,
detectives did a poor investigation; in others, they did only a
cursory investigation. But in most cases, detectives did a cred-
itable and thorough analysis of all leads, yet came up with
nothing because they had only lying witnesses or no witnesses
at all, or their informants provided contradictory accounts or
there were no informants, or local upstanding citizens with
knowledge about specific crimes universally responded to the
police: "Yo no sé!" (I don't know!)

Why is such stonewalling about criminal violence prevalent in Washington Heights? What resentments
does it create among police who are left to clean up the messes?
At about 2135 hours on October 18, 1988, POs Michael Buczek
and Joseph Barbato were patrolling the precinct's sector Charlie, just east of Broadway in the low 160s. They responded to
an "aided" call of a Dominican woman complaining of stomach pains at 580 West 161st Street, Apartment #22. The officers double-parked their car and went upstairs to check on the
woman; the several women attending the sick woman told
the officers that medical help was on its way. Unneeded, the
officers started to leave the building, pausing to talk with EMS
technicians who had just arrived in the lobby. One of the
technicians asked Buczek how undercover PO Chris Hoban
was faring. Hoban had been shot earlier that evening on 105th

Street near Manhattan Avenue while posing as a drug dealer making a buy. Buczek responded: "Not so good."

Just then three Dominican men, one of them carrying a bulky black bag, came down the stairs into the lobby, walked around the officers, and left the building hurriedly. Because the bag looked suspicious, Buczek asked the men to stop, but they quickened their pace and headed west toward Broadway on the south side of West 161st Street. The officers tried to overtake them on foot, with Buczek in front of Barbato. On Broadway, just around the corner heading south, only two of the men were in sight. Buczek grabbed one of them. Barbato came around the corner, saw his partner in a struggle, and tried to apprehend the second. But that man suddenly turned, gun in hand, and began to fire toward both officers. The man Buczek was holding fled down Broadway, his arm bleeding. Barbato dove to the ground unharmed, drew his own weapon, and shot four times at the now-fleeing assailant. But one of the assailant's bullets had hit Buczek in the chest. He fell to the ground face first. Barbato ran back to Buczek. He threw himself on top of Buczek to protect his partner from further harm, but the gesture proved futile. Michael Buczek died at 2231 hours in the emergency room at Columbia Presbyterian Hospital.

The Buczek murder spurred the most highly organized and thorough police investigation in recent memory. It exposed the patterns of violence endemic to the drug trade, and also some disturbing patterns in the Dominican immigrant community. From the start, apart from the usual spate of anonymous calls to Copshot with street rumors and false accusations, investigators received very little cooperation from the mainstream Dominican community in finding Buczek's killers, much to cops' disgust. The essential problem, investigators discovered, was that a great many Dominicans think of themselves precisely, and only, as Dominicans. Although Dominicans have streamed to the United States to escape the grinding poverty of their homeland, less than a third of the large Dominican immigrant population in the Heights ever apply for United States citizenship. Even many second-generation Dominicans, who are American citizens by birth, still nurture, at this stage of their immigrant experience, dreams of eventually returning to their island paradise in the Caribbean, prosperous from high American wages or welfare monies or crime. Dominicans legally repatriate more than $800 million a year to support their families, indeed whole towns of relatives, in the Dominican Republic or to feather future nests.

A Dominican motto is: "Un pie aquí, un pie allá" (One foot here, one foot there). Such a sentiment resonates with American society's current obsession with racial and ethnic identities, complete with social policies that reward particularistic standards of reckoning, providing little incentive for reluctant immigrant groups to abandon quasi-tribal loyalties. In particular, the young men from San Francisco de Macoris, or Santiago, or Santo Domingo, the places of origin of a great many victims and culprits in drug-related homicide cases in the Three-Four precinct, are almost all illegal aliens who fully expect to return to the Dominican Republic as rich men after a few years of hazardous work. The loyalties of these DominicanYorks, as they are called, to American society and its institutions are tenuous at best. Indeed, this sector of the Dominican immigrant community sees American society through the lens of their island experiences. In particular, they look with derision at the fantastically elaborate procedural apparatus that governs the United States' legal system and police. In the Dominican Republic, the residue of its long history of strong-man rule scarcely erased by thirty-odd years of democracy, such institutions are stringently authoritarian. American procedural carefulness, when seen from the ethos of the streets by which such young men live and die, seems downright weak. Echoing Tony Montana, the fearless and ruthless Marielito portrayed in the 1983 version of *Scarface*, a boy from the gutter who made it to the top scoffing all the way at American justice, the typical sentiment among DominicanYorks is: "Ain't nothin' this country can do to me that the DR ain't already done." In short, many young Dominicans live—by choice—in a world apart; others approach American society as predators, looking at every turn for weaknesses to exploit.

In the course of turning the precinct upside down searching for Buczek's killers, investigators also discovered that drug dealers were laundering enormous piles of money generated by their trade, totaling millions of dollars a week, through the local economy of Washington Heights. Indeed, investigators discovered that the stream of clean money heading back to the Dominican Republic was shallow in comparison with the river of dirty cash flowing through upper Manhattan. Early in the 1980s Dominican drug dealers simply used local banks, establishing multiple accounts under fictitious identities, and moved large sums of money back and forth from New York to the Caribbean, where they bought real estate and transformed towns like San Francisco de Macoris and Santiago into typical third-world, split-level, barbed-wire-enclosed paradises surrounded by hovels. The 1972 Bank Secrecy Act prohibited money laundering and required banks to report all transactions of $10,000 or more. But the law was unaccompanied by regulations to make its provisions enforceable. Only when federal prosecutors went after the Bank of Boston in 1984 for not reporting multiple transactions by one person in excess of $10,000 and then the Bank of New England in 1985 for flagrant organizational indifference to the Secrecy Act did banks begin to get religion. Since then, a whole body of federal laws has developed clarifying the Bank Secrecy Act, including the Crime Control Act of 1984, the Money Laundering Control Act of 1986, the Omnibus Drug Acts of 1988 and 1990, and the rider attached to the Housing Act of 1992. Banks now stagger under compliance costs of about a billion dollars per year.

As banks have become somewhat impermeable, a new breed

of ever more intelligent money launderers has emerged. Among a variety of methods, Dominican drug dealers physically haul, ship, or mail money to the island and then bring it back to the United States as "legitimate income" from dummy corporations. Or they set up dummy corporations in the Heights, which front for still other dummy corporations, complete with elaborate business records to justify high cash flow. Or they establish a "trading corporation" in Greenwich, Connecticut, that funnels funds, some legitimate, some illegal, from a host of subsidiary small businesses in New York City to the Dominican Republic. Or they utilize any of the extraordinary number of travel agencies in Washington Heights, sometimes five to a block, to wire money to the Caribbean. Travel agencies also act as brokers for the purchase of luxury goods such as cars, durables of every sort, and jewelry, taking money from buyers in the Heights, issuing them vouchers for merchandise to be redeemed in the Dominican Republic, and settling accounts with sister agencies there. Car dealers accept off-the-books cash payments for the luxury cars crucial to drug dealers' requisite style of life.

Many drug dealers, either directly or more often through middlemen, act as private banks, loansharking monies at fifty percent interest rates to new immigrants to start up legitimate businesses, like jewelry shops, beauty parlors, social clubs, nightclubs, or restaurants. Or they bankroll newcomers' purchase of the bodegas that crowd every street in Washington Heights, sometimes using the stores as fronts to bring in more illegal immigrants for work in the drug trade, disguised as legal employees in the grocery business. The dealers then finance the illegal gambling that operates out of such small groceries, bankrolling pinball machines, the numbers racket, and the Bolita, the Dominican lottery. They require many bodega owners either to hold or deal drugs, or guns, or both, and to accept food stamps as payment for such contraband. Many bodegas also sell illegal green cards and other government documents as well as telephone "blue boxes" that enable one to make international calls without charge. Or they make cash purchases of large pieces of real estate, particularly in northern Manhattan, then empty the buildings of old tenants and fill them with immigrants, who often live three families to an apartment and sometimes become fodder for the street drug wars. Coupled with the demand they create for illegal services, drug dealers are major consumers in their own right, spending and generating lots of cash in the community. In short, crucial sectors of the local small business economy in Washington Heights depend on drug money. That money, Buczek homicide investigators decided, helps buy community-wide silence about drug-related violence.

If the community's vested interest in drug money were not enough, the sheer extent and heartlessness of drug-related violence in Washington Heights, and the seeming inability of authorities to stamp it out, erodes the legitimacy of the forces of order and exacerbates people's natural fear of physical reprisal. Unchecked criminal violence produces a society of bystanders as surely as the state-directed violence of a totalitarian social order.

Although the children and staff of St. Elizabeth's School went to great lengths to console police officers for Michael Buczek's death, police received virtually no help from the larger Washington Heights community in investigating his murder. But after two quick mistaken arrests, marked by a legally catastrophic misidentification of the shooter in a lineup by PO Barbato, scores of the most experienced detectives in the city, spearheaded by Sam Gribben of the Three-Four squad and John Hickey of the Manhattan North Homicide Squad, finally cracked the Buczek case. It turned out that Buczek's killer, Daniel Mirambeaux, spent six months of every year in the Dominican Republic, where he was an important regional player in one of the island's numerous leftist political parties.

During the other six months he ran a robber crew in Washington Heights to finance his political vocation. On the night of October 18, 1988, his whole crew had gone to West 186th Street and Audubon ostensibly to pick up a kilo of cocaine ordered in advance but actually to rob drug dealers Francisco Ulerio and Freddy Then. Freddy owned, among other subsidiary enterprises, a network of bodegas through which he sold drugs and guns, smuggled young illegal Dominican aliens into New York to employ them in the drug trade, and laundered enormous amounts of drug money. But Ulerio and Then didn't show for the scheduled meeting, and Mirambeaux and his crew could not find them that night.

Back at the crew's headquarters at 1770 Andrews Avenue in the Bronx, crew member Juan Jose Alvarez-Salazar aka Rhadames Matos claimed to know from an encounter earlier that day that a drug dealer named Jacinto had just received six kilos of cocaine. Jacinto lived at 580 West 161st Street and was part-owner of El Gigante bodega on the corner of West 161st and Broadway. The crew decided to go and rob Jacinto. While crew member Jose Fernandez-Peralta aka Freddy Parra, a livery cab driver by trade, waited downstairs in his cab, Rhadames met with Jacinto in Apartment #44 at 580 West 161st Street and made a deal to purchase cocaine. Jacinto sent Rhadames downstairs to Apartment #35, the drug-sale location, in the company of his two workers, both nephews. Once they were there, Mirambeaux and two additional crew members (Pablo Almonte aka Emilio and Marcos Jaquez), who had been hiding in the building, burst into the apartment and robbed three kilos of cocaine, all that was left of the shipment, leaving Jacinto's workers and two customers tied up, along with Rhadames, in order not to blow his cover. As the robbers were leaving the third-floor apartment, another customer, a woman, came into the apartment and told the robbers that there were police in the building. After tying her up, Mirambeaux, Emilio, and

Marcos went out together, with Marcos carrying the three kilos of cocaine in a black plastic bag. In the lobby, Buczek and Barbato challenged the men about the package.

When the men didn't stop, the cops followed them the sixty feet across West 161st Street to the corner of Broadway. Marcos fled down Broadway with the cocaine. Buczek, who was in the lead, grabbed Emilio and struggled with him; Barbato came around the corner and started to go after Mirambeaux, who stopped, pulled out a 9-millimeter pistol, and fired several shots at the officers. One of these rounds hit Emilio in the arm and entered Buczek's chest. Both Emilio and Mirambeaux then fled south on Broadway, while Barbato first shot at them and then rushed to aid his partner. The culprits turned left on West 160th, where Emilio discarded a bloody jacket containing a fully loaded .357 Magnum revolver just before Mirambeaux ran into another police officer, whom he excitedly directed to the downed cop just around the corner. The two robbers then met up with Marcos, who had commandeered a livery cab at Amsterdam; they piled into it and fled. In the excitement, Marcos dropped the package of drugs on West 160th Street, much to his partners' fury.

The next day, after being treated for his wound, Emilio flew to the Dominican Republic with his wife. A few days later Mirambeaux followed. Interviews with the robbery victims along with information from a registered confidential inform-ant led investigators to Rhadames Matos and, in turn, to the robbery ring. When police later interrogated Marcos, who had been arrested on an unrelated drug charge, he gave detailed statements about the Buczek murder which implicated his colleagues while completely exculpating himself. Indeed, he removed himself entirely from the scene and put in his own place the brother of Rhadames Matos. In order to clear his brother, Rhadames Matos himself called police from the Dominican Republic and placed Marcos Jaquez on the set, while, of course, exculpating himself.

On January 6, 1989, a Manhattan grand jury indicted Mirambeaux for the murder of Michael Buczek. The District Attorney of New York announced the indictment on April 4, 1989, demanding Mirambeaux's extradition from the Dominican Republic, where he had been incarcerated on an unrelated gun charge. Though the Dominican Republic does not normally extradite its nationals to the United States, President Joaquín Balaguer, under great and highly unusual pressure from the U.S. State Department, announced that he had decided to make an exception in Mirambeaux's case. On June 29, 1989, the day Dominican officials were to hand over Daniel Mirambeaux to American authorities, who were waiting downstairs in police headquarters to take custody, the Dominican government informed the United States that, while securely handcuffed and waist-chained and accompanied by officers of the Dominican National Police, Mirambeaux "leapt to his death" off a third floor landing of police headquarters. Riots ensued in the Dominican Republic at Balaguer's decision and Mirambeaux's death. The NYPD Detective Bureau wished to press the cases against Rhadames Matos, Emilio, Freddy Parra, and Marcos Jaquez but, with the acquiescence of high-ranking police officials, the District Attorney of New York, citing the legal difficulties created by the early false arrests and initial misidentification of the shooter in a lineup, promptly declared the case closed and refused to prosecute any of Mirambeaux's accomplices in the crime. Many police officers have never forgiven DANY officials or high-ranking members of their own department for that decision. Nor have they ever forgiven members of the Dominican community of Washington Heights for keeping quiet when one of their own died on the streets.

Buczek's murder cast a long shadow. Special Agent Joseph Occhipinti, Chief of the Anti-Smuggling Unit of Immigration and Naturalization Services for the New York area—

and one of the most decorated federal agents in U.S. history, with 78 awards or commendations for meritorious service—aided NYPD detectives in the Buczek investigation at the request of Detective Captain Salvador Blando. Once the police investigation had uncovered the aborted rip-off of Freddy Then and Francisco Ulerio as the original targets of Mirambeaux's robbery crew on the night of Buczek's murder, Occhipinti opened his own investigation into Then's bodega network, in Project Bodega. Accompanied sometimes by police detectives and sometimes by Drug Enforcement Administration agents, Occhipinti raided 55 bodegas looking for illegal aliens. In some bodegas, he seized drugs, guns, or money neatly bundled into bricks in the drug-trade fashion, some of it clearly earmarked for the money-laundering operation in Greenwich, Connecticut. Occhipinti received several bribery overtures during Project Bodega, which he reported to the FBI's Corruption Unit. Working with three DANY district attorneys specially appointed to Project Bodega, Occhipinti made 39 arrests, resulting in 25 convictions.

The project generated enormous opposition in Washington Heights, spearheaded and coordinated by the quickly organized Coalition for Community Concerns and especially by the Federation of Dominican Merchants and Industrialists. The Federation was ostensibly a small businessmen's association, originally organized in the early 1980s to mobilize support for political candidates in the Dominican Republic. The Federation denounced Project Bodega, arguing that Occhipinti was violating the civil rights of the Dominican immigrant community through illegal searches and seizures. Occhipinti's bosses became apprehensive and told him to back off. But, with his usual bulldog-like singlemindedness, Occhipinti pressed his inquiries aggressively. Then, on April 4, 1990, newly elected Mayor David Dinkins, who owed his narrow victory to his capture of 70 percent of the city's Hispanic vote, condemned Project Bodega from the steps of City Hall before a screaming demonstration organized by the Federation, which, Occhipinti later claimed, had contributed heavily to Dinkins's mayoral campaign. Dinkins charged that Project Bodega was a "Republican-backed conspiracy" to reduce Hispanic participation in the 1990 census. The Mayor demanded that INS officials shut down the project and that Occhipinti be investigated for civil rights violations. Dennis deLeon, the city's Human Rights Commissioner, echoed Dinkins's charges a week later (April 10, 1990) in an interview for a story in *The New York Times*, indicating that his agency was "looking into allegations of unauthorized arrests, seizures of money and possible human rights violations." The story focused on expressions of outrage against the bodega raids by various "community leaders," including Jose Liberato, Jose Elias Taveras, and Jose Prado, all bodega owners whose stores had been raided, all leaders of the Federation, and all complainants against Occhipinti.

On March 6, 1991, the United States Attorney's Office of the Southern District of New York announced a grand jury indictment of Joseph Occhipinti on 25 counts of violating the civil rights of 12 plaintiffs either by not having probable cause to search their establishments or by not properly obtaining consent to search them, or both, and of making false statements in his reports. The indictment also charged Occhipinti with stealing money seized in some of the searches. Occhipinti asserted that almost all of the plaintiffs had criminal records for possession of illegal firearms and for running illegal gambling operations; moreover, without exception all the complainants were Federation members and several were related to one other. None of the other 43 bodega owners raided by Occhipinti's task force joined the complaint against him of illegal searches, although many of these had been convicted of holding contraband; indeed, several of these owners stated that Occhipinti's actions in searching their establishments had been completely above board.

The case was assigned to Federal District Court Judge Con-

stance Baker Motley, a Lyndon Johnson appointee to the bench
with strong Kennedy-family backing. Motley—a former Manhattan Borough President and a member of the tight-knit political clique, along with David Dinkins, Charles Rangel, and
Percy Sutton, that for many years ruled Harlem's Carver
Democratic Club, the uptown branch of old Tammany Hall—
had a long record of civil rights activism. Assistant United
States Attorney Jeh Johnson helped prosecute the case;
Johnson was Motley's former law clerk.

On May 17, 1991, on the eve of the trial, Occhipinti's lawyer
asked to be excused from the case, claiming that he had just
suffered a nervous breakdown. Judge Motley did not allow
Occhipinti to change counsel, leading Occhipinti to claim in-
adequate representation as one of the main bases of his later
appeal. Judge Motley also prohibited the use of the criminal
records of the complainants/witnesses against Occhipinti to
impeach what he argued was their concerted perjured testimony. On June 28, 1991, the jury convicted Occhipinti of 17
civil rights violations, dismissing the charges of embezzle-
ment. On October 18, 1991, the anniversary of Michael
Buczek's murder, Judge Motley sentenced Occhipinti to 37
months in federal prison.

Both before and after his conviction, Occhipinti made
strenuous efforts to exonerate himself by collecting information on his accusers and the Federation of Dominican Merchants and Industrialists. He gained support from some key
figures. Beginning in October 1991, Staten Island Borough
President Guy Molinari hired former federal narcotics agent
Ray Hagemann as a chief investigator to probe Occhipinti's
prosecution and conviction. In early 1992 Hagemann became
acquainted with one Ramon Rodriguez, formerly on the DEA
payroll as an informant paid by the piece, plus expenses, for
information he provided. Rodriguez told Hagemann that he
had personal contacts and dealings with Jose Liberato, Jose
Elias Taveras, and Jose Prado, as well as with Leonides Libera-

tor and Altagracia Crucey, all key trial witnesses against Occhipinti. Rodriguez provided Hagemann with a sworn affidavit dated April 21, 1992, describing several of these interactions.

Rodriguez had had a conversation with Elias Taveras in November 1991. His affidavit states: "Mr. Taveras was bragging to me how he was responsible in convicting a federal agent from Immigration for stealing money and doing an illegal search of his bodega. He personally admitted to me that he lied to the jury about the theft of monies and the illegal searches. Mr. Taveras also told me that a Dominican woman called Altagracia Crucey, who owns a bodega on Broadway near West 162nd Street . . . also falsely testified against the Immigration officer." In characterizing Taveras and Crucey, the affidavit states that Taveras "is involved in the sale of numbers, gambling, illegal drug money transfers to the Dominican Republic, and also arranging drug sales" and that three Dominican drug dealers all had admitted to him that Altagracia Crucey was their source of heroin.

In the same document, Rodriguez also describes a January 1992 conversation with Jose Liberato in which Liberato, bragging to Rodriguez that he had "fucked the federales," explained that, when INS had raided his bodega, the officers had not discovered 18 kilograms of cocaine secreted in the floor and that he falsely testified against the INS officer in court because the raids on bodegas were hurting his loan-sharking business by arresting people who owed him money. According to the affidavit, Liberato said that he and others organized many of the bodega owners to testify falsely against the officer. Rodriguez referred to his personal knowledge of Liberato's cocaine smuggling, in which he handled as many as 50 to 100 kilos at a time, often secreted in frozen yucca, and described Liberato as close friends with Papito, "a known assassin who owns the El Baturo Restaurant."

At Hagemann's direction, Rodriguez went undercover to tape-record conversations in Spanish with Elias Taveras and

Jose Prado. According to a later affidavit by Hagemann printed in the November 21, 1993, *Congressional Record,* these conversations indicated that Taveras and Prado lied to the grand jury and at trial about Occhipinti. Hagemann submitted the taped conversation with Taveras, complete with a control tape of Taveras in another conversation, to an independent voice analyst in Bowling Green, Kentucky, who reported that the voices on both tapes appeared to be the same. According to the Hagemann affidavit, Rodriguez produced a tape of a conversation which, he claimed, contains the voice of Jose Prado in which Prado admitted receiving $35,000 to testify falsely against Occhipinti. On that same tape, Prado also implicated Jose Liberato, Altagracia Crucey, Rhadames Liberato, and others in perjury.

However, when Hagemann and Occhipinti presented these materials to the Office of Professional Responsibility of the Department of Justice, which handed the matter over to the department's Criminal Division, the department discounted any information coming from Ramon Rodriguez because, it said, he was not a credible witness; Rodriguez had been dismissed as a DEA informant in June 1991 at the insistence of a federal prosecutor because Rodriguez had changed his story about the circumstances of a major drug deal.

In spring 1992, according to his same affidavit, Hagemann worked with reporters from CBS's *Inside Edition,* which, for a national television audience, captured Elias Taveras's admission on camera that he had given false testimony against Occhipinti. Two other men also made undercover forays into the bodegas owned by Occhipinti's main accusers. Hector Rodriguez worked for Molinari's office under Hagemann's supervision and, as he reports in an affidavit printed in the March 17, 1994, *Congressional Record,* discovered illegal gambling in several of the bodegas and narcotics trafficking in the Crucey grocery. Luis Rodriguez worked free of charge for a private investigator laboring on Occhipinti's behalf. His affidavit in the February 23, 1994, *Congressional Record* states that he discovered various illegal activities at the bodegas owned by merchants who testified against Occhipinti, including illegal gambling, selling false documents, drug-trafficking, and illegal wiring of monies to the Dominican Republic; Luis Rodriguez's subsequent affidavit in the February 28, 1994, *Congressional Record* provides specific details of illegal activities of Jose Prado and Elias Taveras, among other merchants. Both investigators claimed to have discovered bits and pieces of information supporting Occhipinti's assertion that he had been framed.

Then in mid-1992, Manuel de Dios Unanue, former editor of *El Diario-La Prensa* newspaper, and at the time the editor of a weekly newspaper called *Cambio*, provided Occhipinti and his allies with an affidavit supporting Occhipinti's claim of a concerted frame-up. This was subsequently published in the September 27, 1996, *Congressional Record*. According to de Dios's affidavit, he had personally interviewed numerous members of the Federation in the course of writing a story on the Occhipinti case and "these individuals confided to me that Mr. Occhipinti had been set up by the Federation and that the complaints against him were fraudulent. These individuals have indicated to me that they are in fear of their safety and as a result would not go public with this information." De Dios agreed to turn over to the United States Congress and to the Department of Justice evidence about Dominican organized crime that, he alleged, corroborated Occhipinti's claims, but he was assassinated before he could do so. His death was attributed to Colombian drug cartels in retaliation for his journalistic crusade against their narcotics trafficking.

Occhipinti had high hopes for his appeal, since Judge Motley had the distinction of being one of the most frequently overturned federal judges in her district. With a new attorney, Steven Frankel, he filed a brief of over 700 pages, including appendices, appealing his conviction.

On the day of argument, in April 1992, there was a noisy

demonstration organized by the Federation on the steps of the United States Court of Appeals threatening riots in Washington Heights if Occhipinti's conviction were overturned. The demonstrators' cry was: "No Justice, No Peace." The demonstration, in fact, burst into the courtroom during the brief appellate proceedings just as Frankel began his presentation. The panel of judges dismissed Occhipinti's appeal within an hour of hearing it. On June 11th—the day before his negotiated date of surrender for incarceration away from the general prison population in a minimum security prison in Memphis— Occhipinti appeared on *The Jackie Mason Show* protesting his innocence. He returned home to find that Judge Motley had ordered his immediate arrest and transportation to Oklahoma's El Reno maximum security penitentiary. After being shackled hand, foot, and body for 12 hours, Occhipinti was put in a holding cell with over 60 prisoners, including several Dominican drug dealers from Washington Heights.

Occhipinti ended up serving seven months before President George Bush commuted his sentence on January 15, 1993, just before leaving office. For several years, Congressman James Traficant, Jr., and later Congresswoman Susan Molinari have entered voluminous materials into the *Congressional Record* supporting Occhipinti's request either for a full pardon or for a new trial, but the Department of Justice, after one review by the FBI, has refused all requests to reopen the case. Those who had labored on Occhipinti's behalf, including Guy Molinari and Ray Hagemann, objected that instead of thoroughly investigating the possibility of a frame-up, the FBI focused most of its attention on trying to discredit Occhipinti's supporters.

These long-festering resentments were in the background in early 1992, when detectives in the Three-Four precinct—each staggering under a load of about 250 cases per year—encountered a bewildering series of violent episodes involving drug dealers in Washington Heights. On January 11, 1992, Detective John Bourges caught a shooting at the Las Vegas Nightclub at 179 Dyckman Avenue, a well-known hang-out for drug dealers who like to flash their green, gold, and girls. Bourges was a 15-year veteran of the police department who came into the Detective Bureau out of the twilight world of undercover narcotics work, where more than once he had had a gun stuck into his ear while making a buy. Bourges knew this particular club well, since on August 26, 1991, he had assisted Detective Marta Rosario (best known for singing the National Anthem in a ringing contralto at political rallies and Christmas parties alike) in the investigation of the attempted murder of Rafael Rodriguez—an up-and-coming minor league ballplayer, who was shot as he left the Las Vegas Nightclub, apparently for flirting with the wrong girl. No witnesses came forward for that shooting; Rodriguez was paralyzed for life. Now in January, according to an eyewitness, a man had tried to enter the nightclub and was rebuffed by the owners. He returned later in the evening and lit up the club, firing several wild rounds and hitting Linda Miner, a girl sitting near the band, in the head. Though seriously injured, Miner miracu-lously survived the assault. On January 17th, Bourges "did an escort" with the eyewitness, driving him around the area in an unmarked van with deeply tinted windows, until the wit-ness spotted the shooter on the corner of 174th Street and Aububon. After radioing for backup, Bourges arrested the man, charging him with first-degree assault, reckless endanger-ment, and criminal possession of a weapon, since the man was strapped at the time of his arrest. He also had a small quantity of marijuana on his person.

Bourges identified the man as Juan Carlos Peña aka Carlito, known to be associated with various drug dealers in the area. Carlito admitted the dispute with the owners of the nightclub, who, he said, wanted him to take off his baseball hat. When he refused, they ejected him from the club. However, he denied any involvement in the shooting. The nightclub owners said they did not see the shooter, but the eyewitness was firm in his identification. Bourges, dubbed The Alienator by his colleagues because his brusque tenacity and total dedication to his work ruffle many feathers, wanted to press the case not only to clear it but to get Carlito off the street, almost always a prime concern for frontline police officers. But when he took the case downtown, Assistant District Attorney Dan Rather argued that arresting Carlito at that point might jeopardize a larger ongoing investigation. Rather felt there had to be more than a simple dissing behind the nightclub incident.

Both detectives and prosecutors knew that Carlito's associate, Ruben Perez, was a marijuana dealer at 174th Street and Audubon who controlled the distribution of "smoke" for the entire area. Detectives had a tip that Ruben was involved in a shoot-out that had become known in the precinct as The Halloween Murder. According to witnesses, at 2000 hours on the previous Halloween, right in front of 629 West 173rd Street, a tall, skinny, light-skinned Dominican man wearing a Halloween mask emerged from a car driven by a dark-skinned, stocky Dominican and began firing round after round at Jose Alberto Rodriguez aka El Gordo, a well-known marijuana dealer. The skinny masked man continued to shoot as El Gordo fled toward Broadway and, badly wounded, tried to take refuge in a bodega at 4101 Broadway. Bursting into the store and, in front of several witnesses, the masked man pumped the last of twenty bullets into El Gordo, as he scrambled frantically up and down the bodega's narrow, crowded aisles. The shooter then fled on foot toward Fort Washington Avenue. Apparently even El Gordo did not understand what was happening to him, since the EMS technician reported that he kept asking, "Por qué? Por qué?" (Why? Why?) all the way to the hospital.

Ruben Perez did not fit the description of the shooter, however, nor that of the shooter's companion. What then was the meaning of the tip to police? Who were the shooters? Had

Ruben hired them as independent contractors? What, if anything, did Carlito know about Ruben's involvement? Instead
of locking up Carlito for the nightclub shooting, could he be
flipped to betray Ruben? While Rather and Bourges were at
loggerheads—a minor skirmish in the ongoing jurisdictional
warfare between precinct detectives and various investigative
units of DANY—the issue suddenly became moot. The eyewitness to the Las Vegas Nightclub shooting disappeared, un-
doubtedly after learning just who Carlito and his friends were.
Bourges's case against Carlito collapsed.

On February 1st, three weeks after the shooting at the Las
Vegas Nightclub, Detective Annie Peters of the Three-Four
squad—a tall, vivacious young black woman—caught a homicide that seemed to originate in the 20 de Mayo Restaurant,
owned by Miguel and Frankie Cuevas. Fat Frankie Cuevas was
a known associate of Ruben Perez. According to a confidential
informant, on January 31st Danny Montilla aka Bumblebee, or
more often Madonna because he constantly munched McDonald's hamburgers, was in the restaurant with two girlfriends.
Lexington Rojas aka Mask, among others, was also present.
After table-hopping to talk with Manny Garcia and Gilbert
Campusano, both of whom were known to be Fat Frankie's
lieutenants, Madonna told his girlfriends that he had to go to
the Bronx to make a drop with Manny and Gil and would be
back shortly. He discouraged the girls from coming along for
the ride because "the car is dirty." After he left, Frankie kept
the girls company. But Madonna never returned. Shortly after
midnight police found his body on the Henry Hudson Parkway
at 177th Street, with two in the head.

Initial interviews produced the following story: Madonna
had bailed his good friend and drug partner, Emilio Bera aka
Nicholas, out of jail to the tune of $12,000, borrowing $5,000
from Frankie Cuevas and $7,000 from Lenny Sepulveda to do
so. But when Nicholas got out, he refused to pay Madonna
back, leaving the latter to face Frankie and Lenny, both of

whom wanted their money. That story quickly collapsed when Peters learned that Lenny was in prison at the time and Madonna had just spent the evening in Frankie's restaurant, under no apparent stress.

When police interviewed one of Madonna's relatives, another story emerged. The relative argued that Madonna had been silenced for two reasons: first, because he knew of Frankie Cuevas's criminal activities and, second, because someone named Tezo had told Madonna that he had "taken care of El Gordo on Halloween because he was competition." Had Madonna been killed because Tezo had talked too much? Or were Tezo's boasts actually threats to Madonna? And who was Tezo? Was he the tall, skinny shooter at The Halloween Murder or the dark-skinned, stocky driver? Moreover, what was Tezo's relationship to Frankie Cuevas and his criminal activities? Was Cuevas also involved in El Gordo's murder? If so, why? And where did the story about the bail money come from? The case stuck in the mud of such queries, and Detective Peters could get nowhere with it.

On the following March 16th, Frankie Cuevas and his driver, Manny Garcia, spent the night on Fordham Road in the Bronx, "scoping girls" and driving past George Washington High School at West 192nd and Audubon, their old alma mater. Near midnight they stopped at a traffic light at 185th Street and Audubon, when suddenly an unknown assailant opened fire on them from another car and then fled the scene. Cuevas, shot in his left arm and wrist, jumped out of his car, ran west on West 185th Street and then down Broadway to the Three-Four precinct station house between 184th and 183rd Streets. He told the police who took him to the hospital that his friend was dead. When police returned to the scene of the shooting, they found Manny Garcia alive but wounded in his arm and spine, and paralyzed from the neck down. A check on the car in which Cuevas and Garcia were traveling revealed an extensive summons record issued to Jose Vizcaino aka Big Cuba.

There were reports of still another car besides the shooter's that fled the area after the shooting, and witnesses got the license plate number for that vehicle.

When Detectives Dugan and Bourges interviewed Cuevas in the hospital, where his girlfriend, Carmen Gonzalez, waited on him hand and foot, he "exhibited," according to Dugan, "a casualness and indifference" to the investigation and to Manny Garcia's serious injury. His attitude was: "We're soldiers and soldiers are meant to fall." Cuevas denied any knowledge of why anyone would want to shoot him. When queried about Madonna's death, Cuevas denied any knowledge of that too, saying only that he and Danny Montilla had been friends.

In a virtuoso display of the fatalism at the core of the ethos of the streets, Manny Garcia exhibited even greater indifference to his own life-threatening injuries. When Bourges pointed out that whoever had shot him was out there enjoying life while Garcia would never walk again, would never have sex again, Garcia simply said: "This is the way it is. This is the way it's going to be. I'll live with it. Frankie will take care of me." Cuevas checked out of the hospital the next night, on March 17th.

Who was gunning for Frankie Cuevas? Since the heavily tinted glass of his car prevented an easy identification of its occupants, someone must have fingered him for the shooters. But who pointed him out? And why? Who were the hit men? By this time, Detective Dugan had begun to develop a remarkably thorough cross-referenced index file on all the players and their associates linked to the Cargill murder, The Quad and The Double, and various assaults in the Three-Four precinct, including The Halloween Murder. But the social organization of the crew or crews at work, and the fault lines that frequently produced violent conflict among them, were still obscure. Dugan had also shared with the Three-Four squad the statement that he had taken from Platano in New Jersey that placed a "Frankie" in the car with Lenny Sepulveda and Raymond Polanco when David Cargill was murdered. If Platano's statement was accurate, and if Frankie Cuevas had been friends with Lenny and Polanco in May 1991, had something happened to break them apart? And had that something set off a drug war?

On the same night that Frankie Cuevas checked out of the hospital, anticrime PO Michael Callahan was sitting with his sergeant and another officer in front of 155 Audubon Avenue at 172nd Street, a notorious drug building. At 0015 hours two men left it, passing in front of their unmarked car. When one of the pair, a stocky dark-skinned Dominican, glanced at the police car, his eyes "bugged out." He quickly reached into his waistband and dropped a weapon in the street. All three officers scrambled out of their car and arrested him and his companion; the latter, after being identified as Gilbert Campusano, was released. At booking, the man who had dropped the gun gave the name Paul Santiago. Later that morning, at his arraignment in criminal court before Judge Laura Safer Espinosa, ADA Richard Chin requested bail in the amount of $2,500, noting that, although the defendant had no record of prior arrests, police had recovered a loaded 10-millimeter, semiautomatic weapon with its serial number defaced. Chin also noted that Paul Santiago "had $388 on him, a beeper, and a phony driver's license." The defendant's lawyer, Barry Weinstein of Goldstein, Weinstein & Fuld, made the following argument:

> He is not charged with the driver's license, he is not
> charged with the beeper, he is not charged with the
> money, the last two not being crimes in this state, at least
> for now. My client has no prior record. He says the gun
> was not found on him. He says he was on the street and
> the cops found the gun underneath an automobile and
> other people ran and he didn't, so he was arrested. He says
> the cops put the gun there. My client has verified commu-

nity ties. I spoke to his wife. He's been unemployed for five months. Prior to that, he was working for Portofena Auto Repair, 101 Featherbed Lane, in the Bronx. He's been unemployed for the last five months because his five-month-old daughter has been ill. He stopped working to take care of his daughter. He lives with his father for the last fifteen years at the residence given. His common-law wife and his daughter live there with him. He's never been arrested. He is 26 [years old]. He has been in this country his whole life and I ask he be released on his own recognizance.

Paul Santiago, known on the streets as Platano, was out on bail in time for lunch.

Later the same day, March 17, 1992, there was another shooting in the precinct. Frankie Gonzalez, whom only a few days before police had caught in a surveillance photograph in a red car with Frankie Cuevas, was sitting in a beige Cadillac with another man in front of 555 West 173rd Street between Audubon and St. Nicholas Avenues, when suddenly an unidentified man began shooting at the car. Gonzalez suffered a minor wound, got out of the car, and began running down the street; his companion fled in the opposite direction. Gonzalez ran into someone he knew only as Mask, who drove him to Columbia Presbyterian and then disappeared. In a statement given to Detective Bourges on April 10th after the hospital released him, Gonzalez said that he did not recognize his assailant and had no idea why anyone would shoot at him. He added that his companion in the car was a man whom he knew only as Tezo, a tall, skinny Dominican. Gonzalez said that he hadn't seen Tezo since the shooting. The police still didn't know who Tezo was, but they now knew from Gonzalez's description that he was tall and skinny. Had he, instead of Gonzalez, been the target of the assault? When police checked Gonzalez's background, they discovered that he had a sister named Carmen. Was this the Carmen Gonzalez attending Cuevas in the hospital? Were Gonzalez and Tezo part of Cuevas's crew? Was Tezo the tall, skinny, light-skinned Dominican responsible for The Halloween Murder of El Gordo?

Three days later, on March 20th, at 0045 hours, Gilbert Campusano, Frankie Cuevas's close associate, walked into Columbia Presbyterian Hospital shot in the face and right hand. Two men escorted him and promptly disappeared. On Campusano's person were papers for one of the automobiles seen fleeing the scene of the shooting of Frankie Cuevas and Manny Garcia on March 16th. Before he underwent an operation that removed part of his brain related to memory, Campusano claimed that he had been beaten by unknown assailants. But police traced a copious trail of blood back to 500 West 174th Street, Apartment 5E, Frankie Cuevas's mother's apartment, where they found blood all over the apartment, a gun in open view on the floor, and several other weapons hidden on the premises. Detectives Dugan and Bourges went up to the roof of the building. It had snowed the night before, and the detectives found a clearly demarcated trail of footprints made by old sneakers and, on the slightly lower roof of the next building, lying in the snow, the gun that had been used to shoot Gilbert. Downstairs, Dugan challenged a man entering the building. The man said he was "on the Job," showing his shield identifying himself as PO Roberto Lazar (a pseudonym); he was a uniformed cop assigned to the Bronx's Four-O precinct. Why was he at 500 West 174th Street, Dugan inquired? Lazar said he was friends with "Franklin" on the fifth floor, had heard that there was trouble, and had stopped by to see if he could help. Dugan found the encounter extremely curious.

Other detectives interviewed Campusano's parents, asking them all the basic questions: Does your son work? Where was he that night? Was he having problems with anyone? To each question, the response was a resounding "Yo no sé!" Yet the Campusano family was clearly shocked at Gilbert's shooting; Garry Dugan spent long hours with them listening to their bewilderment and grief. In the meantime, Frankie Cuevas called in, claiming that he had been at his second home in Orangeburg, New York, at the time of the shooting. He said when he returned to New York City to have dinner with his brother Miguel around 34th Street, Miguel told him to call the police immediately about Gilbert's shooting. Frankie said he had no idea how guns got into his mother's apartment. Detective Dugan invited Cuevas to come into the Three-Four station house to give a statement. When he arrived, he was wearing brand-new sneakers.

The war on the streets continued unabated. On April 7, 1992, Lexington Rojas aka Mask was shot to death at the corner of 173rd Street and St. Nicholas as he sat in the driver's seat of a car with New Hampshire plates. Frankie Gonzalez, whom Mask had assisted to the hospital only a few weeks before, disclaimed all knowledge. Police found the gun that killed Mask a short distance away, but in ballistics tests its bullets matched none of the other crimes ravaging the precinct. Though Detective Bourges pursued a number of leads, very few people seemed to know much about the Dominican man with the unlikely name of Lexington.

The very next day, Frankie Cuevas and Jose Vizcaino were arrested in the Three-O precinct driving a black Nissan automobile with no license plates. Police searched the car and discovered a *clavo* containing three guns. Frankie and Big Cuba disclaimed all knowledge of the guns, arguing that they had simply borrowed the car from a friend. The officers asserted that marijuana was in plain view in the car's ashtray, but because the grounds for searching the car were legally questionable, DANY declined to prosecute the case.

Then, on April 14th, Platano was shot near 191st Street and St. Nicholas. Driving south on St. Nicholas, he spotted a black Nissan Pathfinder with heavily tinted windows. Moments later, while Platano was stopped at a traffic light, a man came from behind a van and approached Platano's car, shooting through his closed window, shattering the glass, and severely wounding him. Platano drove through the light, looked in the rear view mirror, and saw a man known to him as Franklin standing in the street with a gun. He also said that Frankie Gonzalez was with Franklin behind the van. At about 185th Street, he saw a friend named Otis, who drove him to the hospital. The night of the shooting, Detectives Dugan and Dimuro rushed to the hospital and interviewed Platano, who was in great pain with wounds to his stomach, liver, and right arm and was considered "likely," that is, likely to die. When asked what had happened, Platano declared: "Frankie shot me! Frankie, from the Vente de Mayo Restaurant!" He then identified a photograph of Franklin Cuevas in a domestic scene. When asked why Franklin Cuevas wanted him dead, Platano told Dugan and Dimuro: "He's jealous! He's a fat, rich kid who takes advantage of the poor!" In a conversation on April 20th with Detective Bourges, which provided the basic details of the shooting, Platano gave further glimpses into the mayhem on the streets, suggesting that Manny Garcia thought that Platano had done the shooting that had left him paralyzed and had wounded Fat Frankie; that Frankie thought that Gilbert Campusano had set him up to get shot; and that Lexington Rojas was "killed because he stuck up somebody."

Around dawn on April 26th, a wild-west shootout took place only a few blocks from the Three-Four station house. A man by the name of Roberto Peralta, together with his friend Manny Guerrero and two others identified only as Jose and Francisco, were driving east on 181st Street near Pinehurst after a night, Peralta said, of partying and drinking. Suddenly, while Peralta's car was stopped at a traffic light, two men got out of the front seat of a nearby car, two others got halfway out of the back seat, and all began firing machine guns at Peralta. All the shooters were dark-skinned Hispanics with black cloths over their faces, revealing only their eyes. Peralta, who was seriously wounded in the left arm and in the left side of his chest, said he could not identify any of the assailants. Nor could his three comrades. The street was strewn with more than 60 spent shells and some live ammunition as well; four cars and two shops on the street were damaged with gunfire.

The Ford Taurus that had transported Peralta to the hospital contained a 9-millimeter Par machine gun, a 9-millimeter Cobray machine gun, and a .357 Smith and Wesson revolver, as well as ammunition and heroin. An AK-47 was also recovered at the scene. A gray Nissan Maxima abandoned at the scene, inspected by police because it was riddled with bullets, also yielded ammunition and guns, including a 9-millimeter Taurus automatic and a 9-millimeter Cobray machine gun. After the car inspection, Detectives Tony Imperato and Bobby Small went back to the hospital to reinterview Peralta, but he had already checked out. The address he had provided was false. His hospital visitation list included the names of Miguel Cuevas (Frankie's brother) and Carmen Gonzalez (Frankie's girlfriend). Further investigation revealed that the whole incident had originated at Manor and Watson in the Bronx, where men in two cars, said to include "Nelson" and an unidentified big, burly, dark-skinned Dominican, had opened fire on Peralta and Guerrero. No one was hit, but Peralta and Guerrero then chased the attackers' cars back to the Three-Four precinct, where the melee ensued.

Only a few days later, on April 29th, at 0130 hours, three masked men pushed their way into the 20 de Mayo Restaurant, held Frankie and Miguel Cuevas and eight of their patrons at gunpoint, doused the walls with kerosene, set the building on fire, and threatened to shoot anyone who tried to flee the conflagration. But the Cuevas brothers and their customers fled the burning building, guns at the ready, only to find no one on the street waiting for them; everyone escaped unharmed.

Detectives were baffled about the arson and the reasons behind it, and they received no cooperation from anyone associated with the Cuevas brothers' hangout. The Cuevas family immediately rebuilt the restaurant.

Gilbert Campusano miraculously recovered from his head wounds and, after a few months of recuperation with his family in Florida, returned to his old haunts in the Three-Four precinct. It is said that he had begun to regain his memory and that his sudden recollections of times past made old acquaintances nervous. On July 21, 1992, he was hanging out on 173rd Street, when a car approached and someone, through a narrowly cracked window, called Gilbert by name. Gilbert went over and talked to the car's occupants and then told his streetmates that he was going for a ride with friends. He was next seen by a taxi driver, whom he hailed, walking up 133rd Street near Broadway in the Two-Six precinct. He had been shot six times, and he died in the street.

up-
town
murders

Almost as soon as
Assistant District
Attorney Dan Rather
began catching felonies, he
learned that some "really bad guys" had their base of operations in the low 170s between Audubon and St. Nicholas Avenues in Washington Heights. Rather came up through Trial Bureau 60, one of the six main trial bureaus at DANY. Each trial bureau handles both misdemeanor and felony cases. Fresh-out-of-law-school ADAs spend all of their time on misdemeanors in the venue called Criminal Court in New York State until they become seasoned in the intricate procedures of drawing up formal accusatory instruments in the Early Case Assessment Bureau, of presenting their indictments in criminal court arraignment, and finally of negotiating pleas or arguing the interests of the public-at-large in the all-purpose Criminal Court. After such an apprenticeship, young ADAs move on to felonies, arraigning those accused of serious crimes in Criminal Court, obtaining formal indictments from the grand jury, and arguing motions, arranging pleas, or arguing cases before the New York State Supreme Court, which is the State's felony trial court.

Soon after Rather began prosecuting lower-ranking felonies in the Supreme Court, he met Detective Greg Modica from the Manhattan Robbery Squad, a specialized borough-wide unit based on 12th Street just off University Place in Greenwich Village. Modica, like many detectives, was shopping his cases, looking for an ADA with the stomach to "break the fingers" necessary to get robbers off the streets. Dan Rather, like many ADAs, was looking for thoroughness and relentlessness in the detectives that approached him. The two men hit it off, and Modica began to bring Rather his Robbery 3 cases (defined as removal of property by force or intimidation alone), occasionally his Robbery 2 cases (involving use of certain weapons such as knives, boxcutters, claw hammers, baseball bats, chains, or screwdrivers), and eventually the Robbery 1 cases (in which a gun was used), especially those that formed a pattern.

One of the principal tasks of robbery detectives like Modica is to discern emerging patterns of robbery so that police commanders can deploy anticrime units in appropriate locales, hoping to get lucky and be on the spot in the middle of the action or, more likely, be ready to respond quickly when another robbery that plays out a pattern occurs. Once an arrest is made in one robbery, police interrogators can probe further about possibly related crimes, though such thoroughness depends entirely on the willingness of commanders to grant overtime. By contrast, commanding officers in the police department abhor patterns, since linked crimes of any sort, if knowledge of them becomes public, seems to erode whatever trust the public has in the police or at least in particular commanders. Moreover, if a pattern is actually identified, one must do something about it or run the risk of being labeled a bureaucrat instead of a crimefighter. Only detectives with a deep understanding of the ethos of the street can recognize patterns in the first place. Only those relentless enough to continue pursuing leads and eventually suspects in the face of reluctant and skeptical superiors can break patterns.

One day in 1989 Modica brought Rather what seemed at first to be a unique case. A fifth-floor resident of the famous Apthorp Apartments at 2211 Broadway, a landmark building that occupies the whole city block from Broadway to West End Avenue between 78th and 79th Streets, looked out of his window onto 79th Street one evening and saw about 15 youths, who appeared to be Hispanic, milling on the street, conferring periodically with someone in a parked car. Suddenly, all of the youths made a rush for the building's garage. The resident quickly called 911. The police arrived in time to apprehend two youngsters driving the last of a dozen luxury cars that the group had taken out of the garage. The police found the garage attendants bound and stuffed into a car trunk but otherwise unharmed. Both young culprits were Dominican.

Modica quickly checked to see whether there had been other recent garage robberies and whether they resembled the Apthorp job. In fact, robbers had hit garages in Midtown, the upper West Side, and the upper East Side, taking, in all cases, only certain luxury models, specifically Mercedes, BMW, Jaguar, Acura, and Lexus. Moreover, the robbers seemed to be targeting specific makes only if the cars had certain features, such as sun roofs.

The two young Dominicans resolutely refused to cooperate, despite the offer of generous deals. Rather offered one of the culprits, who had no previous arrests, a completely free walk in exchange for information, but to everyone's puzzlement the youngster refused to budge and, along with his fellow robber, pleaded guilty to the top count. The kids were obviously robbing cars on consignment, but they were not about to give up the ringleader.

Then another auto-robbery case landed on Modica's desk. Two anticrime cops in Queens nabbed Rafael Toribio aka Clint from West 174th Street driving an expensive red Mercedes carjacked from a man and his wife in upper Manhattan. The two complainants were unable to identify Toribio in the lineup that followed, so Modica had Clint only for possession of stolen property. Clint, however, gave Modica two other Dominican kids who, he said, had actually carjacked the Mercedes. When police picked up these youngsters, the fingerprints of one of them matched prints discovered on the Mercedes. Confronted with that evidence, the boy confessed and gave up his companion; moreover, in lineups, the robbery victims identified both youngsters as their assailants. But neither culprit would provide further information to the investigators, specifically about who had hired them to rob the car.

Clint also gave someone else to Modica, a Miguel Amador (a pseudonym) who, Clint said, had done a garage robbery at 135th and Edgecombe with a guy named Johnny. Modica grabbed Amador and put him in a lineup, where witnesses to that robbery identified him as one of the culprits. Why did Clint give these carjackers to Modica? Modica suspected Clint of organizing the robberies himself and then giving up his underlings to avoid paying them $1,500, the going rate for car robbery at gunpoint. Later Modica flipped Amador and began using him as a confidential informant after he was released on bail. Amador confirmed Modica's suspicions about Clint, saying that Clint had organized the whole Edgecombe job, ordering the cars, getting the guns, and driving everyone to the garage. But without corroborating evidence, Modica had no way of proceeding against Clint.

In the meantime, Clint, brazen, sophisticated, and streetwise, began to talk frequently with Modica, and then with Rather. He regularly wheeled down to 12th Street and University in his Ferrari, double-parked, and bounded into the Manhattan Robbery Squad to give information to Modica, including the names of people involved in particular robberies. But the information always came after crimes were committed, convincing Modica and Rather that they were dealing with one of the actual instigators of the robberies. Still, with Clint's help, the investigators built a photo book complete with the street names of key players in the garage-robbery ring. With the assistance of Mary Ellen Beekman, an FBI agent with numerous confidential informants in upper Manhattan, they located many of the stolen cars and identified several members of the ring, all low-level operatives.

As it happened, part of the mid-1980s federal crackdown on money laundering involved the arrests of several major car dealers on Eleventh Avenue in Manhattan. The dealers were selling luxury cars for cash to drug dealers who, in turn, had them driven to Miami for export to the Dominican Republic and other points south. The garage robberies, it seemed, were filling a void in the availability of luxury cars for drug dealers that the federal money-laundering crackdown had created. Around the same time, the *New York Post* ran a big story about proliferating chop shops that dismantled luxury cars altogether, providing a steady stream of hard-to-get parts for the underground car trade.

With federal help, Rather and Modica indicted and successfully prosecuted a dozen members of the garage-robbery ring, mostly young Dominicans from between 171st and 174th Streets in Washington Heights. Although Rather and Modica knew that they had caught mostly small fry, they were happy to have the kids off the street because of the disastrous consequences of some of the robberies. One victim, who was driving his wife to Lincoln Center, stopped at a local deli to buy some bananas as a home remedy for an ailment. When he left the car, two kids stealing his make of car on consignment jumped in and pistol-whipped his wife. The man returned at just that point, limping from his poor health, and got into a struggle with the boys. The boys took off in the car with the man holding on to an exterior door handle, and they dragged him for ten blocks before police apprehended them.

The United States Attorney for the Southern District did successfully prosecute one higher-up in the garage robbery ring, Juan Flete aka Baldie, under the federal RICO (Racketeer Influenced and Corrupt Organization) law. And everyone was looking for a Maximo Reyes on the same charge; Reyes, a major drug dealer, later made the FBI's most wanted list. Were Flete and Reyes the real bosses of the operation? The investigators still were not sure who was running the ring. They were also not sure if the garage robberies, apart from their immediate lucrativeness, had some larger purpose. What was happening to all the cash generated by the sale of the stolen vehicles? Was it bankrolling drug operations? Despite Clint's help in the investigation, Rather and Modica felt that they were walking too fine a line. In mid-1990 they ceased using him as an informant, and the investigation seemed stymied.

Then on November 5th of that year, Clint came to the investigators' attention once again. Giordano Pagan, a prototypically hard-working embodiment of the American Dream who had fought his way out of Bronx poverty to build a fleet of armored cars, entered a tobacco distributor's warehouse at 135th and Convent Avenue, opposite City College, with his backup man to make a regular cash pickup of $180,000. As Pagan left the warehouse with the moneybag, a shot from behind him exploded his head "like a pumpkin" and another shot wounded his backup man in the foot. A guard with a shotgun stationed in Pagan's armored vehicle did nothing. A group of five robbers—two Dominicans, two blacks, and one Puerto Rican—jumped into a brown Lincoln Town Car and tried to flee, only to be apprehended two blocks away by anti-crime cops cruising the area. Money was scattered all the way back to the scene of the crime. As soon as Modica heard about the brown Lincoln Town Car, he guessed that Clint was involved, since Clint frequently drove a brown Lincoln. A car matching this description had also been spotted in the vicinity of several carjackings. Indeed, all five culprits named Clint as the organizer of the armored car robbery, saying that he had been at the scene. The getaway driver, Anthony Miner aka Lumpy, who was obviously terrified of Clint, said that he had joined the robbery to pay Clint back for coke taken on consignment.

But again, Modica had no way of independently corroborating the robbers' information. So he picked Clint up the very night of the armored car robbery, hoping to lure him into making a statement. Clint suggested that they take a ride to New Jersey, where, he said, he would show Modica the garages where car robbers whom he knew stashed stolen vehicles until it was safe to get them new papers, good plates, and new vehicle identification numbers. Clint even described how a stolen car salesman proves to a customer that the car being bought has been thoroughly camouflaged. The salesman takes the customer for a ride, spots a police car, runs a red light, and lets the police run the plates through their portable computers, thereby proving that a car is clean and clinching a deal for the price of a traffic summons. Although the evening ride deepened Modica's appreciation of the growing sophistication of car robbers, he still had no way to nail Clint for Pagan's murder.

Three months later, in late February 1991, Modica talked to his confidential informant, Miguel Amador, who had been arrested for yet another robbery. And Amador told Modica about another murder. He said that on January 12, 1991, Anibal Rivera Hernandez from West 242nd Street aka Al or Johnny had robbed and killed a drug dealer from West 174th Street named Delasanto Ferreria aka Chepe in a motel in Newburgh, New York. Chepe had brought money and drugs to Newburgh for Clint, who planned to set up a social club as a front for narcotics trafficking. But following his usual practice, Clint doublecrossed Chepe and ordered Al, along with Amador, Juan Mejia aka Terror or Suicide, and Elvis Aduan aka Macho to kill him, taking the drugs and money. Amador said that Al still had the murder weapon in his possession. Without a warrant, Modica hit Anibal Hernandez's house, gained a signed consent to search it, and turned up the murder weapon wrapped in a brown bag and buried in the snow on a window sill. Anibal confessed to the murder and described how Clint, working for Maximo Reyes, Clint's main customer for the stolen cars, had set up the whole robbery operation to capitalize himself as a big-time drug dealer in Newburgh and Washington Heights.

The investigators understood Clint's flirtation with them. In addition to betraying his underlings for mercenary reasons, Clint, like a lot of hard guys, played both sides of the street, since one never knows when one will need some friends. But by this time Clint, whose patron saint was Clint Eastwood and whose talisman was a huge .45-caliber automatic, was "in the wind" in the Dominican Republic. Though it was said he longed for New York, he did not return, even for the funeral of his brother, who was gunned down in the Three-O precinct in late 1991 while playing basketball.

The investigators remained intrigued by the stony silence of the young garage robbers and most of the young carjackers, since all faced long stretches in state prison, never a pleasant experience. Such silence in the face of harsh punishment betokens fear on the streets. Indeed, the investigators encountered the same silence when they pressed their regular informants for information about the shadowy figures who controlled the low 170s near Aububon. Nobody would say anything, apart from a few references to a "bunch of crazy, wild Dominicans." Only Anibal and Amador went further. Clint's models, they said, were some "really bad guys" from 171st Street who hung out at 174th and Aububon by the names of Lenny and Nelson Sepulveda. Months before the Cargill murder, The Quad, or the drug war in Washington Heights, Rather and Modica began to think that they had stumbled into something big.

But both Modica and Rather had to move on to other cases. Rather was assigned to supervise 17 junior assistant district attorneys in their apprenticeships in Criminal Court. Whenever possible, he took homicide call, where seasoned ADAs catch whatever homicides occur on their watch and work with the detectives who catch the murders. In all the time that he did homicide call, Rather caught only one case below 125th Street. All the rest of the killings were "uptown murders."[1]

---

1. The term's geographical point of reference is Manhattan, but metaphorically it refers to a certain kind of violence throughout the entire city.

Uptown murders are always troublesome. Although often witnessed by a great many people, no one comes forward to testify; no one acknowledges that he knows the victims; no one claims to know anyone involved. Uptown murders take place in deep shadows; few people publicly mourn the victims, not even their own families, or express outrage about the crime, or condemn the culprits; it is as if they never happened at all. Detectives and district attorneys pursue such cases principally because it is their duty to do so.

One case sticks in Rather's mind as the prototypical uptown murder. Harold Thornton aka Hippy and his cousin, Randall Johnson aka Fats, were local bully boys in the Two-Eight precinct in central Harlem—loud, abusive, self-promoting 16-year-old thugs who regularly beat up all the younger kids in their neighborhood and made their living by robbing local drug dealers of their stashes and then reselling the wares in the same location. Kasheem Guiden aka K and Eric Murell aka E, enforcers for a local drug dealer, had warned Hippy and Fats again and again to stop knocking their boss's customers around and especially to stop stealing and reselling his drugs. One busy late afternoon, in full view of more than a hundred witnesses in the densely crowded area, K walked up to Hippy on the street at 133rd and Madison and shot him five times in the head with a .38-caliber revolver; E shot Fats in the back as he tried to flee the scene. The crowd cheered wildly.

K and E ran away in separate directions, but K ran straight into a police radio car while he was still holding the .38; he gave up E, who was then arrested a few hours later. When the police arrived at the scene of the double murder, not a single person came forward. The police didn't understand what had happened. Most of the people on the street didn't understand what had happened, but the crowd treated the occasion as a kind of sport, milling around the corpses and the cops who responded to the scene, continuing to cheer and sometimes jeer. No one wanted to get involved in the investigation, especially since Hippy and Fats were no loss to anybody. While Rather was interrogating K and E on videotape at the station house, there was a raucous street party at 133rd and Madison, celebrating the deaths of the 16-year-old cousins.

The defendants argued to Rather that they had killed Hippy and Fats because Hippy and Fats were going to kill them. The claim makes perfect sense within the intensely personal and practical code of the streets, but in our highly rationalized, abstract legal system such a claim is considered an "anticipatory self-defense" justification, imperfect on its face. K and E each received 6–18 years in prison; not even the victims' families came to the sentencing.

For detectives, uptown murders mainly pose organizational problems. Though the 250 cases detectives in busy squads catch each year refer to flesh-and-blood violence, cases are, first and foremost, bureaucratic entities. Detectives must close all cases that they catch, that is, dispose of them according to bureaucratic formulas. This includes murder cases, although one can readily reopen a homicide if new evidence emerges. Detective sergeants and lieutenants review detectives' cases at regular intervals (7, 21, and 60 days) to keep case loads moving and to measure detectives' effectiveness. When a complainant is unable to identify his assailant, one closes the case with a C-2 label; when one has an uncooperative complainant, one issues a C-3 closure; and, when one has exhausted all investigative leads, one may take a C-4 closure. C closings are frequently unavoidable, but they nevertheless constitute strikeouts in a detective's closely scrutinized batting average. When one catches "nonamenable" cases, that is, cases where investigation is required but an arrest is inappropriate, one can choose from a range of B closings, arguing that a complaint is unfounded or that the case belongs with another unit. B closings are equivalent to walks in baseball: they neither help nor injure one's batting average. Only arrests or their equivalent simultaneously close and clear cases. When one arrests a culprit in a case of one's own, one takes an A closure/clearance; when uniformed officers or other detectives make the arrest, one clears the case with a D closure/clearance; and when one has the requisite proof to arrest and presumably convict a culprit, knows where he is located, but, for some reason beyond one's control, is unable to arrest him (for instance, the culprit is dead or is in a country that does not extradite its nationals), one takes an EC, or exceptional clearance. Only closings that are also clearances count as base hits.

No detective wants cases that he cannot clear. Detectives joke about discreetly moving an uptown corpse across the street into the next precinct so that the case responsibility and the unenviable C closure will fall to another precinct, squad, and detective. Not long ago, the Chief of Detectives himself had to decide whether an uptown corpse found exactly in the middle of the 59th Street Bridge should go to the Silk Stocking district's Nineteenth squad or across the river to Queens's One-Fourteen squad. Uptown murders also become fodder for the nearly constant squad-room bantering and razzing of peers, since everyone knows how difficult it is even to identify the victims, let alone to make the cases because the reticence of witnesses prevents public proof of culpability even when detectives know who the murderers are.

When a detective catches any homicide, except for high-profile murders such as the Cargill case or The Quad, he is taken off the chart for only four days to concentrate fully on the murder, while the trail, if there is one, is hot. After this initial period, he pursues the murder while catching other cases in the normal rotation. Because typical uptown murders draw no public notice and therefore little supervisory attention, detectives often call them "four days and a drawer" homicides, a tag that suggests the eventual disposition of most such cases unless they have "meat on the bone"—investigative leads that will produce specific proof of wrongdoing. When cases are in the drawer, detectives wait for the phone to ring with a tip either from an informant or, more likely, from another detective who has arrested someone ready to give testimony about an uptown murder in return for a deal.

Some detectives just go through the motions, and uptown murders allow slackers who simply want to be "on the tit" ample opportunity to dump cases. As in most large organizations, perhaps particularly in giant municipal civil-service public bureaucracies, about a fifth of the New York City Police Department, not necessarily the bottom fifth by rank, consists of timeservers, an estimate widely shared among veteran policemen. Some of these are "house mouses"—police officers who have seen the horror of the streets and will do anything to avoid it. But timeserving occurs in the Detective Bureau as well. Once a fabled elite corps, detectives used to be selected only by other detectives. In order to gain entrance to the bureau, one proved one's investigative capability or potential to already proven investigators and then underwent an apprenticeship of about five years before one was thought to be a seasoned detective. This selection process was honored as much in the breach (through hooks based on ethnic, kin, or sexual ties) as in the keeping, but only an invitation of some sort enabled one to enter the Detective Bureau.

Now, however, the route to the gold shield is thoroughly bureaucratized, so that, in addition to promotions for merit or by hook, certain tours of duty—say, 18 months in buy-and-bust narcotics operations—guarantee police officers the gold shield, whether or not they have any investigative experience or potential. Detectives themselves are acutely aware of the remarkable variations in skill level and especially investigative desire among their ranks. Some detectives find all witnesses uncooperative and close cases after half-hearted inquiries; in rare cases, some detectives do phantom investigations complete with false written reports documenting interviews that never happened. One aphorism in detectives' world is: "Wanna get away with murder? Do it when [Jones] is catching."

Detectives expend little sympathy on uptown homicide victims, who are seen to have lived in a different world, an alien moral universe. Indeed, detectives refer to the violent deaths of robbers, drug dealers, hit men, and other occupational criminals as public service homicides, a steely notion tempered in the furnace of continual exposure to street violence, where one sees different faces but always the same patterns. For instance, Detective Bobby Small, a tough-as-nails former Army sergeant during the Vietnam war, shed few tears on February 7, 1992, when he found the body of 17-year-old Taj Meyers, bullet in the top of his skull, on the first level of the fire escape behind 504 West 159th Street. The gut-shot body of 23-year-old Elvis Cruz was found in Apartment 3C of the same building, a shabby two-room dive with a scale, other drug paraphernalia, and a makeshift shrine on two juxtaposed coffee tables. The shrine included eight pictures of the Virgin, St. Joseph, and the crucified Jesus, along with seven tall votive candles encased in multicolored, religiously decorated glass; scattered around the shrine were scores of torn one-dollar bills.

Although Small later led an exhaustive investigation that resulted in the arrests of several of Meyers's family in Bridgeport, Connecticut, the main conversation among police at the scene was whether Cruz might have lived long enough before his stomach wound claimed him to get to the window and plug his obvious assailant, Meyers, who was making his getaway on the fire escape. Indeed, some police come to see their role essentially as the geographical containment of violence, allowing "bad guys" like this pair to kill one another. Although some detectives occasionally say, "A life is a life," as a way of legitimating to outsiders their hard work on a difficult uptown case, such sentiments are half-hearted at best and are never argued before peers. In the world of detectives, some human lives are simply worth more than others.

The measure here is perceived decency, that is, law-abiding, hard-working, other-respecting sobriety. Of course, detectives note ruefully that social worth is no talisman against violence. Indeed, detectives, joined by many prosecutors, argue that the amount of force required to kill someone is usually inversely proportional to his social worth. They cite decent women who bleed to death from a nicked elbow in an attempted rape, or police officers who die of trauma from a single bullet wound, as contrasted with drug dealers or robbers who walk out of the hospital under their own steam even though their bullet-riddled bodies resemble Swiss cheese.

Detectives often note with satisfaction that the streets mete out justice to guilty victims far more effectively and unforgivingly than the courts. Squad-room talk regularly features searing stories of street justice, always told in a matter-of-fact, casual manner. Such stories highlight the consequences of violating the law of the streets, often with an overtone of biblical meetness. Thus, rapists get raped in prison; hit men get their brains blown out by other hit men; robbers get robbed; drug dealers get shot in the spine and find themselves paralyzed for life. And, unlike other social worlds where incompetence does not matter and indeed often triumphs, the streets exact a savage price for bumbling ineptitude. Thus, in squad-room dialogue, guilty victims of murder are as likely as their assailants to be called mutts, mopes, skells, dirtballs, knuckleheads, scumbags, or slimeballs.

Victims of personal disputes that turn violent, the everyday stuff of underclass existence, whether emerging out of volatile sexual liaisons, or real or imagined street insults, fall into a more anomalous moral category. Still, detectives see the deaths of such victims as inextricably connected to their chaotic, directionless lives. Sooner or later, it is thought, those drifting in or near our society's undercurrents will get sucked into unpredictable and swirling eddies.

Of course, detectives can make cases without any empathy whatsoever for victims. Indeed, bureaucratic incentives ensure some efforts, often extraordinary efforts, even for victims that detectives think loathsome. Moreover, unraveling the tangle of underworld life, searching for dangerous men, and breaking them have their own powerful fascinations. One penetrates false identities and crooked tales to glimpse savage truths that become fodder for amusement and wonder with one's fellows; one thrills to the chase, with adrenalin coursing and heart pounding, knowing that things might end in bloody chaos; one exults at outwitting and trapping hardened criminals in contradictory statements that might lock prison doors. And, if one possesses and demonstrates the requisite doggedness, one might elicit from peers the highest accolade that one detective can pay another: "I wouldn't want that guy after me." The world of detectives, indeed of all police, is a world of secret knowledge coupled with action.

Still, all detectives want cases with "innocent" victims, those who through no fault of their own have suffered unjust violence, whose lives make their deaths worth investigating and, one hopes, avenging through the legal process. At bottom, detectives see themselves as defenders of the innocent, upholders of the social structures that make innocence possible. Only cases involving innocent victims permit detectives to espouse openly abstract, universalistic principles among their peers, and this only briefly, even as such cases provide detectives with well-lighted arenas to display their skills and to garner public attention for what is usually thankless and anonymous work.

Between the extremes of guilty and innocent victims, detectives sometimes construct quasi-innocent victims out of corpses. When, for instance, prostitutes are sexually violated before being murdered or victims have been tortured or suffered particularly gruesome deaths, detectives drop their hallmark caustic sarcasm and sometimes even the dark humor that impels them to give every case a sardonic name. They speak of such victims with rueful sadness, justifying dogged work on even seemingly fruitless cases by arguing that "no one deserves to die like that."

For the prosecutors who eventually have to dispose of the cases that detectives catch, uptown murders present serious evidentiary problems intrinsically connected to the nature of their work. Prosecutors are officers of the court and the guardians and enforcers of often quite rarified legal procedures. They are caught in a constant contest between detectives' knowledge of criminality, often obtained only by bypassing procedures, and their own (and the courts') demands for legal proof, that is, convincing demonstrations of waywardness that adhere strictly to established and legitimate procedures. Prosecutors have more discretionary power than any other occupational group in the criminal justice system. In major cases, prosecutors decide who gets arrested and who does not, a decision determined by their judgments about the strength of existing evidence. They negotiate pleas, reducing charges and prison time in exchange for admissions of guilt and testimony against other criminals. Most important, they can decline to prosecute because they think that a defendant is not guilty, because the evidence against him is simply not strong enough to withstand the attacks of defense attorneys, or because they think that particular circumstances make prosecution inequitable.

Prosecutors exercise their power in very different ways. At one end of the continuum are zealots, easily spotted by the inflexibility of their plea offers or, conversely, by the cases they choose to try. Even when evidence is overwhelming and a good plea easily obtainable, zealots pursue the top count. Or when the evidence is shaky and a plea bargain is advisable, they insist on trial. Owing to their inflexibility, zealots rarely last long in the finger-twisting, eye-gouging, horse-trading bazaar that is the criminal justice system, an environment uncongenial to moral fervor. Some zealots are careerists in disguise, who stay in the district attorney's office no longer than it takes to become known as aggressive prosecutors; once established, this reputation is easily bartered for more comfortable surroundings in a law firm.

At the other end of the continuum from zealots are prosecutorial technicians who settle all cases quickly in a wholly mechanistic way, losing any sense after a while of the reality of their cases and the humanity of their complainants, victims, and witnesses, let alone their defendants. Such ritualism is a classic response to emotionally draining work where one constantly confronts gore, mayhem, and extreme violence. One cannot even figure out what justice is in specific cases, let alone pursue it, without entering deeply into the violent details and opening oneself to the danger of being ravaged by them. The ritualist applies bureaucratic formulas to protect his self from his work.

In between are prosecutors slogging away at middle-range cases: offering pleas in most, when they have a case at all, in order to clear crowded calendars, all the while hoping that today's plea bargain will not turn out to be tomorrow's Jack the Ripper; or going to trial when plea discussions break down, trying to extract whatever justice can be salvaged from messy, often ambiguous, always troubling fractures of the social order.

When cases do go to trial, prosecutors are expected to win them. At DANY, 90 percent of all felony trials result in convictions. When a major trial comes along, usually one with a high media profile, the stakes are enormous. Loss of a big trial can undermine a prosecutor's reputation, not only at DANY but with detectives, even though everyone knows that trials are crap shoots. Indeed, fear of losing colors prosecutorial work far more intensely than the desire to win. The reward for winning a tough case is to be assigned to even tougher cases.

Uptown murders test prosecutors' nerve, ingenuity, and especially their tolerance for ambiguity. Indeed, to understand uptown murders at all, let alone to resolve them fairly, one must enter into the everglade terrain of the netherworld. In uptown murders, few things are ever certain. One never knows whom to believe, witnesses are almost always suspect, and one resolves a case only when the right fish gets caught in the right net tended by the right fisherman. Uptown murder cases often end in a morass, without any resolution whatsoever. Such quicksandlike affairs typically swallow zealous prosecutors whole and frighten technicians completely out of the mire. Even the most idealistic prosecutors come to appreciate, and share in their own way, detectives' caustic endorsement of the rough justice of the streets.

Many years ago, mirroring detectives' notion of uptown murders as public service affairs, even the best prosecutors at DANY resolved such homicides with the promise of Zip-1 (0–1 year) pleas, giving detectives the ability to clear essentially unsolvable cases. Detectives obtained confessions on old murders from criminals arrested on new charges by assuring the culprits of essentially no prison time on either the old or the new charges in exchange for the truth, a promise that their comrades who had taken such deals and who were already back on the streets could easily confirm. But with the tremendous increase in the city's murder rate in the 1980s, as a result of crack cocaine's democratization of the drug trade, such bureaucratic solutions to uptown murders, however desirable from an organizational point of view, became politically untenable; almost all the characters in uptown murders are regularly from minority groups, and the issue became the perceived equitability of police investigation. Moreover, the explosion in violence, although it was usually confined uptown, became perceived as a dangerous threat to general public safety.

Uptown murders test the commitment of both detectives and prosecutors to the universalistic principles that underpin our social order. Yet, despite all the peer sanctions in both worlds against appearing high-minded, despite sometimes cranky, short-sighted bosses, unsympathetic victims, problematic witnesses, and stories so tangled that one can scarcely ascertain what happened, let alone prove someone guilty of crime, some prosecutors and detectives spend months, even years, on uptown cases, including time without pay, simply to do justice.

Early in 1992 Dan Rather joined the Homicide Investigation Unit with the agreement that he could make a big case and get to the bottom of the mayhem emerging out of the low 170s in Washington Heights. Initially, he focused once again on the garage-robbery pattern, knowing that those robberies had financed drug operations, the key to most street violence. As it happened, Clint's trail was stone cold by that time. But quickly several paths into the bramble opened up almost at once.

First, Jerry Dimuro brought the Cargill murder to Terry Quinn at HIU, telling him that he was looking for Platano, as was Detective Mark Tebbens in the Four-O precinct; Tebbens's investigation into The Quad, with his long-term knowledge of the violence on Beekman Avenue, had yielded a portrait of a gang headed by Lenny and Nelson Sepulveda that was from the Three-Four precinct and was tearing up Mott Haven. Quinn also had notes from an interview with a confidential informant who stated: "Lenny Sepulveda is the worst guy in New York." Quinn contacted Tebbens and told him about Detective Garry Dugan's systematic indexing of the same ring of players. All of this information was passed along to Rather.

Then on January 29, 1992, Platano was arrested for possession of narcotics in New Jersey and named Lenny Sepulveda as the shooter in the Cargill homicide. After the Bronx District Attorney's office refused to issue an arrest warrant for Platano for his participation in The Quad, leading to his immediate release on bail, Rather contacted Tebbens and offered HIU's help in making the case against Platano.

As spring 1992 wore on, and as the street war in the Three-Four precinct escalated, each new homicide and assault deepened many investigators' confusion. But for Garry Dugan, still with the Manhattan North Homicide Squad, each one provided yet another glimpse into the structure of the street violence. His already encyclopedic index files were growing. The warfare began to spill over into the Bronx on May 3rd, when John Soldi was killed and seven other men and women severely wounded after being gunned down in a drive-by shooting of Frankie Cuevas's drug spot at Manor and Watson Avenues. Street rumors had Cuevas as the intended target, with Fat Danny Rincon and Pasqualito from the Red Top crew as the shooters. On the morning of June 21st, Lenny Sepulveda got out of prison. That night, once again at Manor and Watson, Kevin Nazario was shot to death and five other men wounded in a drive-by shooting. Street rumors had Pasqualito and a burly, dark-skinned Dominican as the assailants.

Back in Manhattan on July 12th, at 0015 hours, Jose Reyes, aka El Feo or Moncheche—a diminutive, stocky man with mustache and goatee but, according to street rumors, a widely feared, big-time cocaine and heroin supplier of great personal authority—was on the telephone in his bodega headquarters at 2172 Amsterdam Avenue at 167th Street in the Three-Four precinct, when a single unidentified assailant shot him in the spine, paralyzing him for life. Investigators knew little about El Feo and had no idea who shot him.

Making cases on big-time, sprawling street-criminal operations requires certain habits of mind. If one is to make a case against a gang, one must break through the bailiwick mentality endemic to all large organizations. Few occupational worlds are more bureaucratized than the criminal justice system, the institutional crossroads where the bureaucracies of the police, district attorneys and their investigators, the courts, corrections, probation, and the defense bar all come together around particular cases. Only bureaucratic organizations can bring a semblance of rational control over the seeming irrationalities of the street. Yet, rational organization almost always produces its own irrationalities.

Each of the bureaucracies of the criminal justice system has its own internal hierarchy, its own organizational premiums on specific behaviors, attitudes, and accomplishments, its own internal rewards and prestige rankings, and its own carefully guarded jurisdiction. Each bureaucracy thus creates a self-referential world with its peculiar myopia. Squad detectives, to take just one example, get credit only for clearing and closing their own cases in their own precincts. Perhaps even more importantly, their commanders are judged on their subordinates' clearance rates, providing no institutional incentives for commanders to allow their detectives, especially their star detectives, to get involved in investigations of cases outside their precincts. Meeting internal organizational exigencies, crucial for fostering one's career, often takes precedence over crimefighting or the larger maintenance of public order. But unless one can find a way to harness the dense and intimate street knowledge of detectives, often from different precincts and with different bosses, large-scale investigations founder before they begin; criminal gangs are unfettered by these bureaucratic complexities, although they recognize and exploit them.

One must also find ways around the legal constraints posed by different jurisdictions. While the New York City Police Department has citywide jurisdiction, each of the city's five counties has its own district attorney's office, stamped with its own peculiarities, shaped in part by the style of its courts, itself a reflection of its juries. For instance, the Bronx's and Brooklyn's (Kings County) largely minority juries are famous for nullifying even well-made cases, particularly when police officers' testimony is central. Moreover, prosecutors in the DA's offices in both the Bronx and Brooklyn view the New York district attorney's office with the same jealousy that many residents of the outer boroughs harbor toward bright-lights, big-city Manhattan, and only very reluctantly yield jurisdictional prerogatives, even when prosecuting a case in Manhattan offers the best chance of achieving justice.

These bureaucratic and jurisdictional issues become considerably more complicated when federal prosecutors, federal courts, or federal agents from any of Washington's alphabet soup of law enforcement agencies decide to get involved in state criminal cases. Federal authorities play by their own rules. Federal prosecutors can use uncorroborated accomplice testimony in their cases, sometimes producing variant, and highly suspect, court records that defendants in associated state cases can utilize in mounting the endless appeals intrinsic to our system. Federal agents sometimes pull rank, stealing desirable cases from local police and frequently concealing information from them, even as New York City detectives universally ridicule federal agents' investigative abilities. ("Show me one federal hick who's solved a city murder. How can you solve murders sittin' at a desk?") Clashing jurisdictional claims and rivalries often sidetrack pursuit of the common weal.

Such bureaucratized structures typically produce fragmented knowledge. But making a big case means telling a big story, weaving together threads and patches of information, discrete cases in scattered, competing jurisdictions, into a coherent narrative pattern. Only coherent stories ultimately convince juries; and only big stories draw the media attention coveted in a world that offers few material rewards.

Dan Rather's prosecutorial interests and the Homicide Investigation Unit's philosophy made a nice fit. Not only does HIU deal almost exclusively in uptown murders, but it eschews piecemeal prosecution of individual cases. Instead, the unit prosecutes gangs as cohesive social groups, aiming to destroy whole criminal enterprises at once. The process is brutal and direct. When dealing with narcotics-trafficking organizations, HIU uses undercover cops to put buys into as many gang members as possible, making them either potential defendants or witnesses. The unit takes down (arrests) everybody at once in order to ensure any cooperation at all. Using the penalties of New York's stringent drug laws as a threat, it forces some gang members, in exchange for lesser sentences, to betray their comrades, garnering bits and pieces of the street history of a gang. It focuses in particular on the murders that are part and parcel of the gang's business operations. The warp for the story is New York State's conspiracy laws, which provide a way of linking individual crimes. HIU is also the organizational crossroads for the High-Intensity Drug Trafficking Area Task Force, a federally funded initiative that brings together city and state police, a variety of federal agents, as well as state and federal prosecutors. The unit is in the forefront of cross-jurisdictional investigative and prosecutorial work, and thus at the center of all the conflicts such efforts entail. Finally, HIU is an extremely active unit that always has multiple cases at various stages of investigation or prosecution.

When Rather joined the unit in early 1992, for instance, HIU had a number of other cases in the making or in the very early stages of investigation. Among these were cases against a 15-man East Harlem heroin trafficking ring based in a playground at East 105th–106th Streets between Lexington and Third Avenues (arrests made on April 1, 1992; all pleaded guilty); three separate cocaine gangs involving 25 people operating out of 2011 Amsterdam Avenue and 498 West 159th Street (indicted June 2, 1992; all pleaded guilty); the Purple Top crack cocaine gang of 12 members centered on East 122nd Street (indicted October 8, 1992; all pleaded guilty); the 13-member Avenue C boys, who operated a crack, cocaine, and heroin supermarket between 8th and 12th Streets on the Lower East Side (indicted November 22, 1993; all pleaded guilty); the 64-member La Compania based between 147th and 150th Streets and Amsterdam (indicted September 8, 1994; all pleaded guilty); the 48-

member Young Talented Children from 107th Street between Amsterdam and Central Park West (indicted June 22, 1994; 45 pleaded guilty, 3 convicted at trial); the 33-member Young City Boys, from Columbus Avenue between 104th and 106th Streets (indicted September 9, 1994; 30 pleaded guilty, 3 convicted at trial); and the 22-member Natural Born Killers, from Amsterdam Avenue between 104th and 109th Streets (indicted June 14, 1995; 21 pleaded guilty, 1 convicted at trial).

Constructing the history of a street gang and its crimes is slow, complicated work, filled with contradictions and ambiguity. Those with real knowledge of specific crimes committed by gang members are usually deeply involved in the crimes themselves or are guilty of other crimes, and therefore know to keep their mouths shut, or, especially if they are independent witnesses, are terrified of reprisal. Even when one finds a witness and can force him or her to testify under the threat of prosecution for still other crimes, or gets independent witnesses past the fear of testifying, what initially seems to be direct knowledge often turns out to be hearsay, recycled versions of street rumors intrinsic to a world where a fearsome reputation is one's most valued asset. Established gang members themselves may not know of certain criminal acts committed by their comrades or may know only part of the story. And when criminals become witnesses, they almost always leave themselves out of the pictures they paint, laying the blame for serious crimes on their comrades.

Finally, when one is investigating a street gang that is still on the street, one is aiming at a moving target. In trying to piece together the street history of the key criminal group between 171st and 174th Streets, Rather began by mapping out a skein of major violent events thought to be the gang's work. By mid-March 1992 his list included the Cargill homicide, The Quad, Platano's accidental killing of little Leideza Rivera in front of the Jerome Avenue chicken shop, the attempted murder of the ballplayer Rafael Rodriguez at the Las Vegas

Nightclub, now attributed to Platano for hire, the murder of Danny Montilla (Madonna), the shooting of Frankie Cuevas and Manny Garcia, and the subsequent shooting of Gilbert Campusano.

Rather still had no clear picture of the gang's structure or of the factional splits that had led to the ongoing war on the streets. But he finally learned something of the group's origins. The informant who had initially given Quinn the name "Lenny's Boys" later told Rather and Quinn that many members of the gang had been classmates at George Washington High School in Washington Heights. They played football together and cut classes to hang out on the handball courts in the schoolyard. They did not distinguish themselves as scholars or as models of decorum in high school. Indeed, an exasperated teacher once characterized them as "a bunch of wild cowboys."

cracking
the
case

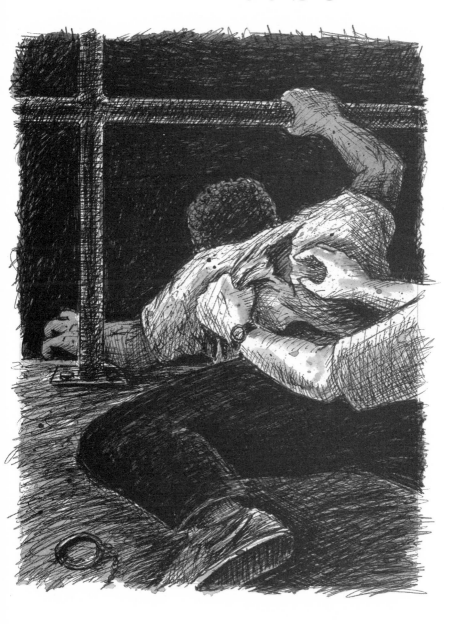

The first big break
   in the Wild Cowboys
investigation came
   disguised as just another uptown
murder. On March 20, 1992, Detective Ruben Gonzalez of the
Four-O Squad caught the homicide of Esteban Clemente aka
English, who had been shot in the lobby of The Hole at 348
Beekman Avenue. Detective Mark Tebbens, who assisted Gonzalez, knew English as a custodian of drugs and night manager
for the Red Top crew. English was married to Fat Iris Cruz, in
whose apartment two floors above the crew stashed sizable
stores of drugs to re-supply The Hole as needed. Bleeding to
death, English struggled up the stairs into his and Fat Iris's
apartment, where EMS technicians found him and took him
to the hospital.

When Tebbens canvassed the building, no one provided any
specific information. Street rumors, however, named one
Marion Frazier aka Boogie as the gunman. Boogie's mother was
Louise McBride, whose third-floor apartment at 352 Beekman,
next door to The Hole, served as another stash location for
the Red Top crew. Boogie also worked for Red Top but side-
lined as a stickup man; it was said that McBride's other son,
Smooch, was also involved with Red Top. Only four days earlier, the Four-O Squad had caught the homicide of Kennedy
Earl Thomas, a customer at The Hole who had been shot to
death after somebody, perhaps Thomas, pulled a knife on
Louise McBride while buying crack from her. Boogie was the
prime suspect in that killing as well. Louise McBride and English were said to have quarreled; perhaps Boogie shot English
to defend his mother's honor, as detectives suspected he had

done with Thomas. Unlike most of the other cases on Beekman Avenue, Detective Gonzalez was able to develop a reasonable amount of evidence against Boogie. On April 6th Tebbens spotted him at 141st Street and Cypress Avenue, hanging
out with Fat Danny, Pasqualito, and a tall, skinny Dominican,
and arrested him for English's murder.

Then on April 22nd Tebbens received a frantic phone call
from Elizabeth Morales, also of 348 Beekman. Morales, the
37-year-old matriarch of the huge Morales-Cruz family of
twelve children plus assorted nonconsanguineous relations,
told Tebbens that she and her entire family had fled Beekman
Avenue in fear for their lives. The Red Top crew was after
them. After staying briefly with a relative in the Bronx, then
in a motel, then in an emergency shelter on Catherine Street
in Chinatown, she was in a Tier-Two family shelter on Dean
Street in Brooklyn. She said she desperately needed help
and that she could tell him about the violence on Beekman
Avenue.

By that time Tebbens was well known on Beekman for his
war cries and his persistently aggressive investigations. Beekman Avenue residents had even assigned Tebbens his own code
name, Seventy-Eight, the meaning of which is obscure to this
day, to alert everybody to his constant intrusions in the neighborhood. The Morales-Cruz family was afraid of Tebbens as
well, fearing that he might arrest them because of their involvement with the Red Top crew. When Tebbens went to
the shelter to see Elizabeth Morales, the children scattered
to the corners of their squalid room, some even climbing out
the window to the fire escape, prepared to make a getaway.
But the family had nowhere else to turn.

Out of scrambled, sometimes hysterical accounts, Tebbens
pieced together the following story. On March 20th English
staggered into his apartment, bleeding profusely; he screamed
at Fat Iris to get a package of drugs and money, which Platano
had given him just that morning to stash in his freezer, out of

the apartment before police arrived. By this time, the entire apartment was crammed with building residents, including several of Elizabeth Morales's children: 20-year-old Angel Cruz aka Tito, 19-year-old Alejandrina Cruz called Ita, 17-year-old Michael Cruz, 16-year-old Little Iris Cruz, and 14-year-old Joey Morales. As her husband lay dying, Fat Iris fetched the package from the freezer and handed it to Little Iris, who passed it to Ita, who gave it to Michael, who stashed it in a washing machine with dirty laundry. Later, after English was taken to the hospital, Edgar Maldonado aka White Boy, married to Elizabeth Cruz (another of Elizabeth Morales's daughters), retrieved the package of cash and eight bundles of crack vials, each bundle containing 100 five-dollar vials. The youngsters divided most of the money and drugs, leaving some hidden in the apartment. Elizabeth Morales admitted to Tebbens that Tito, Michael, and Joey were deeply involved with the Red Top crew, either as pitchers, lookouts, couriers, or errand boys. And she and her daughter Little Iris often joined Fat Iris and Louise McBride in packaging the crack vials for sale, tapping the vials in the process.

But now she and her family were in big trouble. The day that English was shot, Pasqualito, along with Francisco Robles aka Frankie, the chubby neighborhood kid who had risen slowly but surely in the gang's hierarchy, stormed into Fat Iris's apartment, demanding their packages. Fat Iris sent them to Elizabeth Morales, who told them that the packages were lost. Pasqualito threatened to kill Morales and her entire family unless he received the packages immediately. The next day, Pasqualito and Frankie approached Morales's son Tito, who was sitting in a car in front of 348 Beekman. Pasqualito told Tito: "Get the packages or I'm gonna kill you." When Tito claimed no knowledge of the packages, Pasqualito pistol-whipped him through the window, then dragged him out of the car and continued the beating; 25 stitches were required to close Tito's wounds. He then put a gun to Tito's head, and shouted to Elizabeth Morales, who watched, terrified, from her fourth-story window: "Get the packages or your son is dead." Morales took the remaining drugs and money still hidden in her apartment to Fat Iris, who brought them back to Pasqualito and Frankie, but Pasqualito demanded everything back by the next day. At that point, Morales said she also heard from a tall, skinny man named Tezo, who always carried a gun, that the "big boss gave his permission to come and kill" her family. She frantically turned to Battata, a manager for the crew, who suggested that she ask Platano for help.

Morales knew Platano well. He regularly gave her money for groceries and had her cook for him. When he came to her apartment to eat and watch television, he flirted with young Ita, promising one day to marry her. Once, Platano had come to her apartment somewhat agitated and asked her to fix food for him; while he was eating, he told her that he had just accidentally killed a young girl at a chicken shop while shooting at someone else. He regretted the incident, he said, because he too had a daughter and could imagine the pain of losing her. But even Platano couldn't help Morales in her situation.

Pasqualito's fury knew no bounds. When Morales received another death threat, she took her family and fled. She heard later that Pasqualito and Frankie tried to break into Fat Iris's apartment, still demanding their packages; Fat Iris also fled to a city shelter, where she remained for more than a year.

As it happened, police had arrived on the scene right after Tito had been beaten unconscious. When he awakened in the hospital, he told them that Pasqualito had pistol-whipped him. A month later, on April 20th at 1600 hours, Mark Tebbens, along with Detective Jimmy Slattery, who had caught Tito's beating, found Pasqualito in the basketball courts opposite 370 Cypress and arrested him for the assault on Tito. On the detectives' way back to the house with Pasqualito in cuffs, the squad patched through a call from the firm of Goldstein, Weinstein & Fuld demanding that the police not speak to

Pasqualito. After they reached the squad room, Pasqualito's lawyer, Barry Weinstein, called Tebbens again, reiterating that no statements were to be taken from his client. He also asked Tebbens if the police were looking for another suspect in the pistol-whipping. Tebbens responded that they were. Weinstein asked for the name of the suspect, saying that he would arrange for surrender; but Tebbens refused to name Robles to Weinstein.

That evening, Tito picked Pasqualito out of a lineup as the man who had pistol-whipped him. Pasqualito was processed, posted bail, and, within a couple of days, was back out on the streets. On April 23rd, Michael Nedick called Detective Slattery to say that he had heard that Slattery was looking for a client of his named Frankie. When Slattery confirmed this, Nedick arranged for Frankie Robles's surrender later that same day. When lawyers arrange for their clients' surrender, magistrates are more amenable than usual to bail applications because the clients have shown themselves subject to appropriate authority. Frankie Robles also made bail quickly.

The same day that Tebbens heard from Elizabeth Morales, he sat down with Joey Morales and asked him what he knew about The Quad. Joey said that on the night of December 16, 1991, he had been standing right near 320 Beekman Avenue when Platano, whom he also knew as Darkman, along with Stanley and Shorty, came out of a white car shooting at people in the alley. Fat Danny stayed in the same car holding a gun; and Renny Harris, along with a male Hispanic whom he could not identify, came out of a black car shooting. Joey said that, right before the massacre, he had blundered into a meeting on the second-floor landing of 348 Beekman, where all of the shooters, plus some other men, were loading guns. Joey later gave a statement about The Quad to Bronx ADA Don Hill that differed in some details from his statement to Tebbens, and when he testified about the shooting to two Bronx grand juries he gave additional, slightly different, statements. The inconsistencies of his accounts created some apprehension about his reliability as a witness.

Ita told Tebbens a story similar to Joey's first statement, adding Pasqualito and three other men she could not identify to the list of shooters. On April 28th Tito confirmed his siblings' version of the events, adding that Platano and Stanley had bragged to him the day after The Quad about "wasting all them people" on the street. Even though the evidence was given in desperation and therefore sure to be contested, the Morales family's testimony gave Tebbens enough to get an arrest warrant for Platano. He finally made the arrest on May 13th at Columbia Presbyterian Hospital, where Platano was recovering from the serious gunshot wounds he had received on April 14th. The day before the arrest, PO Vasquez, who was guarding Platano in the hospital, overheard him say in a phone conversation to an unknown party: "Supposedly they have a witness that came forward. Find out who it is, find out about it, and take care of it." Tebbens arrested Fat Danny for The Quad on June 10th on the evidence from the Morales-Cruz family.

Joey Morales also told Tebbens that he had witnessed the murder of Edgar Maldonado aka Eddie in St. Mary's Park on November 7, 1991. The police had found Maldonado's body just inside the park near Beekman Avenue with nine stab wounds, seven in the back. The wounds were so gaping that Maldonado's internal organs had gushed out. Joey told Tebbens that, at about 3:45 in the afternoon, Platano, Stanley, and Ulysses Mena aka Dominican Chino confronted Maldonado, a pitcher for Red Top. Platano told Eddie: "Give me the drugs." Maldonado claimed that he didn't have them. Platano stabbed Maldonado with a machete-like knife. Then Stanley stabbed him as well. Dominican Chino followed with a serrated "Rambo" knife and carved Maldonado up, disemboweling him. Once Tebbens located Fat Iris Cruz in the city shelters and persuaded her to talk to him about events on Beekman

Avenue, she told Tebbens that, earlier in the morning of November 7th, she had seen Platano, Dominican Chino, Tezo, Stanley, and some other Red Top members standing in front of 348 Beekman Avenue. Fat Iris said that she overheard Platano and Stanley telling the others that they "had to get this guy." Dominican Chino replied: "I wish you had told me earlier, I would have got him for you."

Tebbens knew that Dominican Chino was a bad actor. The night of December 21, 1990, Loretta Baker aka Winkie of 348 Beekman, who lived with her identical twin Floretta Baker aka Baldie, woke up in the hospital with a bullet in her head. The afternoon before (as Tebbens learned from a confidential informant), Lenny, Nelson, Platano, and Dominican Chino had barged into her apartment on the second floor because, after Platano had slapped her teenaged niece in the face, Winkie had given notice that she no longer wanted her house used as a stash apartment. Confronting her, Platano threw several bundles of crack on the table. Winkie insisted that she no longer wanted drugs in the house. Platano pulled out a pistol, pointed it at her, said: "Pow, Pow. Pow." He placed the pistol on the table. Dominican Chino picked up the gun, waved it at Winkie, and shot her in the head. Later, Chino apologized to Winkie, telling her that he hadn't meant to shoot her, but he laughed and joked about the incident with his own friends, saying that he was tired of Winkie "tapping the bottles." Tebbens had also heard about Chino beating up workers with his fists to keep them in line and threatening to throw one down a flight of stairs. Such outbursts of direct, physical violence punctuated his normal gun-wielding threats and were triggered, it seems, by women calling him a "pussy" for needing a gun to keep girl workers in line.

Ita Cruz also told Tebbens about the murder of Anthony Villerbe, whose riddled body was discovered by police at 0057 hours on January 3, 1992, in front of 610 Beech Terrace. Villerbe was a former Correction officer who had been fired because of his association with known felons connected to a

September 30, 1991, homicide in the One-Fourteen precinct in Queens. His body was hanging out of the driver's side of his car, his back and torso on the ground, his feet still in the car, his mouth frozen in a macabre grin. Villerbe had gone into the crack business, buying and then reselling Red Top crack from Beekman Avenue as far south as Baltimore. Ita saw him leave The Hole at 348 Beekman and get into his car, which he drove in reverse to Beech Terrace. He parked and sat waiting in the vehicle. Suddenly, Nelson Sepulveda came out of The Hole and walked up the block toward Beech Terrace with his hand under his shirt. Ita heard shots. Then Nelson came running out of Beech Terrace, again with his hand under his shirt.

Tebbens's immediate task was to keep the Morales-Cruz family alive; the lawyers could sort out credibility issues later. The family couldn't stay much longer in the Dean Street shelter. With the help of Bronx ADA Don Hill, Tebbens got the family moved to a city-owned apartment on Chauncey Street in Brownsville, Brooklyn, right at the edge of Bedford Stuyvesant. He also arranged for them to receive public assistance. He befriended the children, especially Michael, Joey, and Tito, often giving them money out of his own pocket and spending enormous amounts of time with them, the only adult male ever to have done so.

While members of the Morales-Cruz family were beginning to trust Tebbens, they had little faith in the system as a whole. Family members knew that the Four-O precinct had at least one corrupt cop, namely PO Roberto Lazar (a pseudonym), who grew up with the whole Red Top crew in Washington Heights. They knew that another cop, Marilyn Perez aka Smiley, had become a junkie and, with her sister Nyxida aka Nikki, was pitching crack on Beekman to feed her habit. They had also seen Correction officers Anthony Villerbe and Guy Gaines deeply involved in the Beekman Avenue drug scene. Pasqualito's immediate release after pistol-whipping Tito offered little reassurance.

In early August 1992 Tebbens's own situation became unsettled. He was transferred out of the Four-O squad and assigned to the Bronx DA's office to help make the case on The Quad. Elizabeth Morales and her children had more trouble reaching him, and he had less time to spend with them. Over the summer, the family drifted back into old patterns of association, calling friends in the Bronx, becoming, as is often the case with uptown murder witnesses, their own worst enemies.

Late in the afternoon of August 4, 1992, a wild car chase originated at West 171st Street and Audubon in the Three-Four precinct. Tall, lean, and hard PO Johnny Moynihan of Local Motion, the precinct's aggressive team of anticrime cops whose basic job was to take guns off the street, was riding with Paddy Regan and Artie Barragan when he spotted a powerfully built man with the butt of a gun clearly visible in his waistband getting into the front passenger seat of a dark gray Taurus. The car's driver was also big and husky with closely cropped hair; a third man was in the rear seat. The officers drew their own weapons and started to approach the Taurus when it suddenly took off, heading west on 171st Street. The officers jumped back into their own car and, with Paddy Regan driving, followed closely. The Taurus raced across Audubon and St. Nicholas Avenue to Fort Washington Avenue, where it headed north. At 179th Street the Taurus made a careening left-hand turn, ripping through red lights with abandon and plunging toward the West Side Highway. The car turned north on the highway and quickly reached a speed of over 100 miles per hour, with Local Motion right behind it. The Taurus ripped off the road at the Dyckman Avenue exit at extremely high speed and did an almost immediate 180 degree U-turn around the sharply pointed traffic island separating east- and westbound traffic, swinging back toward the West Side Highway, where it turned south, hitting speeds of 125 miles per hour, weaving in and out of traffic.

Moynihan yelled at Regan to slow down, but Regan, who raced cars as a hobby back in his native Ireland, was already in his own zone, a state of intense, focused concentration that made him oblivious to all distractions. He kept pace with the Taurus, driving instinctively through the maze of startled drivers, some of whom pulled to the side of the road in terror. The cops put it over the radio about the chase in progress and asked for a roadblock to stop traffic. Between 125th and 110th Streets, Moynihan saw the front-passenger-seat man throw a gun out of the window. Traffic finally began to slow at 100th Street because of the roadblock. Suddenly, the Taurus tried to back up on the highway in an attempt to escape, but the car was blocked from behind. The driver then tried to drive up the steep embankment separating the southbound side of the highway from the northbound, but the Taurus couldn't make it up the slope.

The three men leapt from the car and scattered into Riverside Park, now swarming with cops from several precincts who chased the culprits, ran them to ground, and arrested them. All three went the hard way, with Moynihan tackling the rear-seat passenger, who turned out to be Manny Crespo, and subduing him after a prolonged struggle. Crespo had a tin containing a small amount of coke on his person. The driver was Pasqualito, and the passenger with the gun was Lenny Sepulveda. Lenny asked Moynihan if he were part of Local Motion, and said that a lot of cops had chased him and his boys but that no one had caught him before. Give credit, Lenny said, where credit is due.

Local Motion had the car removed to the Three-Four station house garage. Overnight, it was sent out to the police Whitestone Pound in Queens; the car turned out to be registered to 13-year-old Nicholas Bohan of West 171st Street. Garry Dugan had listened to the chase on the police radio back at the Three-Four and, with Bobby Small and Tony Imperato, took a ride downtown in time to see Lenny being arrested. When Dugan came back on duty the next morning, he went to the Queens pound and searched the car. By sheer luck, he hit the right combination of panel controls opening a *clavo*. Inside were a loaded .45-caliber Ruger and a loaded 9-millimeter Smith and Wesson, along with a box of .357 rounds; Dugan beeped Moynihan to tell him about the guns. Moynihan had taken the collars and had hauled Lenny, Pasqualito, and Manny downtown to court, had housed them in the adjacent Manhattan House of Detention, and had begun the paperwork to process their arrests. All three defendants were represented by Michael Nedick. The trio had joked with Moynihan about the whole process, and even started calling him Johnny. After he heard from Dugan, Moynihan took great pleasure in informing the culprits about finding the guns in the *clavo*.

While Moynihan was in the Early Case Assessment Bureau, Dan Rather summoned him upstairs to HIU, with his prisoners, and wrote up the felony complaint for gun possession, reckless endangerment, and resisting arrest. HIU investigators had covered all the identifying signs on the unit's doors with placards reading: Gun-Trafficking Unit. The investigators tried to get statements from Lenny, Pasqualito, and Manny Crespo as possible evidence to be used later in the conspiracy case. But none of the trio had anything to say that was useful in that regard. Pasqualito was particularly belligerent. Finally, investigators took Major Case fingerprints from all three culprits. As a joke, investigators told Pasqualito that they needed him to drop his pants so that they could take prints of his posterior to be matched against imprints on the seat of the Taurus; Pasqualito howled with laughter.

Then Rather told Moynihan privately that, although he was filing a felony complaint for gun possession along with the other charges, HIU wanted the case treated routinely, since a huge drug-conspiracy case was in the making. Moynihan was furious. He argued that the case should be put into the grand jury, thus holding the trio until ballistics came back on the guns; perhaps the weapons had bodies on them. But Rather argued that the case, taken by itself, could only muddy an already complicated investigation. When arrested, none of the three had guns on their persons; an all-night search for the weapon tossed out of the car on the West Side Highway had been fruitless. In addition, the defendants denied all knowledge of the guns in the *clavo*; in any event, the search, conducted without a warrant while the car was firmly in police custody, was problematic under New York's standards for searches, the strictest in the nation. Finally, the defendants said that they had fled when they saw men, whom they did not know to be policemen, coming toward the car with pistols drawn.

Moynihan thought that the ADA's reasoning was wholly without merit. Police are allowed, he argued, to do an inventory search of a car after witnessing a crime, such as the pell-mell car chase. The guns discovered should be enough to keep these obviously dangerous men off the streets while the district attorneys build a case against them. Why had he, Regan, and Barragan risked their lives to apprehend this crew, if the district attorney's office was simply going to cut them loose? What kind of message did that send to other cops? What kind of message did it send to the gang members? But after their routine arraignment, Lenny, Pasqualito, and Manny made bail immediately and were back on the streets by August 6th.

Just eight days later, on Friday afternoon, August 14, 1992, Michael Cruz was sitting in the passenger seat of a car with his half-brother, Edwin Agusto, on Chauncey Street in Brooklyn. Suddenly another car pulled up alongside them and opened fire. Edwin ducked, but Michael was hit full in the face; remarkably, the round circled his jaw and exited his other cheek, leaving him badly injured but alive. As it happened, Tebbens had just gone off duty, and Elizabeth Morales could not reach him. He was finally notified of the shooting on Sunday afternoon but was told that police from the Seven-Three precinct were handling the case. Since his own overtime log was already huge, he was ordered not to come on duty.

When Tebbens started his regular tour on Monday, Michael told him that the shooters were Pasqualito and Lenny Sepulveda. After the shooting, the police had temporarily relocated the Morales-Cruz family to a motel in Queens with nothing but the clothes they were wearing. Tebbens drove Elizabeth Morales back to the city-owned apartment on Chauncey Street to retrieve the family's belongings. From the street, Morales noticed that the curtains she always kept closed were open. When they entered the apartment, they found that every stick of furniture had been broken, every drawer ransacked, every piece of clothing thrown onto the floor, and every scrap of paper taken in an apparent search for information.

Tebbens and Hill immediately arranged for the whole Morales-Cruz family to be relocated to Middletown, a rural town north of New York City, where Tebbens found and rented two adjacent houses for them. The family was now thoroughly demoralized. Once, when Tebbens and Dugan visited them, they brought along a huge order of Chinese takeout food. The entire family fell on the food in a frenzy, grabbing it wildly, fighting each other for choice items, and then retreating, singly, to corners of the house to eat alone, as Tebbens and Dugan watched in wonder. The family's distress was heightened in mid-September when Fat Danny, under arrest for The Quad on the evidence given by the Morales-Cruz children, made $250,000 bail and walked out of jail. Tebbens and Dugan were long used to what they see as the irrationalities of the criminal justice system; the aphorism among detectives is: "That's why they call it *criminal* justice." But the Morales-Cruz family simply could not understand how "known killers" like Lenny, Pasqualito, and Fat Danny could be free altogether or out on bail.

Tebbens almost caught Lenny for shooting Michael Cruz on August 18, 1992. Detective Eddie Benitez of the High Intensity Drug Trafficking Area Task Force had spotted Pasqualito in a pass-by of the gang's hangout on Cypress Avenue, and he immediately called Tebbens. Together with HIDTA detectives Cesar Ortiz and John Saccia, Tebbens took a ride over to Cypress, which was crowded with neighborhood people on the blazing summer day. Pasqualito was nowhere in sight. But there, lounging right in front of 354 Cypress, was Lenny, along with George Santiago aka Seller. Nearby were two Ninja motorcycles. Lenny and George spotted Tebbens and immediately ran inside 354 Cypress. Tebbens called for backup, and the three officers charged into the building after Lenny.

The two wings of the building are linked horizontally to each other at the rear by concrete balconies, and still other balconies link 354 Cypress to the two wings of 370 Cypress next door. Exterior stairs run up each well, and the entire complex is surrounded at the rear by a high metal chain fence topped with barbed wire. The officers scattered inside the building, with Tebbens heading up the staircase. Just as he reached the second-floor balcony, Tebbens came face-to-face with Lenny. The two powerful men wrestled with each other, Tebbens trying to cuff Lenny, Lenny twisting and turning, all the while crawling toward the balcony. With a mighty shove, Lenny threw Tebbens off his back for an instant and dove head-first over the second-floor balcony to the cement floor below. Tebbens reached out and tried to grab Lenny back, but clutched only his shirt, which tore away in Tebbens's hands. Lenny landed on his right knee, and hobbling badly, ran out the rear of 354 Cypress and disappeared into the honeycomb of 370 Cypress.

By this time the backup had arrived. Lenny was trapped. There was no exit from the complex without being seen by the police. The police sat on the house for awhile. But with night coming on and an always-dangerous door-to-door search in the offing, and with overtime mounting, a lieutenant ordered all the police to return to their commands, much to Tebbens's frustration. When he came back a few hours later, the Ninja bikes were gone. On September 5, 1992, while doing a ride-around in the Three-Four precinct, Tebbens again spotted Lenny in a late model Cadillac on West 171th Street. He followed Lenny over to the Bronx but lost him in traffic.

Throughout the fall, Tebbens pressed the Morales-Cruz family on what they knew about crimes involving the Red Top crew. Some of the information was crucially important. Eventually, on October 29th, Elizabeth Morales, Michael Cruz, and Joey Morales all named Pasqualito, Victor Mercedes, and Lenny Sepulveda as the shooters in The Double homicide of September 3, 1989. Elizabeth said that she had just left a grocery store on Beekman and Beech Terrace and walked over to Cypress when she saw all three men shooting a man in a green car that had tried to make a U turn. Then, she said, Lenny ran right toward her and handed her his gun, saying: "Snitches get stitches. Keep it, and keep your mouth shut, or I'll kill you." The evidence naming Lenny as the third culprit allowed Tebbens to reopen that investigation, essentially in limbo since the Bronx court adjourned Victor's and Pasqualito's trial for the murders when the state could not produce its witnesses.

However, some of the information provided by Elizabeth Morales and Tito Cruz proved troubling. In late 1992 the Cargill murder was still unsolved. Morales told Tebbens that, one day in late spring 1991, while she was talking to Platano about damage to one of his cars, Platano bragged about lighting up some white kids on the West Side Highway, saying: "That happens when you fuck with me." Was it possible that Platano had actually been the shooter in the highway murder? On November 27, 1992, Tito Cruz gave a brief statement to Tebbens about the Cargill homicide, followed, on December 9th, with an elaborate statement to Garry Dugan and Jerry Dimuro. Tito described what happened on Saturday night and Sunday morning of May 18–19, 1991, when he and Mask drove to the Palladium on 14th Street near Union Square, where they met up with several crew members, including Platano. Platano got into a "beef" with "three white guys" because they owed him money, and Platano vowed to "smoke 'em." The whole crew left the club and waited outside in three cars: Tito driving a small burgundy Chevrolet, accompanied by Mask; X-Man driving a large burgundy Chevrolet with gold trim, with Lenny in the front passenger seat, Platano directly behind him, Dominican Mickey Mouse next to Platano, flanked by Dominican Chino. An unknown "fat guy" drove Platano's white BMW with blue convertible top, accompanied by Raymond Polanco. They watched as the three white youths left the club and, after putting a white female into a yellow cab, got into a red pickup truck.

A chase began, as the pickup truck fled across 14th Street, followed closely by the three cars; the chase went up and down many side streets, entering the West Side Highway at 57th Street heading north. At one point, Tito said, the large burgundy Chevrolet sideswiped a white Toyota. In the left lane, the white BMW pulled ahead of the red pickup truck, still in the right lane, followed by the large burgundy Chevrolet, which pulled directly parallel to the pickup; Tito and Mask trailed the large Chevrolet, driving in the left lane. Then, Tito said, he saw Lenny and Platano extend their arms out of the side windows, front and back, guns in their hands; both men fired at the pickup truck. Tito swung his car to the far left lane and passed both the large Chevrolet and the BMW; he saw the pickup truck swerving and slowing in his rear-view mirror. The next day, Mask asked Tito to accompany him to get the large Chevrolet fixed; the pickup truck, Tito said, had struck the right front fender of the burgundy car with its bumper during the chase. Tito also said that the Chevrolet had a bullet hole near its other damage. He assumed that someone in the pickup truck had fired at the Chevrolet.

Tito's account varied dramatically from Platano's statement in late January. It placed David Cargill and his friends at the Palladium, made them part of the drug underworld, put a gun with someone in Cargill's truck, had different members of the Red Top crew at the scene, and named Platano as one of Cargill's shooters. The already confused sequence of events became still more obscure a bit later. Megan Reilly (a pseudonym), a close friend of Cargill, who after the highway shooting had spent a lot of time with Kevin Kryzeminski, called Dimuro. She told him that she had asked Kevin if he, David, and John had seen the people who had done the shooting earlier that same night. She said that Kevin had become enraged at the suggestion; she felt that his overreaction was inappropriate. Tito's statement, coupled with Megan's call, gave Dimuro and Dugan pause. Was it possible that so many major players had gathered at the Palladium the early morning of May 19th not just for a night out on the town but for a meeting with the boys from Tarrytown? Coincidences make seasoned investigators uneasy. Still, the detectives suspected that Tito was lying because Cargill's truck, though its windshield was riddled with bullet holes, showed no evidence whatsoever of any collision with another vehicle. Dimuro and Dugan still did not have enough to make the Cargill case.

The discrepancy also worried Tebbens. Was Tito simply making up a story, working from street boasts and rumors, to put himself near the center of big-time action? How much could his word on other crimes be trusted?

Nevertheless, Elizabeth Morales's family had become cornerstones of the legal case against the Red Top crew, as well as potential gold mines of information about the whole Beekman Avenue scene, a fact that Red Top crew members fully understood. On November 9, 1992, while walking home from a store in Middletown, Elizabeth Morales was accosted by two Dominican men, whom she claimed not to recognize, who appeared out of nowhere, pushed her into a wooded area, put a knife to her throat, and showed her a picture of her family taken months before at 348 Beekman Avenue. They told her that they would kill her and her entire family unless she stopped "talking to the cops." Only Tebbens's constant attentiveness and reassurances kept the Morales-Cruz family as witnesses through such incidents.

In the midst of this turmoil, Tebbens had other witness worries as well. On August 28th Lamar Taylor aka L approached Ramon Jimenez near 175th Street and Weeks Avenue in the Four-Six precinct. Jimenez had witnessed part of The Quad and had testified about it to the Bronx grand jury. Taylor told Jimenez: "Stanley got arrested, and snitches get stitches." Taylor punched Jimenez in the face; Jimenez fought back but then withdrew. Taylor pursued him, now with a six-inch knife, which he swung at Jimenez's head. Jimenez blocked the assault with his hand, but the blow nearly severed two fingers and required thirty stitches to close. A crowd gathered. Before Taylor left, he said: "I'll be back and I'm gonna kill you."

By this time, HIDTA had trained its eye on the Beekman Avenue area. In late June 1992 Detectives Eddie Benitez and Al Nieves had driven an unmarked Mustang with heavily tinted windows up Cypress Avenue from East 138th Street toward St. Mary's Park to scout the area. The detectives saw a group of young Dominican men standing in front of 354 Cypress; they slowed their vehicle and Nieves did a "drive-by shooting," that is, he photographed the men with high-speed film through the Mustang's dark windows. The men on the street stared at the strange vehicle and some "got rays," becoming noticeably nervous. The detectives turned left at St. Mary's, circled the block, and came back up Cypress. Most of the men had moved to the stoop of 370 Cypress, but three of the men stood their ground. When the detectives passed for the second time, slowing their car again, two men ambled into the street. In the car's rearview mirrors, the detectives could see the pair, each gesturing with both arms, motioning the detectives to come back. The detectives decided to leave the area. When they developed the photographs, they identified the men who had gestured to them as Lenny Sepulveda and Pasqualito.

Benitez and Nieves returned to the area a few days later disguised as city building inspectors and went into every building and onto every rooftop on East 138th Street, as well as on Cypress and Beekman Avenues, even taking a complaint from one woman unhappy with her kitchen equipment. They established an observation post at East 138th and Cypress, where they installed a camera allowing 24-hour videotape surveillance of the street. They set up regular surveillance of The Hole at 348 Beekman from a rear apartment of 353 Cypress that looked straight down into the drug-sale location. Finally, HIDTA sent in its own undercover cops to make several recorded buys of Red Top crack at The Hole, some for hundreds of vials, as well as several buys of Orange Top crack on East 138th Street.

A murder in Brooklyn led to the second big break in the investigation. On July 14, 1992, at about 0145 hours, Juan Francisco aka Papito, a small-time crack dealer on Brighton Second Place in the Six-O precinct, was shot to death on the street. According to eyewitnesses Cynthia Williams and Pirri Rodriguez, both local drug addicts and sometime street pitchers, a black Nissan Maxima with at least four men stopped in the middle of the street. Two men got out and strolled over to Papito and his boys. One of them, a tall, skinny man, said to Papito: "Do you remember me, Papito? You look like a man at peace." The second man, dressed in shorts practically covered by an extra-large T-shirt, flipped up a partial ski mask to cover the lower half of his face and asked: "Which one is he?" The tall, skinny man pointed at Papito and said: "That's him." The man with the ski mask pulled out a large black gun and shot Papito six times. Both men jumped into the Nissan, which sped away.

When Detective Richard Gwillym, who caught the case, started investigating, he immediately began hearing street rumors about two incidents involving Papito just a few days earlier. On July 10th Papito flagged down a marked police patrol car, pointed out Ramon Madrigal aka Battata near Brighton Second Street and Brighton Beach Avenue in Brooklyn, and told the officers that Battata had drugs on his person. The officers chased Battata and eventually apprehended him after he threw down a bag containing 38 orange-topped vials of crack arranged on a strip of clear tape. Gwillym also heard that on that same day Papito had beaten up a Dominican called Flaco with a stick. Following up on these street rumors, Gwillym checked Battata's arrest record at the Brooklyn Bail Clerk's office and discovered that a Rafael Perez had bailed Battata out on July 11th. Gwillym ran Rafael Perez through the Bureau of Criminal Identification and found that only ten days after bailing out Battata, Perez, with an accomplice, had been arrested in Manhattan in possession of several bundles of green-topped crack and an AK-47 weapon. He showed Perez's picture in a photo array to members of Papito's crew who had witnessed the murder and confirmed that Perez was, in fact, Flaco, the man who had asked: "Do you remember me, Papito?" right before his accomplice murdered Juan Francisco. One of the witnesses also reported hearing Flaco say, the night after he was beaten by Papito: "I'm gonna kill the lil' muthafucka." Apparently, since June 1992 Battata and Flaco had been recruiting local drug dealers to distribute Red Top and Orange Top crack on Brighton Third Place. Papito beat up Flaco to scare him off and then used the police to get rid of Battata. In Perez's criminal file, Gwillym noted that Perez had a pending case on September 11, 1992, in Supreme Court at 100 Centre Street in Manhattan. The detective waited in the lobby there and arrested him.

Before interrogating Perez, Gwillym phoned the Three-Four precinct to see if he could get more information on the gun from Perez's Manhattan arrest; specifically, Gwillym thought it might be the same gun that had been used to kill Papito on

July 14th. Garry Dugan answered the phone at the Three-Four. Dugan was elated when he heard that Gwillym had Rafael Perez in custody. Only two days before, on September 9, 1992, anticrime cops in the Three-Four had stopped a black Nissan Maxima because the car had heavily tinted windows, a violation in New York City. The driver, Fernando Caban, turned out to be unlicensed. When the cops brought the car back to the house, Dugan recognized it immediately as a car known to be driven by Pasqualito and Lenny. Dugan quickly found a *clavo*. In it was a ski mask, perhaps the mask used by the shooter in the murder of Papito. Dugan told Gwillym to call Terry Quinn at HIU. Gwillym did reach Quinn, and Quinn said that he was coming over to Brooklyn immediately. By 2200 hours, Investigators Quinn and Bobby Tarwacki, Detective Mark Tebbens, and ADA Dan Rather were in the wilds of Coney Island in the Six-O precinct station house waiting to talk to Rafael Perez.

They wanted to talk with Perez because they suspected that he was the elusive Tezo. The lead had come less than a month before, on August 19, 1992, when Terry Quinn had interviewed Victor Mercedes. Though Victor had just been released from jail on August 13, 1991, because of the trial postponement for The Double, he seemed unable to curb his temper. On October 18, 1991, accompanied by Fat Danny, he shot Michael Turner in the leg and shot at Turner's cousin, Carolyn, near 354 Cypress. But both Turner and his cousin refused to press charges against Victor. However, when Victor shot Pedro Stevens on Cypress Avenue on November 8, 1991, Stevens did cooperate with police, and Tebbens was able to arrest Victor on a gun warrant. Victor had been in jail ever since. In the course of arguing to Quinn that he, Fat Danny (his half-brother), and Pasqualito had nothing to do with The Quad, Victor had named Nelson Sepulveda, Platano, Stanley, and Tezo as the shooters in that crime. Victor said that Tezo's first name was Rafael; he was tall and skinny with a pushed back fade for a hairstyle.

Moreover, Victor said, Tezo had killed some kids on Halloween night of 1991 on West 173rd Street between Broadway and Fort Washington and, typical of Tezo, had bragged about it many times since.

Then Victor provided the key to identifying Tezo. He said that Tezo had been arrested near the 207th Street Bridge for possessing an assault rifle and more than nine bundles of crack, along with Kiko, the brother of Lenny Sepulveda's wife, Lisi. The investigators found that case. On July 21, 1992, PO Harold Hernandez had arrested a Rafael Perez, along with a Rafael Fernandez, at the corner of Dyckman Street and Seaman Avenue. Fernandez was of medium height, but Perez was listed as 6'2" tall and 183 pounds—a tall, lean man who matched Victor's description of Tezo. Moreover, Barry Weinstein from Goldstein, Weinstein & Fuld represented both Perez and Fernandez. Investigators were elated when Gwillym called, since, they thought, a very big fish had practically jumped into the net.

But even though they knew nothing about the players or the implications of the larger case, the Brooklyn investigators, in yet another skirmish with the boys from bright-lights Manhattan, asserted the priority of the Brooklyn homicide investigation and kept the HIU investigators cooling their heels for hours in a small room in the Six-O precinct. Gwillym interviewed Perez first. In that statement, Perez said that he worked for Pasqualito and that, after Papito beat him up with a crowbar, Pasqualito shot Papito. Perez admitted to Gwillym that he had pointed Papito out to Pasqualito. However, in his subsequent videotaped statement to Brooklyn ADA David Blaxill, Perez denied pointing Papito out to Pasqualito, although he still put the gun in Pasqualito's hands and had Pasqualito saying, after he blew Papito away: "Niggas just can't fuck with me." Perez also said that Nelson and Renny Harris accompanied them in the Nissan.

The HIU investigators finally got to talk with Tezo at 0300

hours on September 12th. Since they needed additional evidence before they could do a fruitful interrogation on The Halloween Murder or The Quad, they did not press him on those crimes. They queried him instead about the killing of Papito, which by then they called The Brighton Beach Murder. They suspected that Tezo had lied to the Brooklyn investigators about Nelson being in the car when Papito was shot; Victor had told Quinn that Nelson had already fled to the Dominican Republic. So whom was Tezo shielding and why? The investigators also focused on the structure of the Red Top crack organization and its relationship to Orange Top. Tezo acknowledged that Lenny Sepulveda was the top boss of the organization, and even when he was in jail ran it by phone. Lenny's brother, Nelson, was second in command. Platano had been the chief enforcer, but since he was shot in April 1992, Pasqualito had moved into his spot. Heavy D was, Tezo said, the overall manager of Lenny's spots, along with Renny and Frankie Robles. Tebbens knew Heavy D as Jimmy Montalvo, a gigantic, billiard-ball-shaped young man and dead ringer for the rap star, whose name became his alias. Tezo also said that "Mickey" did a lot of the cooking and transporting of the crack.

The investigators asked Tezo about a whole skein of incidents, including the murders of Madonna and Mask, and the arson at the 20 de Mayo Restaurant. Tezo gave the investigators bits and pieces of information but not much that was specific, and nothing that could pass as evidence. A lot of the information, in fact, was nonverifiable double or even triple hearsay, such as Tezo's report that he had heard from Madonna, who was now dead, that Madonna had heard that Platano and Lenny "had lit up some niggas on the West Side Highway around 157th Street." But when the investigators asked Tezo about the street war between Lenny Sepulveda and Franklin Cuevas, Tezo stated that the two bosses, each with their own crews, used to work together. Lenny had even set Frankie up in the drug-dealing operation at Manor and Watson in the Bronx after Frankie got out of prison in 1989. But Frankie had tried to move his drugs onto Beekman Avenue, destroying the trust between them.

There were, Tezo argued, other disputes as well. Frankie had given someone close to Lenny a "bad package," and this person was furious. Tezo was careful not to name this man, but he said that he was a boss with a hit man called Freddy Krueger, who hung out at Tremont and University in the Bronx. But at that point, Lenny and Frankie were still friends, and Lenny protected Cuevas from harm. Then, Tezo said, things changed. Gilbert Campusano, Cuevas's lieutenant, set up his boss to get whacked by telling Platano when Cuevas and Manny Garcia would be picking up drugs from Cuevas's supplier, yet another "Papito," on 189th Street and Audubon. And Platano sent Freddy Krueger to do the hit, which wounded Cuevas and paralyzed Garcia.

Who in the world was Freddy Krueger? The case was filled with shadowy, unknown gunmen, most notably at The Quad but in many other incidents as well, including the wild shoot-out on West 181st Street on April 26, 1992, and the drive-by shooting at Manor and Watson on June 21st. Now Tezo named Freddy Krueger as the shooter of Cuevas and Garcia. What was Freddy Krueger's relationship to Platano? Who was Freddy Krueger's boss? If Cuevas was getting his drugs from Papito, who was supplying Lenny with the cocaine for his business?

Thinking that Freddy Krueger must have been caught in some bureaucratic net in the recent past, Tebbens did a computer run of all narcotics-related arrests in the Beekman Avenue area for the previous several years, apprehensions made by the borough-wide specialized narcotics unit that do not routinely come to the attention of precinct detectives. Out of hundreds of cases, one in particular caught his eye. A Freddy Sendra had been arrested on Cypress Avenue on February 27,

1990. Sendra was with Winkie Baker in the lobby of 348 Beekman; Baker was carrying a bundle of crack in her hands. Suddenly, more than a half dozen men charged into the building, identifying themselves as police officers. The officers tried to seize Sendra, but his reflexes were quick. Sendra threw Baker into the officers, ran out the back door of the building, and down one of the alleys leading toward the vacant lot that bridges Beekman and Cypress Avenues directly across from St. Mary's Park. Firing a seventeen-round 9-millimeter Taurus from one hand and a .38-caliber revolver from the other over his shoulders at the pursuing officers, he fled toward 354 Cypress Avenue, where he was captured and arrested. One officer reported that Sendra fired a gun directly at her face from a distance of six feet but missed.

The police also arrested Winkie Baker, who, it turned out, had fetched the bundle of crack from Louise McBride's stash apartment and was being escorted by Freddy to the selling balcony. Sendra told the police about the stash apartment, and they raided McBride's apartment, seizing narcotics and a safe containing more drugs, guns, and money. Sendra pleaded guilty to the top counts: attempted aggravated assault on a police officer and second-degree criminal possession of a weapon. He was sentenced to 6–12 years in state prison. His lawyer was David Goldstein from the firm of Goldstein, Weinstein & Fuld. McBride pleaded guilty to criminal possession of narcotics.

Shooting at the police is a rare distinction for criminals, even in the Bronx, and Sendra's mug shots looked promising. They showed a huge mountain of a man, with hands like catchers' mitts, and a fierce, badly scarred countenance on one side of his face; investigators learned later that the scars were the result of skidding 80 feet on his face while popping wheelies on Lenny Sepulveda's Suzuki GSXR motorcycle after being startled by an unmarked police car. But Sendra had, presumably, been in prison since his 1990 arrest; yet Tezo was linking Freddy Krueger to the assault on Frankie Cuevas and

Manny Garcia in spring 1992. The timing was not right. But Tebbens knew that street time runs on a different clock; maybe Tezo was just circulating unfounded street stories, attributing crimes to someone of legendary stature, even if that person could not have committed them. Someone with a name like Freddy Krueger might know a lot and, if squeezed hard enough, might be able to unravel the whole operation.

Later, the investigators discovered the videotaped statement that Sendra made to a young female district attorney the night that he had shot at the cops, been chased, and arrested. His head was bleeding and swathed in a turban of white bandages that concealed everything but a portion of his face. When the district attorney asked Sendra how he had sustained his injuries, he said simply: "I fell in the snow." Tebbens began to feel sure that this tough, stand-up guy was Freddy Krueger.

Rather had Sendra produced from upstate in the late fall of 1992. Quinn, Dugan, and Tebbens crowded into Rather's office for the interview. When the Correction officers brought Sendra into the room, Tebbens greeted him by saying: "Hey, Freddy. Freddy Krueger, right?" Sendra looked at him and laughed. Then he turned to Rather and said: "I've decided to tell you everything you wanna know."

lenny's boys

Sendra had never heard
of Freddy Krueger. Bu
he had a remarkable
story to tell. The HIU investiga-
tors talked with Freddy Sendra for hundreds of hours. His
narrative ability and his sharp eye for detail enabled the investigators to make sense of strands garnered from their other
sources.

The core group of Lenny's boys—Lenny, Nelson, Fat Danny,
Freddy Sendra, Platano, and later Pasqualito, Victor Mercedes,
and Heavy D—all grew up in Washington Heights between
171st and 174th Streets, except for Freddy and Platano, who
hailed from 184th Street and Audubon. They played street ball
together, football, soccer, and baseball; most went to George
Washington High School and several played on the football
team there. Others went to different schools. But all found
school endlessly boring. Everyone spoke English, some well,
but they generally spoke "Spanglish" with one another. They
cut classes and hung out in George Washington's handball
courts, trading knowledge of street hustles.

Around 1980 they began stealing cars on consignment for
different Bronx garages that specified the year, make, model,
and color of desired automobiles. In pairs or trios, the crew
drove out to New Jersey's Route 4 malls, hotwired targeted
vehicles, and drove them back to the Bronx, getting about $100
per car. Sendra alone stole about 400 cars in 1984–1985, only
an average output among the crew. He finally got arrested in
1985 for stealing a Mercedes 190 from the Bergenland Mall in
Hackensack, New Jersey, and received seven years for grand

larceny auto. While in prison, he was also convicted in the Bronx of possession of stolen property.

Sendra got out in 1987 and, together with some of his old crowd, including Lenny and Nelson Sepulveda, Fat Danny, and Platano, he hooked up with Joe, a big-time marijuana dealer who "started schooling us on the smoke." Joe "showed us all the connections where we could purchase it, where we could buy it in the city, how we could get it direct from the connections down in Mexico [and] Texas, how to break it down, how to bag it up, how to set up a location for selling, how to get the customers." "We bought one ounce, sold that. Doubled that to two ounces. Sold the two ounces. Doubled that. Worked our way up until we got to about five, six, seven pounds. At that time, a pound of marijuana was going for about a thousand dollars. You get 16 ounces. Twenty-eight grams to an ounce. So, you are to bring back at least $200 off an ounce. And you would know, before you even sold it exactly how much you got coming back in."

Initially, the entire crew sold out of a spot on 183rd Street between St. Nicholas and Audubon, only a couple of crosstown blocks from the Three-Four precinct's station house. Soon they were selling ten pounds a week. They split up the business, with each crew member opening his own little spot but still pooling their money to make bulk buys. Eventually, Freddy stopped selling and began to work for Hector Feliz as a transporter because there was more money to be made. Once a week for a year, he flew from LaGuardia Airport to Dallas–Fort Worth, then hopped over to the Midland-Odessa Airport in the middle of nowhere. There he picked up about 120 pounds of Mexican grass, usually paying with cash but sometimes with kilos of cocaine, wrapped the marijuana in Saran Wrap to fool the police dogs, drove back to Dallas, and then flew to New York, where the entire crew split the package for their own outlets.

At the peak of his career in the marijuana trade, Freddy was earning about $20,000 a week, all of which he spent on cars, partying, nightclub excursions, and travel. Freddy ended his trips, however, after a Washington Heights cab driver, whom Freddy was breaking into the business, decided to take the bus from Odessa to Dallas because he was unsure of the driving route. Immigration agents stopped the bus and asked for his green card, but he didn't understand their query. When the agents searched his luggage for identification, they discovered 127 pounds of Mexican grass and that was the "last we seen of him."

Freddy and the whole crew became known throughout Washington Heights as enterprising hustlers who would "do almost anything to make money." At the Friday and Saturday night car races behind the Hunts Point Terminal market in the Bronx or on upper Amsterdam Avenue—two of several gathering spots where drug dealers not only bring their best cars to race, spending as much as $40,000 to soup up vehicles to capture a $1,000 prize, but also come together to gossip, make deals, and talk about the price of cocaine and heroin, or new products hitting the market, or new dealers opening spots, or the virtues of different weapons—Lenny and the crew were regularly offered cocaine on consignment. They took ounces of coke for $300 and sold them for as much as $600, mostly to New Jersey commuters, working their way up to larger consignments and bigger customers.

In the early and mid-1980s, Lenny, Nelson, and Ruben Perez were also pitching for Baseballs, quartered at 522 West 174th near Audubon, where Baseballs's legendary boss, Yayo, had introduced crack in 1985. One of Yayo's employees was Rafael Toribio, aka Clint, Dan Rather's old Ferrari-driving, garage-robbing quarry. Yayo sold out of 145 Audubon at 173rd Street; he had Lenny pitching and then managing at 166th Street and Amsterdam and Nelson first at 145th Street between 7th and 8th Avenues and later on Boston Road in the Bronx. Yayo schooled his juniors in setting up sale apartments, complete with solid steel front doors with small openings, providing safety from robbers and police alike, while also allowing the rapid and anonymous exchange of money and drugs. Yayo took an interest in his charges' success, encouraging them to open up their own spots, always kicking back a percentage to him. Yayo also used the youngsters as enforcers.

In fall 1985 he sent Lenny to burn out a rival's apartment at Jackson and 168th Street in the Bronx. But early in 1986, Capo, Yayo's partner, was arrested in Yonkers with 22 kilos of coke and $700,000 in cash. In summer 1986, according to police, Yayo ordered the killing of a robber who had ripped off one of his spots, telling his hit man, Joaquin, to drive a nail into the man's head after shooting him in Highbridge Park. Then the DEA, acting on tips from informers, found Yayo's Bronx head-quarters and seized ample evidence of his involvement in the drug trade.

Eventually, Yayo fled to the Dominican Republic to which, it is said, he had already shipped $20–30 million. Wherever he went on the island, he was accompanied by four bodyguards with Uzis. He bought several hotels, casinos, and discos with his money. Although he did a prison stretch after an altercation in a disco, complete with gunplay, he claimed in a November 14, 1996, interview with *The New York Times* that he is now retired from the drug trade and is devoting his life to his legitimate businesses and to good works in the Dominican Republic. Moreover, he hopes that the United States can let bygones be bygones, since he longs for New York and wants to be able to send his five children to Harvard.

Nelson Sepulveda tried to branch out on his own. He found a place at 603–605 Beech Terrace in the Mott Haven section of the Bronx, a raggedy, decaying building already host to numerous drug operations. He named his first-floor drug operation "1H" after the number of his sale apartment. Nelson cast around for a supplier and ended up getting "work" on consignment from two brothers, yet another Capo and a Freddy, from Sedgwick Road in the Bronx. The brothers usually supplied Nelson with red-topped vials of crack in bundles of 100, but sometimes gave him different colors to sell. Nelson kept 25–30 percent of all sales. But the operation drifted under Nelson's leadership. Nelson smoked a lot of blunts, Philly Blunt cigars emptied of tobacco and stuffed with marijuana and given a little edge with powder cocaine and sometimes even crack. He didn't maintain firm enough control of the neighborhood youngsters whom he hired to manage and pitch for him. Investigators learned later that, when Nelson chided lackadaisical workers by calling them "Wack," they called him "Wack" in return. Even though it was a joke, the name stuck. Sales began to drop and worker thievery increased. In late 1986 Nelson got pneumonia and the business really began to drift. Finally, he asked his brother Lenny, who after Yayo's departure had gone back into the marijuana trade at 174th and Audubon, to give him a hand at 1H. Lenny readily agreed. He left his grass business in the charge of his very close friend and partner, Ruben Perez, maintaining a Manhattan headquarters at the spot, complete with gun and drug stashes.

Everything changed overnight. Lenny, sometimes called Woolly on the street because of his thick body hair and permanent five o'clock shadow, had an air of command about him. When he was a youngster, his streetmates razzed him about his wandering right eye; but nobody kidded Lenny now. Almost immediately, he took over the whole operation, always ready to use violence to back his authority. In February 1987, for instance, a customer waved a machete at Lenny while making a buy and was gut-shot for his troubles. Nelson, whose authority was fading rapidly, raced out of the building, gun in hand, to help his brother; he got spotted and chased by a cop near the scene. Although he ditched his gun under a car, he was arrested and convicted for gun possession, despite his attempt at intimidation of a hapless crackhead witness. He received five years' probation. Lenny's primal vitality brooked no opposition; others picked up the pieces or took the fall. The watchword on the street was: "Nobody fucks with Lenny Sepulveda."

Eventually, Lenny scared all other drug operations out of 603–605 Beech Terrace. He brought in a whole crew of tough, seasoned street brawlers, all from the old crowd in the Three-Four precinct, including Platano, Victor Mercedes, Pasqualito, Heavy D, and Miguelito Castillo (just returned from Dodgers training camp in Puerto Rico). Lenny rationalized the entire operation, establishing three eight-hour shifts, each manned by one and sometimes two managers. Each manager received a salary that ranged between $500 and $1,000 per week, depending on overall sales. Each manager received "work" as needed on his shift and was responsible to Lenny for the proceeds of any drugs sold on his watch; each manager hired his own pitchers and disciplined them as necessary. At first, Lenny and Nelson continued to receive crack already packaged in vials from Capo and Freddy, but after Capo was arrested, they turned to Jose Reyes aka El Feo, a boyhood gang associate who was beginning a wholesale business in cocaine and heroin at West 167th Street and Amsterdam in Manhattan, 1770 Andrews Avenue in the Bronx near Tremont, and out of the Marisco Del Caribe restaurant in the Bronx. El Feo's heroin brands were Eyewitness News, Red Alert, and High Blue. El Feo sold Lenny and Nelson cooked but unpackaged crack for a couple of weeks; they bagged it themselves for sale at 1H.

But, investigators learned later, Lenny rationalized this end of the business as well. He began to buy pounds, then kilos of cocaine from other boyhood friends—Julio Cesar Romero aka Ace, Freddy, Dominican King, Jose, and eventually coming back to El Feo as his steady bulk supplier. Ramon Tijada, one of Yayo's former workers, showed Nelson how to cook cocaine into crack—that is, how to mix cocaine with "comeback," milk sugar or another substance to cut the cocaine, as well as with baking soda and various additives, such as Bacardi rum, anisette, or lemon juice, to provide flavor or extra kick, and how to boil the mixture into a paste and dry it into a rocklike form.

Lenny and Nelson got an apartment on Aqueduct Avenue in the Bronx and set up a crack kitchen, complete with moveable walls to partition the space both for subterfuge from the police and to provide separate work spaces for the older women they hired to cut the cooked crack, package it in vials capped with red tops, and then tape the vials in a row onto a strip of clear tape, covered with yet another piece of tape, and rolled into a ball or bundle of 100 vials. This manner of bundling not only provided a way of stemming pitchers' practice of tapping the vials but was also a quick, rationalized way of accounting. Each bundle consisted of 100 vials, with each vial selling for $5; a pitcher got $10 for each bundle he sold; lookouts got what their manager paid them. The manager in any event had to return $480 to Lenny and Nelson, wrapped into *cuentas* with thick rubber bands, complete with the manager's signature somewhere on the *cuenta.* To ensure relatively standardized levels of quality between the different home-cooked batches, the crew handed out samples to local crackheads for product testing and advertising.

For a while, Lenny or Nelson transported the packaged crack themselves, taking cabs from Aqueduct Avenue to Beech Terrace to supply their managers. But in yet a further rationalization of the operation, Lenny put Platano in complete charge of transport, took over several other apartments at 603–605 Beech Terrace to stash drugs and weapons and to fool thieves, and established a command headquarters two blocks away, first, at 370 Cypress Avenue in Miguelito Castillo's mother's apartment and later at Mireya Betancourt's apartment at 354 Cypress Avenue. The latter location doubled as an unlicensed social club for the entire gang, complete with hot food, video games, and plenty of neighborhood girls for amusement, an important recreational pitstop since the brothers had instituted a firm don't-live-where-you-work rule for their friends from Washington Heights. Nelson ran the kitchen on Aqueduct Avenue, while Lenny supervised the entire operation from Mireya's apartment, maintaining contact with his managers through beepers and cellular phones. The brothers thus insulated themselves from the riskiest aspects of their enterprise, namely transporting and selling narcotics.

Down the line, managers also insulated themselves from risk, though with fateful legal consequences. Mindful of New York's lenient treatment of youthful offenders and of the byzantine intricacy of the search and seizure laws, managers recruited many local kids under the age of sixteen into their operations, among them Frankie Robles, George Santiago aka Seller, and Angel Cruz aka Tito. They tipped the kids lavishly for running errands, then hired them to carry crack from stash apartments to the selling spots in black school bags, and even to carry managers' weapons. Many kids eventually became pitchers, and some became involved in overt acts of violence against other workers or customers.

Platano recruited Freddy Sendra for the Beech Terrace operation in early 1988. Although Freddy was still occasionally transporting marijuana from Texas, he spent most of his time hanging out at 184th and Audubon. He had just quit a legal job driving a sanitation truck because the union discovered that he didn't have a driver's license. Platano drove Freddy over to the Bronx to meet with Lenny at 1H and to look over the operation. Freddy decided to come aboard, but he worked out an arrangement that enabled him to make a four-to-five-day run to Texas every few weeks, provided that he hired another manager to cover his regular slot, that is, his 4:00 PM to midnight shift, seven days a week. Sendra then recruited Will Caceras, who, after instruction from Lenny and Nelson, hired George Santos aka Scarface Chino to pitch under his tutelage.

Like all the other managers on Beech Terrace, Freddy had a

workaday routine. He reported to Lenny in Mireya's apartment in midafternoon to get the daily report on the whereabouts of the Bronx Tactical Narcotics Team. If TNT was not on the block, he reviewed with Lenny the goings-on of the day: Whom did Freddy have lined up to pitch? Was business brisk or slow? Did Lenny expect any customers in the market for large quantities? How many bundles were on hand? How many bundles did Nelson have already cooked and packaged up on Aqueduct Avenue? How was the traffic and how long would it take Platano to get the work down to Beech Terrace? At 4:00 PM, Freddy went to the spot and relieved Hector Saez, the manager who handled the 8:00 AM to 4:00 PM shift. But before Hector left, Freddy checked the safe at 1H to see how many *cuentas* and bundles were on hand, and phoned Lenny at Mireya's to report the totals. If Lenny agreed with the figures, Hector could leave, and Freddy took a bundle downstairs to give to his pitchers, usually any two of the four Saez sisters, Carmen, Myra, Jasmine, and Lisette, crack addicts all. All other managers followed similar routines. Only managers, along with Lenny, Nelson, and Platano, had access to the safes in the stash apartments and therefore to the drugs and guns that they contained. For most of 1988, the 1H operation made about $30,000 a week, with Nelson taking between $2,000 and $3,000 and Lenny between $4,000 and $5,000, and the several managers $1,000 each. The distribution of the rest of the proceeds is obscure.

For recreation a couple of times a week, Lenny, Nelson, Platano, Hector, Victor, Pasqualito, and Freddy Sendra went up to the roof of 352 Beekman, just down the block from 1H, and took target practice into St. Mary's Park, about 100 yards away. They mostly shot at people and cars, trying to come close to or graze, but not actually hit, their targets. Platano was particularly assiduous in target practice; one day, he fired over 100 rounds, and then paid one of the crackheads to collect the shells. Over time, several people were wounded. Detective

Tebbens caught many of the shooting incidents and put together a fat folder on the strange assaults. One of the victims
was Mrs. Heard, the mother of Gerard Heard, the owner of
Yellow Top crack, a pesky rival group to 1H that insisted on
selling vials at the corner of 141st Street and Beekman Avenue.

During 1988 Platano emerged as the key day-to-day enforcer
for the 1H crew. Pasqualito was a contender for the job but,
after he was arrested for the July 20, 1988, shooting of Guy
Gaines, the corrupt former corrections officer, he spent a lot
of the year in jail until he was acquitted at trial that December.
As a result, he missed most of the action. Platano had already
made his bones. In 1987, it is said, he killed a gypsy cab driver
in the Three-Four precinct after a dispute over the fare; and in
the same year he did a drug hit together with Benjy Herrera in
the Two-Five precinct at 122nd Street and 2nd Avenue, the
first, as far as investigators were able to discover, of his independent contract killings. Platano became widely recruited to
carry out the routine extreme violence of the drug trade. He
was expert in all sorts of weapons, from small caliber handguns
to the 9-millimeter machine guns called street sweepers. He
was also an accomplished wheelman, having been mentored
in the art of souping up cars and getting away by Meow Meow,
who was the brother of Carlito—Ruben Perez's associate who
lit up the Las Vegas Nightclub.

Meow Meow's getaway driving skills were legendary, and
he drove for many major drug dealers and contract killers,
until in September 1993 he got shot nine times by Bogototo
over a girl, after he himself had shot one Rafael over the same
girl. Severely wounded, Meow Meow retired. He unburdened
himself to Garry Dugan and Mark Tebbens, since they were
his only visitors in the hospital. But he still took pride in his
best pupil, Platano, who left cop after cop, including Tebbens,
in the dust during many a chase. And Platano loved his cars
and kept them in sparkling shape. Once, with Freddy Sendra,
Platano drove down the West Side Highway to shop at The

Gap at Broadway and 96th Street. Coming east up the hill on 96th Street toward Broadway, Platano had to swerve sharply to avoid a reckless driver careening west downhill; he sideswiped 11 cars parked on the south side of 96th Street, scraping some paint off his own car. He immediately made a U-turn, and headed back to Washington Heights on the highway where he deposited the damaged vehicle in a garage. He said: "Can't drive around in a car with dents in it." Then with another car, its hubcaps and even its tires newly polished by some local crackheads for $3, he and Freddy went down to The Gap.

Platano did his job methodically and thoroughly. In early fall 1988, when Lenny and Nelson felt bothered by Gerard Heard and his boys, Platano went down the block and sprayed their operation with an Uzi, sending the rival crew scattering, a cause for great merriment later at Mireya's apartment. When local security guards for the federally subsidized Jose de Diego-Beekman Houses, which controls whole blocks of red- and yellow-brick tenements in Mott Haven, complained to Lenny about the large number of crackheads that the 1H operation brought to the area, Platano instituted crackhead patrols and, with a couple of aides, regularly grabbed any loitering addicts, smacked them upside the head, and told them to disappear after buying their crack. Platano also disciplined his pitchers severely if they stole crack on his watch, usually pistol-whipping them but sometimes shooting at them. But Platano himself, who as the crew's transporter had first access to newly cooked and packaged crack at the kitchens, regularly clipped two bundles a day and had Freddy Sendra sell them on his shift. The friends split the proceeds.

Platano's wild side gave him an unpredictability important to a fearsome street reputation. Particularly after snorting cocaine, he stomped around Mireya's apartment, bending at the waist, pumping an arm, saying: "Gonna keeeeel somebody tonight!!!" He regularly dressed the gang's pit bull in a heavy flak jacket, took it up to the roof of 352 Beekman, and shot the animal, laughing uproariously when the bullets knocked the beast off its feet. At night, he often lay on the same roof, training a laser rifle at police officers who came to the block, shining the tell-tale red dot on their hearts, creating both fear and rage in the officers who knew, as Platano wanted them to know, that he could kill them anytime he wished. More than once, Platano stopped traffic on the Cross Bronx Expressway near Yankee Stadium to spray bullets into several large green directional signs over the highway, creating holes that are still visible. And one night in the summer of 1991, while he was driving a beige Toronado to Lenny's apartment at Davidson Avenue and Fordham Road, Platano got into a road dispute with two black men in a new car at Fordham Road and Sedg-wick Avenue. He fired several shots at them and then fled up Sedgwick.

Platano also frequently claimed credit for work done by other gang members. For example, on February 24, 1990, Nelson Sepulveda shot pitcher Lourdes Bonilla aka Lulu in the leg for tapping vials and selling dummies in what investigators later named The Lulu Shooting. Lulu was 17 weeks pregnant at the time. A few days later, Platano bragged to Freddy Sendra that it was he who had shot Lulu and, moreover, that he had shot her in the stomach, knowing that she was pregnant. In the shifting status markets of the streets, one's reputation for transgressiveness, however firmly established, demands constant embellishment.

After 603–605 Beech Terrace burned in late 1988, the City of New York, which owned the building, demolished the shell, leaving only a rubble-studded vacant lot that quickly became littered with garbage. The 1H operation sold its crack on the street for a time, according to Freddy Sendra. Then several pitchers began selling on the first balcony of the courtyard of 348 Beekman Avenue, christening the new spot The Hole. Lenny and Nelson knew a good thing when they saw it. They quickly made deals to obtain requisite stash spaces, paying

Elizabeth Morales, Fat Iris Cruz, and Winkie and Baldie Baker at 348 Beekman and Louise McBride, Brenda Blair, and Yolanda Jordan at 352 Beekman for the use of their apartments. The geography of The Hole enabled the Sepulveda brothers to rationalize their business, now called Red Top, still further. Managers stayed out of sight in one or another of the stash apartments; pitchers came to those apartments to re-up, that is, get a new bundle of crack. When managers did leave the building, they could move clandestinely through the building's maze of cubby holes and doorways. Lenny and Nelson made the operation more secure by posting lookouts in the street in front of 348 Beekman and on the roof of 352 Beekman. The operation was virtually impregnable except to undercover police officers. When uniformed cops or the easily spotted Bronx TNT came onto the street, the lookouts alerted the managers by walkie-talkie or with calls on cellular phones to beepers, and the managers shut down the operation by pulling the pitchers into the stash apartments. Or, more simply, the managers sometimes just let the pitchers get arrested to placate the police; crackheads were thought to be completely expendable and replaceable.

The Hole began to make money hand over fist. Twenty-four hours a day, seven days a week, the lines of customers stretched from the catwalklike selling balcony, down the metal stairs, around the dark courtyard, through the 30' X 30' tunnel-like basement passageway, back up another flight of metal stairs, and out to the sidewalk. The customers' faces were almost all brown and especially black—the number of the latter being Dominican drug dealers' street index of a successful crack business. But Tebbens, in his drive-bys, often saw white customers in three-piece suits standing in line, one with his whole family waiting nearby in an out-of-state car while he copped his crack. Red Top steerers cut the line off at the street entrance and herded excess customers across the street until the traffic in the tunnel and courtyard thinned. Once they had made their purchases, customers were directed to a door that led into the actual lobby of 348 Beekman, from which they could exit to the street. The Hole began to gross between $100,000 and $160,000 per week. Nelson was now taking home $8,000 a week; Lenny, $13,000. The Dominican boys from upper Manhattan, who commuted to the South Bronx for work, had created a vast, efficient money-making machine.

The trouble began with the murder of Miguelito Castillo, the homeboy from 171st Street and would-be Los Angeles Dodger. Recruited by Lenny, Miguelito had worked the morning shift at Beech Terrace with Heavy D. But Miguelito, Victor Mercedes, and Lenny, in conjunction with El Feo, had a heroin business on the side up at Marcy Place; the other major figures at Marcy Place were Chico and Tito. After Beech Terrace burned down, Miguelito worked at Marcy Place most of the time, although he still frequently hung out with the old gang at Mireya's on Cypress Avenue. When Miguelito's body was found in Eastchester, New York, on May 31, 1989, the two crew members who were the last to see him alive—David Polanco and Renny Harris—had some explaining to do. Some gang members suspected that one of them might have accidentally killed Miguelito while fooling around with a gun. But David and Renny convinced everybody that they had in fact dropped Miguelito off at Marcy Place.

At Mireya's apartment, on Beekman Avenue, and over at the 174th Street and Audubon Manhattan headquarters, there were endless discussions among David Polanco, Lenny, Nelson, Victor, Pasqualito, Fat Danny, and Platano about who killed Miguelito. Finally, Lenny and Nelson decided that, since Marcy Place was the last place where they could pinpoint Miguelito alive, the responsibility for his death rested with those who controlled that block, namely Chico and Tito. Then they heard street rumors: that Chico owed Miguelito a lot of money, so Chico had killed Miguelito to cancel his debt; that Miguelito had cut Chico out of some business so Chico killed him to save face. But whatever actually happened, all fingers pointed to Chico. The law of the streets was clear: the guys from Marcy Place had to pay in blood for Miguelito's death. So Lenny, Nelson, Platano, and Victor, with Fat Danny driving, began to stalk Marcy Place regularly. One night in late June 1989 a group of Marcy Place guys spotted their car and began to walk away; the gang opened up on them, with Victor and Lenny firing first. But if anyone was seriously hurt, word of it didn't get back to Beekman Avenue. Then, on September 3, 1989, Chico and Tito were shot to death on East 141st Street and Cypress in The Double, and three weeks later Tebbens arrested Victor and Pasqualito for the murders. By this time, Goldstein, Weinstein & Fuld regularly represented the Red Top crew. Freddy Sendra recalls that Nelson had paid the firm up-front cash retainers of $25,000, $15,000, and $10,000 to be on hand in emergencies, an idea that Nelson borrowed from the movie *Scarface,* but also a fairly widespread practice in the hazardous drug trade. Freddy himself, when he was selling grass with Hector Feliz at 184th Street and Audubon, used to ride his motorcycle over to the Grand Concourse every other month to deliver a paper bag stuffed with $10,000 in small bills to Goldstein, Weinstein & Fuld.

Lenny and Nelson had Goldstein, Weinstein & Fuld represent Victor and Pasqualito, but only through their arraignment for murder; the Sepulveda brothers did not put up bail money for their comrades-at-arms. Victor and Pasqualito, who stayed in jail until mid-August 1991, awaiting a trial that never took place, did not give up any of the other shooters in The Double. But their rage at being abandoned by Lenny and Nelson festered.

Why did Lenny and Nelson abandon Victor and Pasqualito? It seems that Nelson never liked Victor. Victor was a wise ass, who called Lenny Doodoo Man behind his back, because every sentence, almost every phrase, that Lenny uttered was punctuated by "and shit." Moreover, when Victor was managing at

Beech Terrace, he couldn't keep his hands off the local girls on the street and was thus often away from his post, a fact which aggravated the businessminded Lenny. Still, Victor and Pasqualito were part of the gang. Why had they been left hanging high and dry for shootings that avenged Miguelito and protected the gang's honor to boot?

Events back on the streets aggravated the situation. Fat Danny, Victor's half-brother, had been pestering Lenny for a piece of the action. After conferring with colleagues at the Hunts Point races, Lenny began to supply Fat Danny with crack to open a spot on 138th Street and Cypress and later on East 141st Street. Lenny made $400 on each and every bundle (worth $500) that Danny sold. Not only was Danny not making much money, especially after he paid his pitchers—youngsters like Luis Villanueva aka Little Louie, Israel Rios aka Junior, Elizabeth Santiago aka Yvette, and Enrique Mejias aka Ricky—but he had to come to Freddy Sendra, hat in hand, every time he needed a new bundle; sometimes he got what he needed, sometimes not. Adding insult to financial serfdom, Lenny insisted that Fat Danny use orange tops instead of red tops in order not to jeopardize the main operation on Beekman.

Lenny and Nelson had known Fat Danny all their lives, but they did not have a high opinion of his business acumen. Danny had an unfortunate habit of not paying his debts, and he also constantly made mistakes on the street. For instance, on April 28, 1990, at his spot at 600 East 141st Street, he shot at a customer who was fist-fighting with his workers. But Danny missed the customer and ended up shooting Lourdes Bonilla aka Lulu in the head, the pregnant woman whom Nelson had shot in the leg only weeks before. Still, despite his failings, Fat Danny was a presence on the streets; by keeping him on a short leash, Lenny and Nelson offended him grievously and contributed to the growing perception of themselves as arrogant.

In late February 1990 Sendra himself ended up in the Bronx

House of Detention after his shootout with narcotics officers near St. Mary's Park. One day, Victor spotted Nelson visiting Sendra. Hollering in a loud voice, Victor accused Nelson and Lenny of letting him and Pasqualito rot in jail; he threatened to kill Nelson once he got out and vowed to take over The Hole. Nelson then asked Freddy to arrange a contract on Victor with the Black Muslim Brotherhood, and he put $500 in Freddy's commissary account for that purpose. The encounter caused Freddy to begin to reflect on his own situation. Freddy felt that his lawyer, David Goldstein, was strongly urging him to plead out quickly to the top count of shooting at police officers. Although Freddy kept his mouth shut all the way through his sentencing of 6–12 years for that crime, he wondered if Victor's rage might not be justified. He never set up the contract on Victor. But he also never received further visits from any gang members, nor even any care packages.

It was nearly three years later that Freddy walked into Dan Rather's office and announced his cooperation. Sendra had always seen himself as a big-time drug dealer, a player equal to Lenny, Nelson, or Platano. Yet he got jammed up for doing his job, for protecting the spot, while his former friends walked away. He came to think that Lenny and Nelson had sent Goldstein essentially to sell him down the river, to make sure that he didn't blab to prosecutors then and there. And his friends rewarded him for being a stand-up guy by forgetting that he existed.

At the same time, Sendra claimed that he was not like the rest of the gang. Sure, he admitted handcuffing Lisette Saez for three hours to a basement railing of The Hole until she repaid him for a theft of crack; and he did take target practice from the roof into St. Mary's Park; and he had shot at the cops chasing him, though he scoffed at the cops' accounts of the incident, saying that if he had intended to harm the officers, he could scarcely have missed from short range and in tight alleyway quarters. But Sendra thought that the gang's violence had gotten out of hand, had indeed gone "over the top." "I don't think it's right a lot of people should lose their lives over selling drugs. When I worked there, we, I myself never had to actually hurt anyone when we were in business. And as it went on, during other shifts, a lot of problems occurred, a lot of people were getting shot for nothing, for no reason really whatsoever." People in all walks of life, including those in criminal pursuits, draw moral lines that others cross at their peril.

Sendra's story gave investigators the main frame to make the case against the Red Top crew. But street knowledge is even more kaleidoscopic than other kinds of knowledge in our society. Freddy's understanding of the gang was limited, and he knew nothing about events since his arrest in late February 1990. While the investigators were interviewing Sendra in fall 1992, Charro (a pseudonym), who was incarcerated at Attica prison for a homicide, called the Bronx District Attorney's office, offering to trade information about Lenny Sepulveda and his Bronx operation in exchange for early parole. The Bronx DA's office never pursued the issue; Garry Dugan heard about the offer and made arrangements for Charro to deal with DANY.

Charro had worked for Yayo and confirmed much of the detail investigators had already gathered about the legendary figure. But investigators were particularly interested in his stories about Frankie Cuevas, since Cuevas was at the center of the spring 1992 mayhem in the Three-Four precinct. Cuevas, who was five years older than Lenny, had been with Yayo from the beginning of Yayo's emergence as the main man in Washington Heights in the late 1970s. On August 25, 1981, when Cuevas was nineteen years old, he was burglarizing an apartment at 247 Audubon, when he was interrupted by its occupant, an 81-year-old woman. He assaulted her violently. The woman later died from different causes, but not before she

picked Cuevas out of a lineup run by detectives for the Senior
Citizens Task Force. Cuevas got heavy time, 5–15 years, for
the burglary and assault. When he finally got out on parole in
November 1989, he found that people like Lenny and Nelson,
who were just kids when he went away, were now big-time
dealers and had gotten rich from the trade. Yayo remembered
his former worker, however, and from the Dominican Republic
told Lenny to help Franklin out. Lenny and Nelson fronted
Cuevas a kilo of cocaine to help him get started and then set
him up at Manor and Watson Avenues in the Bronx. In return,
Cuevas was expected to buy wholesale only from Lenny, who
in turn used El Feo as his steady supplier. At the same time,
Lenny introduced Cuevas to the gun dealer Raymond Polanco,
and Cuevas bought $40,000 worth of weapons from him to arm
his spot. Cuevas made lots of money in a hurry, and used part
of it to buy the 20 de Mayo Restaurant on St. Nicholas Avenue
at 173rd Street. He brought his own crew together: Manny
Garcia, Roberto Peralta, Gilbert Campusano, Danny Montilla
aka Madonna, Manny Guerrero, and his two enforcers, Jose
Vizcaino aka Big Cuba and Andres Carela aka Smiley.

Cuevas came from distinctly middle-class origins that set
him apart in many ways from the rougher-hewn Sepulveda
brothers and their crowd. But Frankie and Lenny, despite differences in social origins and years, were kindred spirits, both
vibrant, powerful figures who exuded authority and com-
manded respect and deference from everyone around them.
They began hanging out together, frequenting after-hours
clubs, key gathering places of the drug underworld. These establishments attract a racially mixed set of participants and
are contained social worlds complete with their own status
hierarchies—from drug dealers generous with free cocaine,
players with fancy girls, lucky numbers winners out for a big
night on the town, boosters (shoplifters), dippers (pickpockets),
and other assorted hustlers who come together to socialize
with their crimeys, all the way down to chumps working
straight jobs who just like brushing their wings against the

flame. Each group practices its own etiquette, with premiums on coolness, elegant attire, engaging sociability, and sexual *savoir faire* with complete strangers.

Lenny and Frankie also liked to hit the big downtown clubs, in particular the Limelight on West 20th Street at Sixth Avenue (closed by federal authorities in 1996), the Ten-Eighteen Club at Tenth Avenue and Eighteenth Street (closed after a wild shootout in which the Red Top crew routed the dealers who ran spots in the nearby Hudson Guild Projects), and the Palladium on East 14th Street near Union Square. All of these gathering places were models for media caricatures of the drug scene—always packed wall-to-wall with dealers from every corner of the city, silk shirts open to the navel, gold jewelry adorning their necks and hands, luscious cocaine whores by their sides, gunmen guarding them at all times, Dom Pérignon on every table. According to Freddy Sendra, while she was still on the Job, Marilyn Perez regularly carried the crew's guns into the clubs by displaying her NYPD shield.

Lenny and Franklin had even shared combat of a sort. At 0400 hours one morning in early 1990, Lenny and Franklin, along with several Bronx girls, closed the after-hours Mars Club near the West Side Highway at 4th Street in the Sixth precinct. As the crew headed toward the highway, two strangers in another car, in the big town for a big night, forced and pushed their own vehicle through traffic, cutting off Lenny and Frankie at the highway's entrance. In a dress rehearsal for the Cargill affair a year later, Lenny shot and wounded both occupants of the vehicle with his .380 handgun.

Powerful personalities, hair-trigger tempers, class differences, abundant access to weapons, constantly shifting loyalties, and obsessive status consciousness are a dangerous mix. Shortly after this shooting episode, born of boisterous camaraderie, a series of events occurred that led eventually to the open street warfare of spring 1992 in the Three-Four precinct and the Bronx.

El Feo, even as he wholesaled cocaine to Lenny for resale

to Frankie Cuevas, noted the rapid growth of Cuevas's business at Manor and Watson Avenues. So he opened a retail spot in the same area to catch some of the action for himself; other dealers began to do the same. Cuevas, furious at the encroachment, confronted El Feo on the latter's home ground at 167th Street near Amsterdam sometime in the spring of 1990. Cuevas arrived with two cars, both with windows heavily tinted and packed with his gunmen, his intentions clear. But Nelson Sepulveda happened to be with El Feo that day. With great courage, Nelson stepped into no man's land, persuaded Cuevas not to get out of his car, and prevented bloodshed. Clearly, Cuevas had not known of El Feo's association with Lenny, nor of El Feo's role as the source of the coke that Cuevas himself peddled at that time. But regardless of misunderstandings, Cuevas's impulsiveness had made him a mortal enemy on 167th Street.

Cuevas was still determined to thwart further encroachment on his territory by other dealers, so Lenny agreed to help him out. One day in late spring 1990, Platano drove Lenny and Smiley, Cuevas's gunman, over to Manor and Watson to hunt for poachers. Smiley was in the front passenger seat, Lenny in the rear. Through the driver's side window, Smiley spotted one of the dealers suspected of poaching. But when he tried to shoot the poacher, he accidentally shot Platano in the back of the head. Lenny rushed Platano to the hospital. Platano suffered amnesia for some weeks and, according to several of his associates, was never quite the same person afterwards. When he got out of the hospital, still in rocky shape, he went to visit his friends, who had begun hanging out at Cuevas's 20 de Mayo Restaurant, which was only two blocks from the 174th and Audubon headquarters. Platano was greeted with jubilation by Lenny, Frankie, and his other comrades, but Smiley slighted him by turning away quickly and being inattentive. When the party broke up, Platano took Lenny aside out in the street. Why was Smiley acting this way? Something must be wrong, Platano argued, for Smiley to disrespect him in public. Frankie broke into the conversation, arguing that nothing was wrong, that Smiley was simply acting stupidly. Platano's shooting, he said, had been entirely accidental.

In the meantime, Smiley was frequently on loan to Lenny Sepulveda from Frankie Cuevas. One day he was at Cuevas's spot at Manor and Watson; the next day, he was on Beekman Avenue. Some of the gang thought that Frankie was sending Smiley to infiltrate Lenny's operation. But at the time Smiley's role and loyalties were murky. On October 23, 1990, at 0115 hours, Smiley, angry at Fat Danny presumably for not letting him shoot out the street lights on Cypress, took his target practice at Fat Danny instead, shooting him seven times and landing him in the hospital.

Was the shooting just another instance of uncontrollable rage? Or was the shooting calculated? If the latter, who ordered it and why? Platano seized on Fat Danny's shooting to argue to Lenny that he had been right about Smiley all along. Smiley was Cuevas's man, and he had tried to kill first Platano and now Fat Danny; Lenny had better act before Cuevas got rid of everybody. So Lenny gave Platano the go-ahead to kill Smiley. On November 10, 1990, Platano shot at Smiley on Wheeler Avenue in the Bronx as he arrived to attend a birthday party, but the bullet only grazed Smiley's head. Smiley kept a low profile for the next several months, but on June 4, 1991, his luck ran out. Meow Meow drove Platano and Freddy Krueger in one of Lenny's big four-door cars over to Wheeler and Westchester Avenues, where Smiley had been spotted. The trio circled the block for three hours until, around midnight, Platano saw Smiley and pointed him out to Freddy. Platano told Meow Meow to wait in the car until he heard shots. Then both Platano and Freddy Krueger got out of the car and, each with two guns blazing, shot Smiley to pieces, critically wounding Edwin Battista aka Fresh in the process. Meow Meow roared up the block, the shooters piled into the car, and they all fled the scene.

Lenny later told Mark Tebbens that it was he who had

ordered Smiley to shoot up Fat Danny and then had Platano kill Smiley to cover his tracks. Despite the steady money Lenny earned off the wholly owned subsidiary Orange Top operation, Lenny wanted Danny out of the picture because he was "getting too big for his britches." But Lenny was also worried about Cuevas's ambitions. Frankie and Lenny were still nightclubbing together on May 18–19, 1991, the night of the Cargill murder, according to Platano's statement to Dugan and Dimuro. And Platano still did business with Cuevas as late as early summer 1991 when, according to Lenny, Cuevas gave Platano a $5,000 contract to kill a crack thief named Watusi who had been plaguing his operation at Manor and Watson. But, from Lenny's standpoint, allowing Platano to kill Smiley was a useful reminder to Cuevas of just who was boss. It also meant one less gun to worry about if things reached the breaking point. The point was not lost on Cuevas. He saw Platano, and therefore Lenny, trying to get at him by killing Smiley.

In the late summer and early fall of 1991, several events brought the breaking point closer. Victor Mercedes and Pasqualito finally got out of jail on August 13th on The Double's adjournment, and they were seething with resentment at having been abandoned by Lenny and Nelson after they had helped avenge Miguelito's death. At the time, Fat Danny was still getting his crack already packaged from Lenny and Nelson with the proviso that he sell only on East 138th Street and East 141st Street. But Fat Danny, Victor, and Pasqualito began to sell Orange Top crack on Beekman, right in front of The Hole, a clear insult to the Sepulvedas. Frankie Cuevas saw his chance and he approached all three, inviting them to work for him and promising them a steady supply of cocaine. Initially, the three agreed. But then Platano and Nelson, speaking for Lenny, threatened to kill them if they went with Cuevas. Fat Danny, Pasqualito, and Victor decided to stick with Lenny. In return, Lenny promised to continue supplying the trio with Orange Top crack, provided that they kept off Beekman.

Lenny had good reason to make the truce. He had pleaded guilty to a gun possession charge earlier in the summer and was about to begin an eight-month prison term in mid-October, leaving Nelson and Platano in charge of Beekman Avenue. Without his formidable personal presence to hold things together, loyalties might shift; without his relentless single-mindedness, backed by whatever violence was necessary, his hard-won domain might crumble.

Soon after Lenny was locked up, Frankie Cuevas became bolder. He announced that he would no longer buy his cocaine from the Sepulvedas, breaking the implicit alliance that economic ties in the drug trade forge; he also tried to expand his operations over to Beekman Avenue. From prison, Lenny warned Cuevas of the consequences of such a break and of Cuevas's attempts to muscle in on Lenny's home ground: "There can only be one rooster on the block." Then, Cuevas crossed the Rubicon. In late fall 1991 he ran into Lisi, Lenny's wife, through whom he regularly relayed instructions about the business for Nelson and Platano. Lisi berated Cuevas for the problems he was creating. Cuevas told her to shut up and threatened to kill her. When he heard the news, Lenny called Cuevas from prison and told him that if he wanted a war, he had a war.

June 20, 1993, was Garry Dugan's last night on the Job. He had decided to retire from the police department in order to accept an offer from DANY's Homicide Investigation Unit as a Senior Rackets Investigator. Officially, he was on vacation but he had worked the previous three 0000 to 0800 hours tours in the bag, trying to accumulate as much overtime as possible to maximize his last year's income as a police officer, the salary base for calculating his pension. On June 19th, Dugan had collared up at the end of his tour at 0800 hours and then spent the entire day downtown arraigning his prisoner. At 1900 hours on the 19th, he went back to the Three-Four to grab a couple of hours sleep before hitting the streets again at midnight in the precinct where, 25 years before, he had begun his police career and where, that night, he would end it.

Dugan's relentless investigation into the war on the streets in the Three-Four precinct and the Bronx throughout 1992 had pointed again and again to Lenny Sepulveda and Frankie Cuevas as the key instigators or targets of the mayhem. Police had never been able to nail Cuevas nor, of course, to gain his cooperation. On February 4, 1993, Dugan thought he had him. A terrified man came into the Three-Four precinct in the morning and told Dugan that he feared for his life. He said that he had been working as a waiter in the 20 de Mayo Restaurant. When he was hired, he said, he was shown the wine cellar, the walk-in refrigerator, and an office that contained several safes. He was told that he could go anywhere he wanted in the restaurant, but he was forbidden to go into the office with safes. But on the evening of February 3rd, while fetching a bottle of wine in the cellar, he saw the door of the office standing wide open. He decided to go in and look around. There, stacked on the table, were an enormous amount of cash and several kilos of cocaine. He abruptly left the office, but on his way out he bumped into Miguel Cuevas, Frankie's brother and partner. The waiter immediately left the restaurant and decided to go to the station house the following morning. On the basis of the man's story, Dugan spent the day getting a search warrant. That evening, together with the Emergency Service Unit, Dugan raided the restaurant. The police found $50,000 in cash and two guns in one of the safes, which Emergency Service forcibly opened. Dugan arrested Miguel Cuevas on gun charges. But Miguel took the full weight of the charges, leaving Dugan with nothing on Frankie.

Dugan wanted Frankie Cuevas. Though Dugan expected to continue his investigation into the violence in upper Manhattan and the South Bronx with DANY, he went into his last tour of duty as a New York City police officer with the sense of a job left undone, of a quarry not yet run to ground.

The call came shortly after midnight. There had been a shooting on West 177th Street between Broadway and Fort Washington Avenue. All available radio cars and squad cars rushed to the area. Dugan had no transportation to the scene so he stayed at the station house reminiscing about his long career with some brother officers, his white-haired head swiveling, owl-like, toward whoever was speaking to compensate for his nearly deaf right ear. From time to time, the police radio squawked out sketchy details of the scene. A man in dreadlocks, perhaps a wig, approached another man leaning into the window of a gray Lincoln, talking to the Lincoln's driver. The dreadlocked man began shooting at the man outside the Lincoln; as the victim tried to flee, the shooter followed, drilling the victim with several more shots in the neck and torso until he fell to the ground. The shooter then shot at the Lincoln; someone got out of the back seat of the car, tried to flee, and was badly wounded. The Lincoln's driver squealed the tires and while trying frantically to pull away crashed the car into a van and then disappeared. The shooter ran toward Fort Washington Avenue, where he jumped into a waiting dark van that sped away.

At 0400 hours Dugan and his partner for the evening, PO Kermit Collins, finally managed to get a radio car and took a ride down to West 177th Street. On the way to the scene, at 180th Street, Dugan spotted Manny Garcia in his wheelchair, looking, Dugan thought, very glum. Dugan attributed Garcia's demeanor to the severe difficulty of living street life in a chair. But Garcia's plight reminded Dugan of all the other fatal and nearly fatal casualties of the street war that had been his own constant focus for the past eighteen months: El Gordo, Madonna, Mask, Gilbert Campusano, Roberto Peralta, Platano, and Frankie Cuevas, who was wounded the night Manny Garcia was paralyzed. On the street, the meat wagon had already removed the dead victim's body; EMS had taken the surviving victim to Columbia Presbyterian Hospital. The NYPD garage had already claimed the wrecked van. The specialized Crime Scene Unit had finished its work and headed back to its offices in the Bronx near Fordham University. The crowd that always clusters around extreme violence had dispersed. Only blood-stains in the middle of 177th Street reflecting the dim light of the street lamps suggested the night's events. A uniformed cop stood sentinel at the end of the block. Dugan asked him who had been shot. The cop shrugged and said: "Some guy named Frankie."

the
take-
down

The takedown came on
    September 15, 1993.
 Police grabbed 28
    members of the Red Top crew,
bringing them one by one into HIU's offices to join those
already in jail. Warrants were issued for seven others, including
Nelson and Pasqualito, both known to be hiding in the Dominican Republic. The District Attorneys from New York,
Bronx, and Kings counties, Robert M. Morgenthau, Robert J.
Johnson, and Charles J. Hynes, respectively, the Special Narcotics Prosecutor, Robert H. Silbering, and the New York City
Police Commissioner, Raymond W. Kelly, took center stage in
a massive press conference complete with the usual law enforcement visual aids: stacks of crack vials, weapons, and cocaine seized from the gang.

The DAs proudly announced the arrests of the Wild Cowboys, or *Los Vaqueros Salvajes*, as the gang became known
in the Spanish press. The name caught the fancy of the media
and became the gang's universal handle, except in official court
proceedings, where the DAs, pressing their case of overarching
organizational conspiracy, called the crew the Red Top and
Orange Top crack organization. Gang members promptly
adopted the popular name and afterwards often introduced
themselves to other law enforcement officers by saying: "I was
with the Cowboys." The DAs also issued a 58-count grand jury
indictment that charged all the gang members with conspiracy
to traffic in narcotics in both the first and second degree;
first-degree conspiracy in New York State involves engaging
children under the age of sixteen in serious criminal acts, a
crime punishable by 25 years to life in prison. Gang members

were also charged, variously, with weapons possession, assaults, and murders.

Dan Rather skipped the press conference. Over the previous eighteen months, he had fashioned a chronology of the gang's major violent incidents out of sprawling materials gleaned from hundreds of interviews and crosschecked with voluminous police reports. Working closely with Bronx ADA Don Hill and Brooklyn ADA Lori Grifa, a cooperation forged early in 1993, Rather had presented this material to a special narcotics grand jury during the summer of 1993. The grand jury indictments became the legal basis for the mass arrests and later the warp of the People's case at trial. But just after the takedown, amid considerable organizational turmoil, Rather left HIU to become chief of DANY's Firearms Trafficking Unit.

ADA Dan Brownell of HIU returned from Nairobi, Kenya, in mid-October to find a message on his home answering machine from Nancy Ryan, chief of DANY's Trial Division and the then-boss of HIU's chief, Walter Arsenault. She asked Brownell to meet her at her office on Columbus Day, a quasi-sacred New York holiday. The tall, lean Brownell, whose dark, sharply featured face bespeaks his maternal French-Canadian background, came up through Trial Bureau 80. There, among many other cases, he successfully prosecuted a reckless homicide charge against Robert Ray, the Transit Authority employee who, while drunk on duty, crashed his train at Union Square Station on August 26, 1991, killing four people and injuring six others. Transit Police detectives who worked that case, like Tommy Burke and Jeremiah Lyons, still rave about Brownell's complete mastery of case materials and especially about his relentless dedication and remarkable discipline, virtues honed by a year in a Jesuit novitiate in his youth.

Brownell, like Rather, also had plenty of experience with uptown murders. After his promotion to HIU in late 1992, Brownell handled the prosecution of Alex Sime of Rivington, New York, for the murder of Johnny Morillo at 500 West 190th

Street on July 1, 1992. Morillo and a friend named Daniel Suarez aka Francisco had gone shopping on Delancy Street on the Lower East Side; Francisco had purchased a television and an air conditioner and Morillo a rowing machine. After a cab ride uptown, Morillo was helping Francisco move his electronic equipment upstairs to the latter's apartment when three male Hispanics, one with gun drawn, approached the pair, called Francisco by name, and announced a robbery. Francisco leapt over the still-boxed television into his apartment, where his wife closed the door, while Morillo hit the gunman with his rowing machine. As Francisco's young son, Jovanny, watched through the peep hole, Alex Sime, whom Francisco knew, shot Morillo to death.

Police arrested Sime immediately on Francisco's identification and Jovanny's eyewitness testimony; the Seventh squad also "liked" Sime for a series of similar felony murders all originating on Delancy Street, including the wanton double murder of an elderly couple beaten to death with a fire extinguisher. Two weeks later, while Sime was on Rikers Island, a gunman named Leonida Cuella, a drug dealer from Rego Park, Queens, killed Francisco with the same gun that killed Morillo. With Jovanny's testimony, a lively lad whom Brownell grew quite fond of, Brownell put Sime away for life. On November 30, 1992, Leonida was killed in front of 184 Dyckman by Ralphie Suarez, Francisco's brother.

When Brownell met with Ryan in the deserted DA offices on Columbus Day 1993, Ryan told him that Jovanny himself was dead, killed accidentally only a few days earlier by drug dealers fooling around with guns in the lobby of his building. Ryan then told Brownell that she wanted him to prosecute the Wild Cowboys case.

Brownell knew a once-in-a-lifetime case when he saw it. He dug into it immediately, assisted by Mark Tebbens, Garry Dugan, and Terry Quinn. Before he left HIU, Dan Rather had managed to get Tebbens transferred to the NYPD's Major Case

Squad and assigned to DANY. Rather had also hired Dugan as a Senior Rackets Investigator when he retired from the NYPD. Tebbens and Dugan now called themselves "The Dominicans," and they delighted in dazzling, and initially befuddling, Brownell with their story-on-top-of-story accounts of the gang's exploits. Detectives prize dense and intimate knowledge of the street and an understanding of its peculiar logic. Their thickly illustrated narratives simultaneously display their abilities to their peers, test others' wits, and challenge others' persistence. But Brownell quickly leveled the field. He plowed through all the case records available on Red Top and Orange Top. To get a handle on the case's Russian-novel-like cast of characters, he made flash cards of all the players, criminals and witnesses alike, with photographs on one side and names, street names, and relationships to specific crimes on the other. Every other day, Terry Quinn drilled him like a schoolboy until Brownell recognized the players immediately.

Once grounded in the basics of the case, Brownell spent the late fall of 1993 doing systematic interviewing, first, to deepen his knowledge of the social structure and relationships of the gang; second, to build a case around particular crimes; and third, to assess for himself witnesses' credibility to a jury. He held detailed conversations with the whole Morales-Cruz family, particularly with Michael Cruz, with whom he immediately established rapport. He decided early on not to use Elizabeth Morales on the witness stand, lest her child-rearing record prove a bonanza for defense attorneys. He talked with Fat Iris Cruz, and with all the other "independent" witnesses, that is, those only marginally implicated in the gang's crimes. He interviewed Freddy Sendra at great length, and then some minor players, like Louise McBride, Winkie and Baldie Baker, and Martha Molina, who already had or were likely to plead guilty to drug possession charges. Only when he knew, or could plausibly pretend to know, as much as the actual players themselves—the *sine qua non* for successful interrogation of criminals who have everything to hide—did he begin to interrogate the indicted members of the gang. These interviews usually took place under the DA's "Queen for a Day" use-immunity agreement, which stipulates that: (1) the state will not use any statements made by a defendant at such a meeting against him in its direct case; (2) the information gained from the interview can, however, be used to gain other leads. Prosecutors may use any evidence resulting from these leads and, should the defendant testify, may also use a defendant's statements and all evidence resulting from them in cross-examination and rebuttal. Defendants use these conversations to assess the strength of prosecutors' case against them and to determine whether they should cop a plea or roll the dice by going to trial.

Brownell looked initially for the weak links, for those most likely to crack under pressure, confess or admit to their own crimes, and give up their former comrades. But even under the whip of plea bargaining, confessions were scarce at first. Gang members had already beaten so many raps that they had no reason to believe they could not beat this one. More importantly, Nelson and Pasqualito were still out there, as was the gang's supplier, El Feo, and his still-mysterious hit man, Freddy Krueger. What might happen to those gang members who rolled over? Further, even if Brownell got some gang members to cooperate, he faced the paradox of all criminal investigation: those with the deepest knowledge of violent crimes gain their knowledge only through some degree of complicity in the crimes themselves. As witnesses, they are morally suspect and often untrustworthy to a jury.

Brownell knew that he had to simplify the sprawling case to make it comprehensible to a jury. Just as detectives in the course of their work translate criminals' accounts of the chaos they wreak on the streets into orderly vocabularies of excuses, justifications, and explanations, so do prosecutors further rationalize such accounts for the legal system. Above all, ADAs craft a straightforward, intelligible narrative for court presentation. In the Wild Cowboys case, this meant showing that the gang's violence was a byproduct and furtherance of a conspiracy to traffic in drugs and thus fell under New York State's two-tiered conspiracy laws. Brownell had to break through the bureaucratization of the criminal justice system and show that seemingly piecemeal cases actually joined together to form a pattern.

But as the lead prosecutor, Brownell inherited a lot of problems. He saw immediately that a great deal of work still needed to be done on some key crimes, particularly The Quad, The Double, and Cuevas's murder, by now called The Fat Frankie Homicide. Despite Tebbens's and the Bronx prosecutors' considerable efforts on The Quad, investigators were still in the dark about many crucial details of the crime; and its probable instigator, Nelson Sepulveda, was at large. Complicated legal problems haunted The Quad. The informant Charro—who in early fall 1992, in an interview at Attica prison, had given a great deal of useful information about Lenny Sepulveda and Frankie Cuevas to investigators still trying to piece together the story—had once been on Rikers Island at the same time as Platano. He had spoken with Platano in the yard, and Platano had, according to Charro, admitted to several crimes, including his participation in The Quad; still later, Platano gave Charro other versions of The Quad. After the Attica interview established his relationship with the authorities, Charro relayed Platano's admissions to detectives and prosecutors in a series of subsequent talks. But then Charro, who had been looking to trade with prosecutors, decided to forget about cooperating because he couldn't get a good enough deal; moreover, the investigators had become suspicious of Charro's information.

Platano's lawyers at the time, Goldstein, Weinstein & Fuld, argued that Charro was a state agent and that Platano's right to counsel had been violated under the *Massiah* case [*Massiah v. United States*, 377 U.S. 201 (1964)]. At a hearing before Bronx Judge Ira Globerman, the lawyers claimed that prosecutors had sent Charro to Platano to get a confession to The Quad. Eventually, Globerman ruled that a *Massiah* violation had indeed occurred, entailing the suppression of all information from Charro after the supposed violation took place, a ruling that travels with a case whatever the jurisdiction. As a result, prosecutors could use essentially none of the information that Charro provided unless they derived the same material from wholly independent sources and could demonstrate that they had done so.

Similar legal problems plagued The Double. Neither the police nor the Bronx DA's office had conducted lineups for it (the Manhattan aphorism is: "The Bronx does things differently") and the case was beginning to grow hair. Although prosecutors now had the statements of Elizabeth Morales and several of her children about The Double, they were still trying to locate the surviving victims and witnesses, drug dealers Anthony Lopez and Rodney Baines, and Clifford Halsey, their cab driver.

Brownell had two witnesses to The Fat Frankie Homicide. Manny Guerrero, Cuevas's right-hand man, had been the passenger in the back seat of the Lincoln, the surviving victim of that shooting. When interviewed at the hospital by Dan Rather the day after the shooting, Guerrero named Pasqualito as the shooter. He clearly saw Pasqualito, whom he had known for years, suddenly appear at the hood of the Lincoln wearing a dark shirt. Pasqualito began firing at Frankie, following him as he tried to get away. Then Pasqualito turned the gun on the Lincoln, shooting Manny as he tried to get out of the car.

Cuevas's girlfriend gave another name to Three-Four Detectives Hank Primus, who caught the case, and Joe Montuori, the legendary soft-spoken veteran of hundreds of murder investigations in upper Manhattan's killing grounds. Montuori was a Brooklyn boy, the sole survivor of his circle of boyhood friends, all long dead from heroin or street violence. The night of the shooting, Evelyn Vargas, a high school student, had been

sitting on the stoop of her building on West 177th Street waiting for her younger sister to come downstairs. Vargas got a
clear, unobstructed look at the shooter's face as he approached
Cuevas, and she picked Pasqualito's picture out of a photo
array. Both witnesses testified before the grand jury during
summer 1993. Vargas's testimony would be invaluable at trial,
provided that she could be kept out of harm's way. But Guerrero was part of Cuevas's gang, and a jury might suspect his
testimony. Brownell needed more to nail Pasqualito for this
killing. Moreover, right after killing Cuevas, Pasqualito had
fled to the Dominican Republic.

Brownell also inherited marked jurisdictional rivalries between the DA offices of Manhattan and the Bronx, and between Manhattan and Brooklyn. The histories of The Double
and The Quad, now joined to the Wild Cowboys case, were
extremely tangled. First, the Bronx DA's office had always
intended to try both crimes in the Bronx, where the crimes had
occurred. But the date to restart the adjourned trial of The
Double came and went and still the prosecution witnesses
were nowhere to be found. Second, Bronx prosecutors Don Hill
and Eric Hirsch had pressed Justice Ira Globerman to try The
Quad as soon as possible in fall 1992 because they greatly
feared for the safety of the witnesses to that crime. Prosecutors'
apprehensions deepened in October 1992 when, after an exhaustive search of the entire homeless shelter system, Mark
Tebbens found Janice Bruington hiding in Manhattan. The only
surviving victim of The Quad now dropped her initial story of
recognizing no one at the murders and admitted to Tebbens
and the prosecutors that Stanley Tukes, whom she had known
for many years, shot her when she stumbled into the slaughter
on Beekman Avenue. After she crawled under the car to escape,
she saw Stanley, Platano, and Fat Danny, guns in hand, running
back to the white car on the scene. Shortly after The Quad, at
her son's insistence, Bruington placed a phone call to Brenda
Blair of 352 Beekman Avenue and, after a while, Platano came

onto the phone, apparently patched into the call or on an extension. Platano told Bruington that she would be taken care of if she didn't testify. Later, again at her son's request, Bruington called Platano's lawyer, Michael Nedick, who said that he would like to speak to her at his office on the Grand Concourse. Bruington decided not to go back to the Bronx to see the lawyer. Later, Yolanda Jordan told Mark Tebbens that Bruington had been offered $15,000 not to testify. The calls had an effect; Bruington had since lived in terror, expecting the gang to find her at any moment.

ADAs Hill and Hirsch argued to Justice Globerman that Bruington's experience, particularly when coupled with Chubby Green's recantation of his testimony on The Quad in Howard Ripps's office, should remind the court that the Red Top and Orange Top organization specialized in intimidating witnesses. But when prosecutors made a pretrial motion to allow evidence of intimidation that would suggest the lawyers' involvement, Globerman denied the application, suggesting instead that the defense attorneys resign from the case and thus remove the problem from his court. They did, in fact, resign in January 1993, and the court adjourned the trial on The Quad for three months to give the defendants' new lawyers time to prepare. Globerman's refusal to allow evidence of witness intimidation convinced the Bronx prosecutors that Globerman was also unlikely to allow evidence of the drug-trafficking conspiracy that linked together most of the gang's individual violent acts. The Bronx prosecutors feared the outcome of a trial before a judge who seemed to construe the admissibility of evidence according to the old Bronx adage: "If something is helpful to the prosecution, it's not admissible."

An unlikely event spurred cross-jurisdictional cooperation. On February 4, 1993, almost unbelievably, Lenny Sepulveda walked into a Manhattan courtroom. Dan Rather had tracked Lenny's and Pasqualito's records closely on the gun felony complaint filed against them in connection with the wild car chase on August 4, 1992. Pasqualito had made his requisite court appearances on that case and was scheduled to appear again on February 4th; in all likelihood, Pasqualito would ask the court to dismiss the gun charge against him because the People had failed to try him promptly. Lenny had not made any court appearances, and Rather had issued a warrant for Lenny's arrest for jumping bail.

The chances that Lenny might keep the court date on February 4th were small indeed. But smart criminals like Lenny have a well-developed sense of the fragmented, bureaucratized state of the criminal justice system. It made sense to try to get rid of the gun case in Manhattan through routine dismissal under the speedy trial provision in order to avoid an additional Manhattan bench arrest warrant. Rather asked the ADA on duty in the second-floor courtroom to notify him immediately if either Pasqualito or Lenny showed up for the court date. Rather reasoned that whoever represented Pasqualito and Lenny that day would present Pasqualito first. If the court dismissed Pasqualito's case, it might agree with arguments to dismiss the case of Pasqualito's co-defendant, Lenny.

Show Pasqualito did, accompanied by Barry Weinstein; his case was routinely dismissed. The coast was clear for Lenny. The ADA on duty called Rather, who immediately told Quinn that Lenny might show as well. Quinn grabbed SRIs Angel Garcia and Bobby Tarwacki. Avoiding the impossibly slow elevators of 100 Centre Street, the three, with Rather following, raced down the thirteen flights of stairs to the second floor. But when they reached the courtroom, Lenny was nowhere in sight. The detectives ran downstairs one more flight to the gigantic first-floor entrance hall of the building and saw Pasqualito heading toward the exit. They enlisted court officers to detain him. Then, looking upstairs to the second-floor balcony, they spotted Lenny still hobbling with a full plaster cast on the leg he had injured when escaping from Mark Tebbens in August 1992.

Quinn, Garcia, and Tarwacki headed back upstairs and, in a wild melee, arrested Lenny. Even after he was cuffed, the physically powerful Lenny ceased struggling only when Quinn jammed his middle knuckle up Lenny's backside, claiming it was a gun and threatening to blow Lenny's genitalia to kingdom come unless he went quietly. Lenny was dumbfounded at his arrest and indignant at Quinn's behavior. But he was most chagrined to learn that he had been caught by the same "gang" that had brought down the Gerry Curls, among others.

The next day, Lenny was brought before Justice Leslie Crocker Snyder of the New York State Supreme Court and was remanded for jumping bail on the old gun case. Lenny cursed at the judge on his way out of the courtroom, but Justice Snyder declined to cite him for contempt.

Lenny's apprehension, and the perceived necessity to find a way to keep him in jail, created the opportunity to break through the criminal justice system's bailiwick mentality and its concomitant fragmentation of both knowledge and authority. Strictly speaking, Dan Rather had Lenny only for jumping bail on the gun possession charge that grew out of the car chase of August 4, 1992—a problematic case at best, given New York's search laws and the vagaries of New York City courts. The Bronx had never indicted Lenny for The Double, even after Tebbens had gotten testimony from the Morales-Cruz family in fall 1992 about Lenny's participation. And despite Michael Cruz's clear identification of both Lenny and Pasqualito as his assailants on August 14, 1992, Brooklyn had indicted only Pasqualito for Cruz's shooting.

Frantic at the thought of losing Lenny, Rather called Brooklyn ADA Lori Grifa, who, under Brooklyn's "community-based prosecution" program, had caught the Cruz shooting because Chauncey Street, where the assault occurred, fell within her geographical area. Rather explained to Grifa the urgency of holding Lenny and argued for the desirability of a cross-jurisdictional prosecution. Rather also called Don Hill, urging him to indict Lenny on The Double. On February 8th, in a superseding indictment, the Bronx indicted Lenny, Victor, and Pasqualito as co-defendants for The Double of 1989. On February 9th Grifa obtained a superseding indictment adding Lenny to the indictment already accusing Pasqualito of the attempted murder of Michael Cruz. On February 10th Dan Rather obtained an indictment against Lenny for jumping bail on the August 4th gun case.

But Rather did not have the same luck holding Pasqualito. Not only had Pasqualito's gun case been dismissed just before his apprehension, but, remarkably, he was out on bail for the shooting of Michael Cruz. On August 25, 1992, Detective Eddie Benitez had spotted Pasqualito on East 138th Street and followed him over to the Beekman Avenue area. Benitez and his partners, Cesar Ortiz and Al Nieves, surrounded Pasqualito at the corner of East 141st Street and Cypress Avenue. Encouraged by a large street crowd that pressed in to aid him, Pasqualito went the hard way. Later, he told Benitez: "Gotta fight, man. Gotta fight." Benitez took Pasqualito over to Brooklyn for arraignment. Even though he was accused of shooting a state-protected witness to The Quad and was also awaiting the adjourned trial for The Double, Judge Angelo Tona, then sitting in Brooklyn's night arraignment court, refused to put him in prison; instead he set a $25,000 cash bail, an amount Pasqualito made in 10 minutes.

In the months that followed, Pasqualito used his bail time well. At the end of May 1993 he blamed Jose Rios aka Corky, who was delivering between ten and thirty bundles a day from the gang's kitchens to various locations, for ten missing bundles. He took Corky to 171st Street and Audubon and, in front of a large street audience, savagely beat him in what became known as Corky's Beatdown. And then on June 20, 1993, Pasqualito tangled for the last time with Frankie Cuevas before fleeing to the Dominican Republic.

With Lenny firmly in custody, Rather suggested to Bronx prosecutors that they had a better chance on The Quad, and indeed on The Double, by bringing the cases to Manhattan as part of a cross-jurisdictional prosecution. At the same time, he suggested to Lori Grifa that Brooklyn join the effort by bringing the shooting of Michael Cruz, as well as The Brighton Beach Murder of Papito, to Manhattan. Grifa, already a seasoned prosecutor, went to the assistant district attorney who had caught Papito's murder and persuaded her to cede it. Hill, Rather, and Grifa finally met in March 1993 and began to work together.

Manhattan's cooperation with the Bronx was almost immediately derailed. The first time that Don Hill met with HIU representatives, he clashed with Terry Quinn. Quinn argued for flipping Platano, unanimously identified as one of the shooters in The Quad, in order to use Platano against Lenny Sepulveda to clear the Cargill homicide. Hill vehemently opposed the suggestion. First of all, the idea posed formidable legal difficulties, since it was still not clear whether Platano was an accomplice in the Cargill murder. More to the point, were uptown murders, such as those in The Quad, less important than the murder of an "innocent victim" like David Cargill? Did clearing one college boy's death count for more than properly avenging the murders of four crackheads in the South Bronx? The conflict was also fraught with the underlying resentment of outer-borough officials, who usually labor in complete obscurity, toward those who work in bright-lights Gotham, the nerve center of the media.

Later, in June 1993, the conflict took another turn when Hill and Rather strongly disagreed about the timing of the takedown. Hill had good information that Fat Danny was about to flee to the Dominican Republic, and he wanted the arrests made then and there to make sure that all the known shooters at The Quad were brought to justice. But because of the past vagaries of the case, Rather wanted to put things together more tightly and present the case fully to the grand jury over the summer. Bosses, and bosses' bosses, got involved in the fight, with ruffled fur on all sides.

While Brownell was fighting the case's ghosts on one front, Tebbens, Dugan, and Quinn were working at cross-purposes with him on another. The detectives had hunted this gang for years, had already documented a vast array of crimes linked to it, and kept uncovering still more details of its violence. They created a timeline of all the crimes thought to be the gang's handiwork, a picture blurred in many places but clear enough to reveal at least shadowy sketches of key gang members in action. After the takedown, some witnesses breathed more easily, talked more freely, and brought many of these sketches into bold relief. The detectives' powerful, occupationally-shaped curiosity, honed by first-hand exposure to the savagery of the streets, led them to continue to widen their own inquiry and to try to broaden the forthcoming issues at trial.

They argued strongly that the heinousness of some of the crimes demanded further investigation and prosecution. Specifically, they pointed to the January 10, 1991, murder of Quincy Norwood, who had robbed crack from one of Red Top's pitchers. One of the gang's enforcers abducted Norwood from the corner of Jackson and St. Mary's Park and set him on fire; half of his leg burned off as he was dying. The detectives also pointed to the attempted murder of Jenny Platero. On March 4, 1991, Platero, a deaf-mute crack addict, created a disturbance on the street trying to make herself understood to other addicts while she was waiting in line to purchase crack at The Hole. Someone on the roof of 348 Beekman Avenue threw a metal barbell weight at her, striking her in the head and leaving her in a vegetative state. The detectives also argued that the wild shootout of April 26, 1992, in the Three-Four precinct and the June 21, 1992, drive-by murder and assault in the Four-Three precinct so exactly illustrated the menace to public safety caused by drug-related violence that the incidents had to be investigated and prosecuted. But Brownell, as the lead prosecutor, argued just as strongly that he had to circumscribe the already sprawling case in order to make it manageable and comprehensible to a jury. From this standpoint, knowledge of criminal activity is useless unless one can convincingly prove that knowledge in open court. He could not pursue, nor encourage the detectives to pursue, still other crimes, even if this meant that some crimes that cried out for vengeance might end up legally unrequited.

The detectives' desire for knowledge and the prosecutor's striving for proof eventually came together when key gang members began to crack. The first to talk, surprisingly, was Lenny. He sat in jail for most of 1993 and said nothing until early December, when his lawyer requested a meeting with prosecutors under the Queen for a Day agreement. Terry Quinn, Garry Dugan, and Mark Tebbens crowded into HIU's interview room to speak with Lenny, although they had no expectation that the use-immunity conversation would lead to full cooperation. Even in hand and leg irons, Lenny Sepulveda exuded authority. He remained silent until everyone was paying strict attention. He reframed questions to his own liking. And he glared at anyone interrupting him. To everyone's amazement, just ten minutes into the interview, Quinn emerged to tell Walter Arsenault and Dan Brownell that Lenny might cooperate. Quinn went back into the interview room and told Lenny that he and the other detectives had worked for years to make sure that Lenny died in jail. With that, the floodgates burst. Eventually, Lenny gave up the narcotics conspiracy and The Double, naming himself, Victor, and Pasqualito as the shooters. He confessed that he and Pasqualito had shot Michael Cruz in Brooklyn. Later, he described many other murders throughout the Bronx in which he had either been a participant or had direct knowledge, often naming Platano, Freddy Krueger, or both as the shooters. He admitted driving the car for The Brighton Beach Murder of Papito, saying: "Who else would drive but me?"

Tebbens and Dugan had already uncovered witnesses that named Lenny as the shooter in at least two other crimes, both drug-related: the July 14, 1990, slaying of Rafael Delvalle and the April 27, 1991, killing of Pedro Sotomayor. The detectives also had street information involving Lenny in the September 13, 1991, attempted murder of Miguel Guzman. But having had no time to investigate these crimes in detail, the detectives were hesitant to raise them with Lenny without being completely sure of their ground. Lenny made no reference to them in his statements. But they had to raise the Cargill murder, even though under New York State law they had no case. Because Lenny clearly understood the legal issues involved, and, investigators think, because of the nature of the crime itself, he was extremely reluctant to speak about his activities on May 18–19, 1991. Only when Brownell and Arsenault made Lenny's confession to the Cargill homicide the price of accepting any plea at all from him did he confess to the wanton shooting. Garry Dugan, accompanied by Mark Tebbens, took the following statement from Lenny about the events on the West Side Highway.

> This is in reference to May 18–19, 1991. I'm not sure of the day of the week, but it was on a weekend. I was at the corner of 174th Street and Audubon Ave. with Franklin Cuevas and Wilfredo de los Angeles (Platano). Raymond Polanco came up to me and told me that he had the fully automatic Uzi available for me that I had agreed to buy for $2,500.00. Since April of 1991, I had already purchased five or six other fully automatic Uzi machine guns from Raymond for $2,500.00 each. He told me that he had to go to get it, so I told Platano to give Raymond the Buick Regal (2 door). This car belonged to Platano, and it had two secret compartments in it which we call *clavos*. The com-

partments were located in the rear seat area, on each side, behind the armrests. They were electronically activated to open and close from the area under the dashboard. There were three metal prongs sticking out that were very close to each other. If a coin was placed against the two right prongs, the *clavo* on the right side would open. By touching the two left prongs with the coin, the left *clavo* would open. They would close by touching the same prongs again. They could only be activated if the motor was running. Raymond took this car to get the Uzi and he agreed to meet me at the Palladium later on to pick it up and test it.

We went to the Palladium later on. I was there with my brother Nelson, Platano, Franklin Cuevas, Ruben Perez, Danny (Madonna), Carlito (Meow Meow's brother), Edward Herrera, Edward's brother (Benjy), and Papo. We got there at about 1:00 AM, and stayed until closing. We came out of the Palladium at about 4:15 AM and Raymond Polanco was parked in the Buick in front of the Pizza Place next to the Palladium. He called me over to the car and told me that he had the Uzi. So I got into the car to check it out. Raymond said: "You can test it out on the highway." He drove the car to Second Avenue, and turned south to 13th Street, where he turned again westbound. He had the left rear *clavo* opened in case any cops were around, so that he could quickly put the gun away. He pulled the Uzi out from under his seat and handed it to me. He said: "It's not fully loaded! There are only a few rounds in it!" From the other fully automatic Uzi guns that I had bought from him, I could see that it had the same thirty round clip. I took the clip out of the gun, and saw that it was about one half full. I could tell this from looking at the holes in the side of the clip. These holes revealed that the clip was about half full.

Raymond drove along 13th Street to 6th Avenue and then turned north. We went past the Limelight Club at 20th Street, and kept going north. At this time, Platano was driving his white BMW convertible with my brother, Nelson, on the passenger side. Also, Madonna was driving the burgundy Chevrolet with Franklin Cuevas on the passenger side and Edward Herrera in the back seat. We all continued up 6th Avenue together. We went up to 57th Street and west, towards the West Side Highway.

We traveled along 57th Street and Platano was ahead of us. When he turned north to go up the ramp to the West Side Highway, he nearly had a collision with a red pickup truck which was traveling northbound through the intersection. The pickup went ahead and up the ramp. Platano slowed down and waited for us. As Raymond and I pulled up next to him, Platano said: "Did you see what that muthafucka did?" We said: "Did he hit you?" Platano said: "That muthafucka almost hit me!" Knowing that we had guns, Platano said: "Let's light him up!" (There was also a black .44-caliber revolver in the right rear *clavo*.) Raymond and Platano stepped on the gas at the same time. The Buick was fast and we were in the lead. Raymond reached under his seat and pulled out the Uzi that I had given back to him after examining it. He said to me: "Go ahead! Test it out!" We raced up the highway and caught up to the truck. As we pulled up to it, I aimed at the driver and pulled the trigger, but it didn't go off. I said: "It don't work!" Raymond said: "Give it to me! I'll fix that shit!" I gave him the gun and I held the steering wheel. He pulled out the clip, adjusted something, and slid it back into the gun. He gave it back to me and sped up to the truck again. I held the gun, aimed it at the driver, pulled the trigger, and the gun wouldn't go off again. I said to Raymond: "This shit's not working again!" and I handed it over to him and I grabbed the steering wheel. Again, Raymond pulled out the clip, adjusted something again, slid the clip back into the gun, and gave it back to me. Raymond sped up to the truck again. I aimed at the driver and pulled the trigger. This time the gun went off, and all the bullets emptied out of the gun. The truck immediately began to slow down and we sped ahead. Raymond said: "I think you hit him!" I said: "I think I hit him too!"

We continued up the highway to the Cross Bronx Expressway. I put the Uzi on the floor in front of me. We headed for the El Elegante Club at Webster Ave. When we got there, Platano had another near accident with another guy. They quickly began to argue and Platano ran over to the Buick to get the .44-caliber revolver. This gun was his. He was having trouble getting it out of the right rear *clavo*, and when the guy saw Platano doing this, he quickly drove away. Once we got into the El Elegante Club, Raymond Polanco was saying to me: "I told you that gun would work!"

I told Raymond to take the Buick that night with the Uzi. I told him to get the gun to Ruben Perez so that he could swap it off with someone else. A few days later, Raymond swapped this gun with Ruben at his spot at 189 Audubon Avenue, 2nd floor, and I got a different fully automatic Uzi in place of it.

Raymond sold the gun that I used on the West Side Highway to Bogototo. Since the night of this shooting, I bought many 9-millimeter semi-automatic handguns and .380-caliber handguns from Raymond Polanco.

Lenny pleaded guilty before Justice Leslie Crocker Snyder on May 18, 1994, the date deliberately chosen, in a sealed courtroom with only court officials, detectives, and the Cargill family present. In his allocution admitting his guilt, Lenny reiterated a version of the statement given to detectives. The detectives thought that, at last, they had the definitive account of the Cargill murder. However capricious and therefore difficult to accept both for the Cargill family and investigators alike, David Cargill had simply been at the wrong place at the wrong time. For Brownell, it meant that he could not use Tito Cruz at trial; Tito's self-dramatizing account of the shooting differed so markedly from Lenny's that it undermined his credibility as a witness to anything.

Lenny blamed his downfall on Nelson's decision to order The Quad. Far from ordering the operation, Lenny had warned Nelson against taking any drastic action against Gerard Heard's Yellow Top operation on Beekman. For a person like Lenny, it's better to knock off rivals one by one. Then different detectives catch the several cases; in the legal system, the left hand doesn't know what the right hand is doing; no one gets the big picture. We scare or kill the witnesses to the individual crimes; we get our lawyers to make the cops look like liars; we beat the raps; and we stay in business. But a wholesale slaughter makes everyone stop and think.

Despite Lenny's shrewdness and air of authority, and the wealth of inside information about the gang that he provided, Brownell feared using him as a witness against his former underlings because his thoroughgoing criminality made him perfect fodder for defense lawyers' arguments. Also, if one uses the worst to indict the bad, the bad might not seem so bad to a jury. Brownell needed other bricks to build his case.

Brownell found plenty of materials in early 1994 when other gang members pleaded guilty (see table). Each co-operator provided pieces of the enormous jigsaw puzzle that the case had become. First, Juan Abarca aka Charlie, who had been arrested holding a kilo of raw cocaine, described how for $500 a week he cooked and packed both Red Top and Orange Top crack in kitchens on Sedgwick Avenue, Kingsbridge Road, and Creston Avenue in the Bronx, and on West 171st Street in Manhattan. Pasqualito recruited Charlie for kitchen work when he was thirteen years old, along with Corky Rios and Corky's girlfriend at the time, Sarap Majid. He also recruited another youngster, Nicholas Bohan, of the notorious Bohan family of West 171st Street, long-time neighbors of the Sepulvedas. The elder Bohans were easily recognizable on the street, when they were not in jail, both because they were among the last Irish in Washington Heights and because they evinced the effects of heavy cocaine use. Depending on the quality of raw cocaine, Charlie cooked and packed from each kilo between 80 and 100 bundles, each consisting of 100 vials of crack. Kilo

Negotiated Pleas, Red Top Crew

Juan Abarca aka Charlie	4–life
Loretta Baker aka Winkie	1.5–4.5
Frank Blair	1–3, concurrent with 8.5–25
Jude Ann Bohan	1
Stephen Bohan	1
William Caceras	2–6
Allen Checo	7.5–15
Manuel Crespo aka Manny	7–21
Rafael Fernandez aka Kiko	1.5–4.5
Juan Gonzalez aka Lace	8–16
Miguel Gonzalez aka Mickey Tex	7.5–15
Robert Lopez aka Rob Base	10–life
Ramon Madrigal aka Battata	2–6
Louise McBride aka Smokie	2–4
Enrique Mejias aka Ricky	2–6
Ulysses Mena aka Dominican Chino	10–life
Jimmy Montalvo aka Heavy D	8–24
Marilyn Perez aka Smiley	2–6
Nyxida Perez aka Nikki	2–6
David Polanco aka Dominican David	6.66–20
Marcos Reyes aka Rocky	3–9
Israel Rios aka Junior	2–6
Francisco Robles aka Frankie	5–15
Siro Rodriguez aka Zero	3–9
Teddy Rodriguez	8–16
Nester Salaam aka Funi	5–15
Edd Sanchez aka Eddie OD	4–12
Elizabeth Santiago aka Yvette	3–6
George Santiago aka Seller	4–12
George Santos aka Scarface Chino	1.5–4.5
Freddy Sendra	6–12
Lenny Sepulveda aka Lenny Rodriguez	25–life
Nelson Sepulveda aka Wack	22–life
Lamar Taylor aka L	1 year
Luis Villanueva aka Little Louie	2–6

prices varied, sometimes dramatically, but, when supply was normal, the cost was $18,000 a kilo. At $5 a vial, each bundle brought back a *cuenta* of $480, after deducting $10 for the pitcher's wages and another $10 which the manager used to pay lookouts or line his own pockets. Thus, according to Charlie, a kilo, when cooked into crack, produced net receipts of between $38,400 and $48,000, or a profit of between $20,400 and $30,000. Charlie was supervised mostly by Pasqualito, but on occasion by Lenny or Renny.

Then Corky confirmed Charlie's account. He also put Heavy D at all the kitchens. And he documented Pasqualito's central role in the main operation beginning around the spring of 1992, asserting that he often saw Pasqualito leaving El Feo's van with a kilo of coke in a brown paper bag. Corky also told investigators that Pasqualito had several subsidiary drug spots in the north Bronx.

Marcos Reyes aka Rocky, who was hired in 1991 by Victor Mercedes to be a manager at the Orange Top operation at 613 East 141st Street, gave investigators an eyewitness account of The Double, placing Pasqualito, Victor, and Lenny on the set. He recalled seeing Pasqualito shoot Chico at East 141st Street and Beekman, while Victor, gun in hand, chased Tito toward Cypress. Later, Rocky saw George Santiago, Michael Cruz, and George Quinones surrounding the green car in which Tito was shot to death. Quinones, Rocky said, had also led the torching of the 20 de Mayo Restaurant on April 29, 1992, that had almost killed ten people. The plan was to enrage Frankie Cuevas, lure him to the Bronx, and kill him on the street. As soon as Quinones returned to Beekman Avenue and announced the torching, Fat Danny, David Polanco, Frankie Robles, Heavy D, Siro Rodriguez aka Zero, Pasqualito, and Freddy Krueger went up to the roofs of 348 Beekman and 600 East 141st Street, where they lay in wait for hours, wearing bulletproof vests with guns at the ready to shoot Cuevas. But Cuevas never came. Reyes's story helped investigators understand why, only a couple of weeks after the arson, police in the One-O-Nine precinct found, in front of the Whitestone movie theater, George Quinones's body with two in the head.

Rocky's statements opened the door for George Santiago aka Seller. George grew up on Beech Terrace; both his father and his mother dealt heroin, providing George with early training in the drug trade. George began several years of extensive psychiatric treatment at the age of seven. He started working for Red Top crack as soon as Nelson opened up shop on Beech Terrace, and his career with the operation typifies that of other neighborhood kids. Initially, he bought rubber bands to wrap the *cuentas* and ran other errands to local stores. He moved up to acting as a lookout and carrying crack from Cypress Avenue to Beekman in a black bookbag. Next, he began pitching crack in one of the spots. Finally, he became one of the managers of 600 East 141st Street for Fat Danny, Victor, and later Pasqualito. George witnessed, fell victim to, and inflicted the routine violence that gang members carried out in Mott Haven. He saw an enraged Victor take a two-by-four board and smash the knuckles of Mono, a pitcher who had tapped crack vials; he was beaten by Fat Danny for losing money; and he himself stabbed a pitcher for tapping and once shot at a threatening customer. George always armed himself during work hours because there were guns, drugs, and danger everywhere on the street. He also smoked five or six blunts every day.

George gave investigators a clear description of The Double, implicating both Pasqualito and Victor and admitting that he himself had flipped the quarter onto Tito's lap as he lay dying. George also told investigators about the murder of Oscar Alvarez. George said that he was asleep after hosting a party of about fifty people at his house at 600 East 141st Street on May 12, 1991, when Linwood Collins and Zero banged on his door. Zero said little, but Linwood told George that he had killed Oscar Alvarez, and demanded that George do something. George went up to the rooftop and looked for Oscar's body. At first, he couldn't find it in the darkness. He hollered downstairs to the fifth floor where Linwood and Zero were waiting, asking for directions, and finally located Oscar's body on the side of the roof of 592 East 141st Street immediately adjacent to his own building. George went down into the street with Linwood and Zero. There, they ran into Shrimpo, Oscar's best pal, who had, Linwood thought, absconded with money, thus precipitating Linwood's shooting of Oscar. Linwood fiercely demanded his money, and Shrimpo gave him $250, half of what he owed. Linwood pocketed the cash and said: "Your friend is on the roof."

With the information from George, investigators broke Zero Rodriguez, a prototypical wannabe gangster, who whiled away dead time in an interview room reciting Tony Montana's lines from *Scarface*. Zero had been a heavy drug user while growing up on Cypress Avenue, financing his habit by robbing local crackheads using a starter pistol. He was introduced to Fat Danny by Rob Base, who managed Orange Top at 600 East 141st Street. Eventually, Fat Danny hired Zero, though both Danny and Pasqualito were Zero's bosses.

Zero gave investigators another account of Oscar Alvarez's death, by now called The Rooftop Murder. On May 12th Zero got high at George's party. Afterwards, he went with Linwood to look for Shrimpo. Linwood found Oscar instead, on the roof of 592 East 141st Street. Linwood pointed the gun at Oscar and demanded to know the whereabouts of Shrimpo. Zero said: "Shoot him." Linwood gave his gun to Zero and threatened to beat up Oscar with his hands; he then opened the door to the roof and threatened to throw Oscar down the air shaft. Though shaking with fear, Oscar refused to divulge any information about his friend Shrimpo. Linwood shrugged and took his gun back. He wandered away from the scene to the rooftop's edge where he hollered down to the street at Boogie Frazier, asking him if he had seen Shrimpo. When Boogie said no, Linwood walked quickly back across the roof and, from a distance of 10 to 12 feet, shot Oscar seven or eight times. At that point, Linwood and Zero crossed over to the roof of 600 East 141st Street and ran down different sets of stairs to George's apartment, where Linwood told George that he had shot Oscar. Later, disguising his voice, Zero anonymously called 911 because, he said, the spot couldn't open with a body on the roof. After the encounter with Shrimpo, Zero walked Linwood home. Linwood told Zero: "You're the only guy that can hurt me."

Zero also gave investigators another murder that had not yet been connected to the gang. Zero said that, in mid-May 1993, he and Rob Base were at the Orange Top spot at 600 East 141st Street when Fat Danny roared up and told them to get in his car, that he had just spotted the man who had shot El Feo, talking on the telephone at East 148th and Jackson Avenue on the northern edge of St. Mary's Park. El Feo was offering $10,000 for the murder of the assailant who, on July 12, 1992, had shot him in the spine and paralyzed him for life. Fat Danny wanted that money. With Danny driving, Rob in the front seat, and Zero in back, Danny stopped at 370 Cypress to get a gun, which he gave to Rob, and told him to do the shooting. When they reached Jackson Avenue, the man was still on the phone. Rob got out of the car and pretended to use the phone next to him. When the man finished and got into his car, Rob rushed to the driver's side window and shot him five times.

Exultant, Danny, Rob, and Zero drove to West 171st Street in Manhattan. When they saw Pasqualito, Fat Danny declared: "My son got one." Pasqualito congratulated Rob. Then El Feo's van pulled up, and Fat Danny and Pasqualito got into it; Rob and Zero waited in Fat Danny's car, since they were not allowed to approach the bosses. A week later, while giving Rob $2,000 from daily receipts, Fat Danny told him that they had shot the wrong guy. The victim was not the man who shot El Feo but was instead, it was said, the assailant's cousin. Investigators identified the victim as Elvis Matos. They knew little about him and nothing at all about his so-called cousin.

As the close relationship between El Feo and the Sepulvedas became clearer to investigators, they began to assume that Frankie Cuevas had El Feo shot as part of the street warfare of spring 1992. Indeed, the informant Charro told them directly in November 1992 that Cuevas had shot El Feo. But Lenny Sepulveda later told Garry Dugan that El Feo's shooting had nothing whatsoever to do with his troubles with Cuevas. Instead, it was the result of a war on another front, against an entirely different enemy. Fat Danny's mistake added to his own reputation as a "fuck-up." But investigators now had him and Rob Base Lopez, though only on as yet marginal evidence, for what they called The Telephone Murder.

Finally, Frankie Robles flipped. Frankie grew up at 605 Beech Terrace in Apartment 1K, right down the hall from Apartment 1H, which began business before he was in his teens. He finished eighth grade, though he won no awards for good attendance. He saw Nelson, David Polanco, Miguelito Castillo, and Lenny running 1H in 1986, joined by Victor, Pasqualito, Fat Danny, Heavy D, Shorty, and Platano in 1987. After 603–605 Beech Terrace burned in 1988, he watched the opening of The Hole and the creation of stash apartments at 348 and 352 Beekman. Along with other neighborhood kids, he gradually became involved in the drug operation. In 1989 Fat Danny hired Frankie as a pitcher for Orange Top.

Frankie was on the street the day of The Double and saw Lenny and Pasqualito running, guns in hand. He saw the green car smashed up on Cypress, a dead man riddled with bullets behind the wheel, George Santiago and Rocky Reyes watching nearby, and the huge detective Tebbens and a host of other cops marching onto the crime scene about five minutes after the shooting. Frankie worked his way up the organization to become an Orange Top manager, along with Rob Base, Zero, George Santiago, Teddy Rodriguez, Allen Checo, Miguel Gonzalez aka Mickey Tex, Renny Harris, Linwood Collins, Juan Gonzalez aka Lace, and Shorty. He worked not only for Fat Danny but also for Victor and Pasqualito when they got out of jail in 1991. He heard Tezo whining to Lenny and Pasqualito about getting beaten up in Brooklyn by a guy with a crowbar, the same guy who set up Battata Madrigal for arrest. Later, he heard Tezo telling Battata about the murder of Papito in Brighton Beach.

By spring 1992 Frankie Robles was no longer just a run-of-

the-mill manager. Increasingly, he and Pasqualito were insepa-
rable, and he began to be seen as one of the bosses. Together,
they pistol-whipped Tito Cruz over the packages missing from
Fat Iris's apartment. Frankie was also on the street the night
George Quinones bragged about torching the 20 de Mayo Restaurant. He lay on the roof with other gang members waiting for Frankie Cuevas, and he was on Cypress Avenue when
Pasqualito bragged about "making a ghost" of Cuevas. He
claimed to be home when The Quad went down, but he admitted that, just before the shooting, Fat Danny told him to
tell anyone he saw on Beekman Avenue to leave the area. Only
a few moments later that same night, he ran into Nelson,
Platano, Mask, and Tezo on Beekman Avenue, and Nelson
asked him if he had seen Gerard Heard, the owner of Yellow
Top. Finally, he heard Lenny, Nelson, Pasqualito, Fat Danny,
and Victor speak, with great respect, about El Feo. He watched
Pasqualito and Danny go hat-in-hand to El Feo's dark van,
where the softspoken, wheelchair-bound drug king sat, always
accompanied by his fierce bodyguard, Freddy Krueger. In short,
Frankie outlined the whole conspiracy story with partial reports of key acts of violence.

But investigators noted that Robles conveniently down-
played his own role, or absented himself altogether from important episodes, a typical editing process in criminal admissions. His cooperation caused friction between Dan Brownell
and Don Hill. Brownell wanted to use Robles's testimony.
Hill, a former Florida and Connecticut cop, distrusted Robles,
arguing that Frankie was more violent than he claimed. In
addition to Robles's participation in the drug conspiracy and
his admitted assault on Tito Cruz, Tebbens and Dugan had
unearthed two homicides in the Four-Six precinct for which
Robles was at least present: the February 19, 1990, murder of
Norman Wade and the July 27, 1993, killing of Rey Alejandro
Rivera. Nester Salaam aka Funi, who together with Rasheed
Rice and Angel Quinones aka Pachulo formed a stickup crew

that regularly ripped off crack customers in the Beekman Avenue area, probably shot Wade and certainly shot Rivera; Dugan's and Tebbens's investigation revealed information that the first shooting was done at Platano's request, the second at Pasqualito's. Each time, Frankie Robles and Rob Base Lopez went along for the ride. In the end, Brownell and Hill brokered their differences over Robles, allowing him to plead guilty. His coming-of-age narrative exactly illustrated both the personal meaning and the long-term social consequences of engaging underage children in serious criminal acts—the definition of conspiracy in the first degree in New York State.

The legal case against the Wild Cowboys had begun to come together, but with Nelson and Pasqualito still at large in the Dominican Republic, its final shape remained unclear.

Investigators found Pasqualito first. In late March 1994 Stacey Scroggins, the mother of two young children fathered by Pasqualito, told everyone in town that she was heading down to the Dominican Republic to see him. One of those who heard about the trip was Zia (a pseudonym), a neighborhood girl (one of many) who was close to George Calderon, the boss of the Dead on Arrival heroin organization based on Brook Avenue, just north of Beekman and Cypress. This was another wide-open drug market, with spots selling heroin, coke, crack, and guns on every corner and in almost every building. Calderon was also an extortionist with a small army, indeed a kind of commando team, that he sent to all the drug spots in a five-block radius around Brook Avenue, demanding about $2,000 a week for protection from his own hit men. In effect, Calderon rented both public and private spaces to other drug dealers. Calderon also ran a robber crew. Indeed, two of Calderon's crew had robbed Mark Tebbens's uncle, his Puerto Rican mother's brother, in July 1983, shortly after Tebbens came on the Job. Tebbens's uncle had closed up his travel agency on East 138th Street and Alexander and was carrying his daily receipts home to East 139th Street when two men grabbed him and then, when he went for his own weapon, shot and killed him. While still in uniform in the Five-Two precinct, Tebbens was allowed to work the case with Detective Clarence Williams of the Four-O squad; it was his first exposure to Mott Haven.

Calderon had watched the Red Top money machine grow steadily in the Beekman Avenue area. He demanded protection payments from the crew in late summer 1991, but Lenny, Nelson, and Fat Danny told him, "Fuck you. You wan' us, come an' get us." So Calderon assaulted 348 Beekman. But the gang had some warning of the attack. They cleared the streets of all their own workers and civilians, oiled all their weapons, and waited for Calderon. When Calderon and his boys came, he was greeted with a barrage of semiautomatic fire out of 348 Beekman toward Oak Terrace. The two sides fired hundreds of rounds, but only one official complaint was recorded, and that was taken by police at Lincoln Hospital from Frank Blair, Brenda Blair's brother, who had come to the emergency room because one of his eyes was nicked, he said, by a ricochet off his wall as he watched television. Blair claimed no knowledge of the street shootout. No one called 911. As it happens, PO Roberto Lazar (a pseudonym) was on duty that day, but, as the gang expected, he stood by and did nothing during the gunfight.

In the end, the battle was a stand-off, with Calderon retreating. The cops eventually arrived and swept up the shell casings, pushing many into the sewers. The shootout became instant street legend. But years later, when investigators heard about it from witnesses who linked Lenny, Nelson, Dominican Chino, Stanley, Mask, and Manny to the melee, they couldn't find the case. The cops hadn't bothered to write up vouchers for the shell casings they had collected. So, officially, the shootout hadn't occurred. Then Mark Tebbens thought to check the complaint record for property damage to automobiles. Indeed, on September 14, 1991, multiple criminal mischief complaints had been filed for insurance purposes on Beekman Avenue, all claiming gunshot damage. Thus The Great Calderon Shootout moved from street lore to official reality.

An unknown assailant, probably Dead on Arrival's second in command, shot Calderon to death on May 21, 1992, on East 160th Street near the state parole office in the shadow of Yankee Stadium. Neighborhood mourners crowded St. Ann's Episcopal Church to pay tribute to a man who scattered flocks of money on Brook Avenue on holidays, who helped his poor neighbors bury their dead, and who gave out fresh needles and bleach to keep the clientele for his heroin alive and well.

During one of the many police investigations into Calderon's operations, detectives had cut Zia a break and she owed them information. Zia knew that the whole world was looking for Pasqualito, and she saw a chance to work off a big part of her debt. She called her detective contact about Stacey's trip to the Dominican Republic. On March 23, 1994, at 1530 hours, that detective, in turn, notified Tebbens that Stacey was leaving the next day.

At 0545 hours on March 24th Tebbens and Detective Kevin Byrant set up surveillance in a Lincoln Town Car with heavily tinted windows near Stacey's house at 164 St. Ann's Avenue. Another vehicle containing Detectives Eddie Benitez and Ray Aguilar was posted several blocks away. At 1045 hours, with one child in tow and the other in a pouch at her breast, Stacey took a waiting livery cab across the Triborough Bridge heading toward the two New York airports. The cab bypassed LaGuardia and went on to Kennedy Airport, followed closely by the two cars of detectives. The detectives half-expected to see Pasqualito waiting at Kennedy. But Stacey went through the stultifying international check-in line, so Tebbens stood right behind her, pretending, as nonchalantly as possible, to be another bored customer. When she finally reached the American Airlines counter at 1135 hours, Stacey was told that she had already missed her flight to the Dominican Republic. She exchanged her ticket for a place on a later flight. Tebbens discreetly followed her away from the counter and over to a bank of phones; he eavesdropped as she telephoned a friend, asking her to call Pasqualito. The friend was to inform Pasqualito about the later flight and to tell him not to leave the Santo Domingo airport, since Stacey spoke no Spanish and didn't want to be stranded there with their children.

Tebbens called Terry Quinn, Dan Brownell, and Pat Lafferty in the HIU office. They, in turn, called Kevin O'Brien, an agent with the Drug Enforcement Agency stationed at the American Embassy in the Dominican Republic, who agreed to contact Dominican officials about apprehending Pasqualito. Quinn faxed O'Brien Pasqualito's New York City birth certificate, clearly indicating that he is an American citizen, and the warrant for his arrest. At 1600 hours DEA agents, together with agents from the Dominican Dirección Nacional de Control de Drogas, confronted Pasqualito in Las Americas Airport in Santo Domingo. He pulled a gun and tried to flee, but Sergeant Francisco Ortíz of the DNCD threw him to the floor and arrested him. Garry Dugan and Jose Flores, who were in Puerto Rico doing surveillance on Pasqualito's mother's house, flew immediately to meet Tebbens in Santo Domingo. Over the next several days, the detectives and DEA Agent O'Brien negotiated with General Julio César Ventura Bayonet to extradite Pasqualito along with the 9-millimeter Smith and Wesson he had wielded in the airport. Upon reaching agreement, they finally brought Pasqualito back to New York on March 29th, after informing the Dominican officials that they wanted Nelson Sepulveda as well. At Kennedy Airport, Pasqualito and the investigators deplaned while the aircraft was still on the tarmac. Pasqualito took great delight at being greeted by a small army of heavily armed cops and federal agents, sent as a response to threats to free him by force.

Since Pasqualito was under indictment, the detectives could

not ask him questions nor later use any information he spontaneously offered as evidence against him. But Pasqualito finds common conversational ground easily, perhaps especially with long-time opponents who share his own deep interest in street affairs; moreover, he has a sense of humor, laced with irony. He told the investigators how he was raised as a Jehovah's Witness and, as a youth called "Little Easter," had gone with his mother from door to door distributing *The Watchtower.* While handcuffed and in leg irons, he razzed Tebbens about his cop's salary. "Hey, Tebbens, I bet you make five grand a month, right? Shit, man, I make five grand a week." He asked Eddie Benitez: "Man, just tell me one thing. Why the fuck did they let me out after you caught me for shooting that kid in Brooklyn?" He told investigators that he stayed in New York for a day after killing Cuevas in order to get tattooed with a red-and-blue emblem displaying a skull with snakes crawling out of every orifice, a ritual he performed after every murder. Although several such tattoos were emblazoned on his body, Pasqualito took particular pride in murdering Cuevas. But apart from the little that he said in ebullient spontaneity, prosecutors learned nothing more from Pasqualito.

Investigators had hoped to hear about a new operation that Pasqualito, along with Allen Checo, Teddy Rodriguez, and Heavy D, was trying to open in the Hudson Guild Projects in Manhattan's Chelsea area. The former owners of the spots that Pasqualito was muscling into were due to come out of prison, memories of their humiliating defeat in the battle of the Ten-Eighteen Club still fresh in their minds, and cops in the Tenth precinct feared a war. But investigators did learn later from a confidential source the reason for Pasqualito's preening about Cuevas's murder. Cuevas had gone completely out of control. Only two weeks before his death, Frankie had stormed down the middle of West 171st Street with a Desert Eagle 9-millimeter assault rifle in hand, bellowing out Pasqualito's name and challenging him to come out and fight. Although

Pasqualito stayed out of sight that day, he couldn't ignore the challenge without dire consequences to his street reputation. So he grabbed one of Cuevas's inner circle and persuaded him to set Frankie up by threatening to murder his entire family. The man did set Cuevas up, phoning Pasqualito to tell him that Frankie was hanging out at West 177th and Fort Washington with Manny Guerrero.

As soon as Pasqualito was in custody, Manny Guerrero showed up in Brownell's office with Roberto Peralta in tow. Peralta, it turns out, was yet another eyewitness to the Cuevas murder. Roberto said Manny Guerrero, along with Cuba and Rafael, picked him up in New Jersey on June 20, 1993, in the gray Lincoln. Cuevas beeped them and told them to meet him at 177th Street and Broadway. When they got there, Cuba and Rafael went to eat. Frankie wanted a man called Jackson to pick up money from his spot at Manor and Watson. Roberto got into the driver's seat of the Lincoln, with Jackson in the front passenger seat and Manny in the rear. As Roberto started the car, Frankie leaned on the Lincoln and began talking to him. Roberto noticed a black van parked near the corner of Fort Washington and West 177th Street. Suddenly, Pasqualito appeared right in front of the Lincoln on the driver's side and began shooting at Cuevas. Roberto saw Pasqualito shoot at Frankie and then he ducked down; Jackson and Manny fled from the car. After the shooting, Roberto drove off in a hurry, hitting a van in the process, parked the Lincoln in a garage on Broadway, and then returned to West 177th, where Frankie lay dying on the street. Prosecutors now had three eyewitness accounts of Pasqualito's murder of Franklin Cuevas.

As soon as the detectives arrived in New York with Pasqualito, they learned that officials had arrested Nelson Sepulveda in the Dominican Republic. Once Tebbens and Dugan brought him back to New York, Nelson quickly agreed to cooperate. He corroborated much of what investigators had pieced together from Freddy Sendra and others about the beginning of the crack operation in Mott Haven in 1986 and its roots in the Baseballs crew headed by Yayo. However, to investigators' bafflement, he denied knowing Freddy Sendra until the latter began working at Beech Terrace in 1987. Nelson insisted that he was not a part of the car-theft-on-consignment ring nor part of Sendra's marijuana trade. Instead, Nelson said that he got his own start as a member of the Royal Playboys, a local Washington Heights teenage street gang. Although Nelson struck investigators as smart and articulate, he told his story without narrative sweep, in fragmented bits and pieces, with nearly complete inattention to dates.

When Nelson was about thirteen, he met El Feo while writing graffiti on subway trains, where he also did knife and strongarm robberies, punching victims, including women, in the face when they didn't comply. At George Washington High School he played middle linebacker on the football team, but earned real neighborhood fame in a two-hand-touch street football league where he played with Fat Danny, a long-time boyhood friend from West 171st Street. When football was not in season, he sold crack for the Baseballs operation after school. He assaulted two or three of his teachers, once throwing a garbage can at a "pain-in-the-ass" female substitute teacher who tried to control the classroom. When he was sent to the disciplinary dean, he punched out the dean. When he got kicked out of school for that offense, he started selling drugs full time. He regularly carried two handguns, along with a sawed-off shotgun that he concealed in a sling holster constructed with hangers. Once a woman leaned out her apartment window and hollered at him on the street, chiding him for selling drugs, so he shot several rounds at her.

Nelson said that he spent little time with his younger brother Lenny while they were growing up. But Beech Terrace was going nowhere under his leadership; Nelson had begun using crack, then caught pneumonia, and in his weakened condition lost control of his workers. He turned to his brother for help because the lionlike Lenny instilled fear in everyone. Between Beech Terrace and The Hole, in addition to living high, Nelson invested money in real estate in both Manhattan and the Bronx. He also saved about half a million dollars which he, his other younger brother, Robert, his uncle Jose, and a girl named Myra laundered by smuggling it back to the Dominican Republic. There, he bought a house for his mother, land for other relatives, and a farm for himself, complete with servants and an eight-foot wall around his property. He also opened a satellite dish business.

Nelson told investigators the whole story of The Quad. Almost as soon as Lenny went to prison on a gun charge in October 1991, crack sales at The Hole and at the East 141st Street Orange Top locations began to plummet. Gerard Heard's Yellow Top crew was selling treys ($3 a vial) at 320 Beekman, and their crack was just as good as Red Top's and Orange Top's at nickels ($5 a vial). Managers' income decreased with declining sales. Renny, Tezo, and Linwood all complained that they would be getting paid better if Lenny were still in charge. A couple of times, Nelson sent Platano, Stanley, and Linwood over to beat up or rob Yellow Top workers, but Gerard Heard just didn't listen to reason. Nelson went upstate to talk to Lenny. Lenny opposed anything drastic and told Nelson that, when he got out of jail in June, he would personally take care of any problems on the street. But Nelson felt that he had to act in order to save face with all the Red and Orange Top managers. He planned the assault.

Ruben Perez got him a white Cadillac for the job, which Fat Danny drove from 174th Street in Manhattan to Crimmins Avenue in the Bronx. With Tezo, Nelson drove his own Monte Carlo to the Bronx and parked on Cypress Avenue. Platano and Freddy Krueger, the latter loaned to Nelson by El Feo, drove over in a black Taurus, which they parked on Cypress Avenue. They all convened at Brenda Blair's "house" on the third floor of 352 Beekman. Nelson then went out onto the street with Platano, Tezo, and Freddy Krueger and looked for Gerard Heard, but without success. Nelson stopped by Cypress to alert Fat Danny to get his people off the street. The whole group went back to Brenda's apartment. After a while, Nelson took Stanley, Platano, Freddy Krueger, Tezo, Mask, and Renny up to the roof of 352 Beekman, then across the roofs all the way down Beekman Avenue to the alleyway next to the Mi Ranchito Grocery at 320 Beekman. Nelson had dressed carefully for the night: black pants, black jacket. He carried a knapsack filled with an Uzi and four handguns, all purchased from Raymond Polanco. From the rooftop, Nelson looked down on the Yellow Top operation and saw Amp Green talking to Gerard Heard. Nelson told the crew that he wanted to set up a crossfire, with a couple of guys shooting into the front of the alley from Beekman, and a couple of guys shooting into its rear. But Freddy Krueger, more experienced in such matters, explained the dangers of that scheme.

According to Nelson, Freddy Krueger kept the coolest head of the whole crowd that night. As a prelude to the butchery, everybody else worked themselves up into a lather about the sheer effrontery of the Yellow Top crew, but Krueger unsuccessfully urged the gang not to act in the heat of passion. Suddenly, Linwood called the crew on the walkie-talkie, warning them that police were making routine rounds in the area. They returned to Brenda's house and waited until the police left. Then the same crew, plus Fat Danny and Shorty, went back upstairs to the roof to meet a second time and review the plan. Nelson had already decided not to participate in the shooting. He talked briefly with Platano, who said: "Leave it to me." Nelson gave Platano the knapsack with weapons and said: "I leave it in your hands."

Nelson left the roof of 352 Beekman, went downstairs to Brenda's apartment, and picked up the day's cash receipts. He left her place and hurried down the stairs, jamming *cuentas* into his pockets on the way. He stopped on the stairs to roll a blunt; as the sweet-acrid smell of marijuana filled the stairwell, he looked out across the trash-filled vacant lot toward the darkness of St. Mary's Park. He wanted to hear the shots. Just as he reached the basement, the volleys shattered the crisp silence of the bitter winter night. He hurried across the vacant lot to Cypress Avenue, got into his car, and drove to his house on Huntington Avenue in the Throgs Neck section of the Bronx.

The next day, Nelson telephoned Platano and told him that he had made the lead story on television news. The day after that, he called again, telling Platano to meet him with the weapons used in the shooting. Platano and Tezo picked up Nelson in the Taurus, and they went to Ruben's marijuana spot on West 174th Street where they copped a couple of bags of weed. Then they drove over to the George Washington Bridge, parking the car on the street near the bridge. They retrieved the weapons from the car's *clavo.* After telling Platano to wait in the car, Nelson walked with Tezo out to the middle of the bridge and dropped the knapsack filled with guns into the Hudson River.

Following information from Alejandrina Cruz, investigators pressed Nelson on the murder of Anthony Villerbe. Nelson admitted killing him, arguing that this was his only "body." Villerbe was a regular customer, buying five or six bundles at a time. On January 3, 1992, Renny and Stanley found Nelson at Brenda's house and got Nelson's clearance to sell Villerbe his normal buy. But when they returned with the money, Nelson thought some of the bills were counterfeit. Taking Stanley with him, Nelson went out into the street and caught up with Villerbe in front of 610 Beech Terrace. Stanley accused Villerbe of jerking the crew. Villerbe denied it. But Nelson and Stanley each shot him several times anyway; Stanley then reappropriated the five bundles of crack. Nelson returned to Brenda's to play Nintendo games.

Nelson also gave Pasqualito up to investigators. He described a social affair in El Feo's stepfather's backyard in Santiago, Dominican Republic. Speaking English in a crowd of a dozen uncomprehending Spanish speakers, Pasqualito bragged to Nelson how, disguised in dreadlocks, he approached Franklin Cuevas, who was leaning over a car at 177th Street and Fort Washington. Pasqualito waited until Cuevas saw him and, as Frankie looked at him, Pasqualito "saw the ghost in his eyes." Then he shot Cuevas and his friend Manny Guerrero. As El Feo repeatedly tried to get him to stop talking, Pasqualito went on to describe how he jumped into El Feo's van, where Manny Crespo, El Feo, and Freddy Krueger sat waiting. They all drove off to celebrate the death of their enemy.

down-
town
justice

The seventeen-story, grimy-granite Manhatta. Criminal Courts Building at 100 Centre Street and Hogan Place towers over Chinatown's tangled, twisting sprawl immediately to its east. To its north, separated at ground level by a plazalike parking lot but interconnected through an underground honeycomb of tunnels where zones of authority between the Police Department and Correction are clearly demarcated by white lines painted on the floor, is The Tombs, the Manhattan House of Detention. It is a new building with a name that dates back to the original late 1830s structure on the same site modeled after an Egyptian mausoleum, and it is always jammed with unsentenced prisoners awaiting trial.

To the south of the Criminal Courts Building, at 80 Centre Street, stands the squat seven-story Louis J. Lefkowitz building, filled with the overflow of district attorneys from DANY's main offices across the street in the Criminal Courts Building, though DANY has a separate entrance at 1 Hogan Place. Farther to the south, still on Centre Street, are the Greek-temple-like gleaming white marble Federal Court buildings and—off St. Andrew's Plaza jutting to the east of Centre, the frieze of its red-brick Catholic church proclaiming *Beati qui ambulant in lege Domini*—the dingy-gray, bunkerlike building that houses the offices of the United States Attorney's Office, Southern District. Beyond it, at One Police Plaza, are the sallow-brick headquarters and puzzle palace of the NYPD.

One enters the Criminal Courts Building at 100 Centre Street from the west side, with tiny Collect Pond Park—always filled with down-and-outers and brazen pigeons in equal numbers—at one's back. The queues at both the north and south entrances to 100 Centre Street usually stretch well out of the building into miniplazas made funnel-like with ten-foot walls angled toward the vaulted entrances, creating wind tunnels at the revolving doors. Waiting in lines that often stretch all the way back to the street, the crowds need only look up a bit to read aphorisms chiseled into the granite. On the walls of the south entrance, one reads: *The Just Man Enjoys Peace of Mind. Every Place Is Safe to Him Who Lives in Justice. Be Just and Fear Not. Why Should There Not Be a Perfect Confidence in the Ultimate Justice of the People?* And *Where the Law Ends There Tyranny Begins.* On the walls of the north entrance, one reads: *Good Faith Is the Foundation of Justice. The Only True Principle of Humanity Is Justice. Justice Is Denied No One. Impartiality Is the Life of Justice as Justice Is of Good Government. The People Are the Foundation of Power.* And *Equal and Exact Justice to All Men of Whatever State or Persuasion.*

But standing in the lines of those waiting to enter 100 Centre Street, one usually hears other sentiments buried in stories: the tale of a man who was cut up and thrown from a roof, dead before he hit the ground, because he had offended his fellow homeboys; the anecdote of a man getting a $100 summons for littering in a city where trash often swirls ankle deep; or the story of cops approaching disruptive white youths from New Jersey with guns holstered, but, in similar circumstances, shooting a black youth to death. Occasionally, while standing in line, one hears the old street saw: "Justice? Or Just Us?"

Inside, one joins yet other lines to pass through sensitive metal-screening devices and scanners, put into place after an armed Jamaican hit man stalking a witness was apprehended by sheer luck in a courtroom. Beyond the metal detectors, one gets caught up in the swarming traffic directed by burly white-shirted court officers, who screen everyone coming into the building, uniformed police escorting handcuffed prisoners to arraignment in Criminal Court, detectives in snappy suits with neckties draped but unknotted, assistant district attorneys in somber grays or blues befitting ministers of justice, paddy-wagon-chasing defense lawyers along with some of the most eloquent advocates of our times, and confused citizens trying to find their way to the jury pools. Every day, 100 Centre Street hosts the dance among the elephantine bureaucracies of Correction, Police, District Attorney, and Court, as well as the clash between the universalistic claims of our system of justice and the intensely personal, highly particularistic ethos of the streets.

All the proceedings in the Wild Cowboys case went to Part 88, the cavernous, 30-foot-ceilinged, oak-pewed courtroom of Justice Leslie Crocker Snyder. Justice Snyder started her quarter-century career in the criminal justice system as an assistant district attorney at DANY, where she founded and headed that office's, and indeed the nation's, first specialized Sex Crimes Unit. After a brief two-year stint as a defense attorney, she returned to DANY as a prosecutor. Then, in March 1983, Mayor Ed Koch put her on the Criminal Court bench, where judges try, by day and night, to impose order on lives ringing with the clang of the streets. In January 1986, along with a cohort of five other judges, Governor Mario Cuomo appointed her Acting Justice of the New York State Supreme Court, seated in Manhattan.

Justice Snyder gathered her staff. She picked the trim and engaging Rocco DeSantis, whom she knew as a court officer during her stint in Criminal Court, to be the clerk of her "part," not only for his meticulous organizational skills but for his remarkable bonhomie that makes a sometimes acrimonious venue inviting to all parties. She chose as her court attorney Alex Calabrese, who had often appeared before her in Criminal Court during his several years as a legal aid attorney. Calabrese's widely admired grasp of the law and his subtlety of argument in countless, pointed briefs on issues petty and grand is complemented by his fierce commitment to Notre

Dame football. His office is festooned with pictures of the Golden Dome, Touchdown Jesus, posters from the motion picture *Rudy*, and, in a prominent place, a glossy color photograph of Lenny Sepulveda, taken on the day he was apprehended, wearing, to Calabrese's delight, a University of Miami teeshirt.

Justice Snyder also chose the fresh-out-of-law-school bright and vibrant Teresa Matushaj, both as a court attorney and as her personal assistant to help manage her 500 ongoing cases, all at various stages of completion. With her floor-length dresses accentuating her constant motion, Matushaj quickly became a fixture at Part 88, writing detailed legal memoranda and knitting together the multiple social relationships that make the court function, supervising the part's regular parade of college and law-school interns, and sitting on the bench next to the judge during trials.

At her appointment to the Supreme Court, along with her entire cohort of new justices, Justice Snyder was assigned to drug cases, work not highly prized then or now. Among other things, drug cases require a judge to be on call twenty-four hours a day to authorize wiretaps and surveillance and to issue search and arrest warrants at the odd hours typical of undercover police work. To her own surprise, Justice Snyder found the drug cases that came her way filled with interesting characters, defendants, witnesses, and police officers alike. Even in the fun-house world of 100 Centre Street, where truth almost always outdistances fiction, one does not find in every courtroom, to take only Justice Snyder's first narcotics case, mobbed-up defendants making drug drops with wife and newborn infant in tow. So, when Justice Snyder was offered a chance to go to other kinds of work, she chose to stay with drug cases. Then the violence endemic to the trade escalated in the late 1980s, especially with the ascendancy of the Jamaican and Dominican gangs. Drug-case work provided glimpses of the minotaur at the center the labyrinthine violence of the streets and the chance to help slay the monster before it devoured a generation of young men and women.

By 1994 Justice Snyder had presided over a series of celebrated drug-gang cases in which she gave lengthy sentences to groups such as the several Martinez brothers, heads of the Gerry Curls gang, who got, variously, 50, 75, 100, and 213 years to life for drug-trafficking and murder. Indeed, assisted by Calabrese and later by Matushaj, Snyder made several rulings that helped shape emerging case law governing appropriate procedures in such cases. These included provisions for *in camera, ex parte* reviews of probable cause underlying search warrants, thereby protecting the identities of confidential informants, as well as rulings that shielded the identities of witnesses until immediately before their testimony in cases with evidence of witness intimidation.

Justice Snyder had become something of a legend to all the street warriors, cops, district attorneys, and drug dealers alike. Undercover cops—tough, stubble-faced, pony-tailed, their working-class awkwardness accentuated in the presence of the widely celebrated, ash-blond, Radcliffe-educated woman—found that when they approached her through her bodyguards for warrants, whether in chambers, in restaurants, or at chic East Side parties, they received not only the requisite signature but arm squeezes and eye-to-eye admonitions to take care. District attorneys counted on her no-nonsense vigilance for public safety in making their arguments in her courtroom, even as they expected detailed critiques of their public performances, based on her vast experience as a former DA.

Drug dealers invented a street-based explanation for the harsh sentences she regularly imposed on them and their business associates. In their view, Justice Snyder's stringency toward drug dealers stems from a vow they claim she took to avenge the death by heroin of her only daughter. As it happens, Justice Snyder has no daughter, nor has anyone in her family died from drugs. But on the street, personal vengeance makes perfect sense; adherence to abstract principles is absurd.

In the end, nine members of the Wild Cowboys chose to go to trial on September 7, 1994. Several of the trial defendants had refused plea offers from Brownell. Each of the nine had his own attorney financed by New York State and appointed by the court from a pool of seasoned members of the defense bar to be advocates for felony defendants who claim to be without means. The defendants and attorneys were:

Daniel Rincon aka Fat Danny, represented by Donald Tucker

Jose Llaca aka Pasqualito, represented by Valerie Van Leer-Greenberg

Wilfredo de los Angeles aka Platano, represented by Robert Soloway

Rafael Perez aka Tezo, represented by David Tougher

Stanley Tukes aka Trigger, represented by Steven Kaiser

Victor Mercedes, represented by Sol Schwartzberg, assisted for a time by Robert Beecher

Linwood Collins aka Cool Water, represented by Robert Dunn

Daniel Gonzalez aka Shorty, represented by Robert Katz

Russell Harris aka Renny, represented by Richard Wojszwillo

Fat Danny, Platano, Stanley, Shorty, and Renny were charged with The Quad. Victor and Pasqualito were charged with The Double. Tezo was charged with The Brighton Beach Murder. Fat Danny was charged with The Telephone Murder. Linwood Collins was charged with The Rooftop Murder. And Pasqualito was charged with the Fat Frankie Homicide. Each defendant was also charged with first- and second-degree conspiracy to traffic narcotics, and with individual acts of violence that, the People argued, furthered the overall criminal enterprise.

On the eve of trial, prosecutors discovered that Ulysses Mena aka Dominican Chino could not have participated with Platano and Stanley in disemboweling Eddie Maldonado in the

St. Mary's Park Stabbing, since he was in jail on November 7, 1991. Prosecutors' prime witness for this murder was Joey Morales, also a key witness for The Quad. Prosecutors felt that Joey's misidentification of Dominican Chino so compromised the case on the St. Mary's Park Stabbing that it could not be presented successfully. Moreover, prosecutors had to acknowledge Joey's error in the stabbing during his direct testimony and hope that jurors didn't discount his evidence on The Quad as well. How had Joey gotten it wrong? Investigators could only surmise that "Satan," Dominican Chino's look-alike twin brother, was involved, but they had no proof whatsoever of this. Reluctantly they dropped this murder charge against Stanley and Platano. Dominican Chino pleaded guilty to the conspiracy and received a sentence of 10 years to life.

Chino also confessed to a double murder, but the bureaucratic vagaries of the criminal justice system thwarted fixing his guilt legally. Manuel Lugo aka Supra worked for Lenny opening up a spot at 2138 Vyse Avenue at 181st Street in the Four-Eight precinct; Wilfredo Roman worked for Supra. Carlos Ventura, the already well-established big man on the block, refused to stop selling his own brand of crack out of the same building. So Supra turned to Lenny for help in persuading Ventura. On December 30, 1990, Lenny took Rob Base, Lace, and Dominican Chino up to Vyse Avenue, where they waited until Supra signaled to them that Ventura had arrived on the block in his car. Lenny asked his boys: "Who's gonna do it?" And Dominican Chino said: "I will." Chino ran over to Ventura's car and shot Ventura in the head. But also in the car was Marilyn Colon, Ventura's girlfriend, seven months pregnant, terrified and wide-eyed. So Chino shot her too. Supra and Roman were tried for the murders in the Bronx. Supra was convicted; Roman was acquitted. Then Chino, in a fit of remorse, poured out his story to Mark Tebbens, Dan Brownell, and Don Hill, and even agreed to take a 20-years-to-life plea to the murders. As part of his own plea agreement, Lenny admitted his role in the murders and named Chino as the shooter. But when the investigators contacted the Bronx District Attorney's office and the Four-Eight detective squad with the news, they received chilly receptions. Were the boys from Manhattan once again trying to outshine the Bronx by unmaking a made case?

Prosecutors also decided to drop one serious charge against Shorty. Sometime around late summer or early fall 1992, Shorty propositioned a female Red Top pitcher inside the Baker sisters' stash apartment, offering to trade crack for sex. The pitcher refused, telling Shorty that she wanted money for her work as a pitcher. Shorty pulled out a gun and forced her into the bedroom, where he gave her both money and crack, raped and sodomized her at gunpoint, and then took back the money and crack. Although her testimony in the grand jury brought an indictment against Shorty, the woman's inability to date the attack with any exactitude made prosecutors uneasy about including it in an already tangled case.

The entire legal process leading up to trial and the trial itself were raucously contentious from start to finish. Authorities learned from prison records, hospital reports, and monitored correspondence that the defendants had resurrected old rivalries and were quarreling savagely among themselves. Fat Danny pressured Platano to leave him out of The Quad and indeed to take the fall for all accused of those murders. Platano refused. Then somehow Pasqualito got into Platano's cell and beat him badly. To avenge the assault on his close friend Platano, Nelson Sepulveda then confronted Pasqualito in August 1994 and tuned him up, breaking Pasqualito's hand in the process. Pasqualito was also enraged at Tezo for naming him as the shooter in The Brighton Beach Murder, even though there was insufficient corroborative evidence to charge Pasqualito with that crime. And on November 7, 1994, Fat Danny, Victor,

Renny, Stanley, and Shorty spotted Glen Stretching, a former Orange Top worker, in the holding pens on their way into court. Stretching had pleaded guilty but had not cooperated with authorities. But Renny showed Stretching a copy of the indictment and asked him: "If your name is in the indictment, how come you're not on trial?" Victor chimed in, asking: "What, you think we're stupid?" The gang members beat Stretching within an inch of his life.

At that point, Justice Snyder called Hillel Bodek, a consultant to the New York State Supreme Court and a master of the organizational idiosyncrasies of Correction, the Police Department, Parole, and the Court itself. She ordered him to work with Pat Lafferty of the HIU staff to get all the warring factions of prisoners and, of course, incarcerated witnesses housed separately, but still accessible for timely, segregated transport to court, where they were to be kept in separate holding units. All of these were formidable logistical undertakings for command bureaucracies used to doing everything in batches.

Once it became clear that Lenny and Nelson had cut some kind of a deal with the district attorney, even though the details were unknown, Fat Danny threatened to kill the whole Sepulveda family, according to an HIU informant. The same source said that Fat Danny, Victor, and Pasqualito also threatened to kill any former gang members such as Frankie Robles or Zero Rodriguez, or bit players such as Louise McBride or Loretta and Floretta Baker, who cooperated with the authorities and testified at trial. Some gang members took such threats to heart. When, for instance, authorities arrested and charged Ruben Perez with arranging The Halloween Murder, Brownell was willing to offer Ruben a generous deal provided he name the shooter in that killing, who everybody knew by that time was Tezo. Had Perez been willing to testify against Tezo in that case, Brownell could probably have extracted a guilty plea from Tezo for The Brighton Beach Murder, thus greatly simplifying the main trial. But, though Perez pleaded guilty, he refused to cooperate. At his sentencing, he told Justice Snyder that his relatives crowding the courtroom still lived in Washington Heights, and he feared for their safety. Of course, all independent witnesses, such as Fat Iris Cruz and the children of Elizabeth Morales, were under constant threat.

Then, on October 14, 1994, Tebbens got a call from Taco [a pseudonym], a soon-to-be-released prisoner who had been housed with Pasqualito on Rikers Island. Taco told Tebbens that Pasqualito had offered him $30,000 and a stake in several crack spots set up according to Lenny's formula to kill Dan Brownell, in the courtroom if necessary. Pasqualito also wanted Taco to kill: the eyewitnesses to Franklin Cuevas's murder; Clifford Halsey, the driver at The Double; the man in Brooklyn who gave Pasqualito the car for The Brighton Beach Murder; and Nelson and Lenny, who were cooperating. Pasqualito told Taco that he was planning something special for Justice Snyder. Alarmed by the threats, HIU investigators pressed their other confidential informants and intensified their monitoring of defendants' phone calls from jail. They learned that El Feo, the gang's long-time cocaine supplier, was distressed at the plight of his former comrades-at-arms, particularly that of Pasqualito, who, from the time of his release from jail in August 1991 until his apprehension in spring 1994, had distinguished himself by his alacrity to commit violence. The informant said that El Feo put out contracts on key officials associated with the case. These included Justice Snyder and her entire family; the judge's highly visible assistant, Teresa Matushaj; ADA Dan Brownell; and Detective Mark Tebbens.

Justice Snyder's courtroom turned into an armed camp. Sharp conflicts broke out between the court officers regularly responsible for courtroom security and NYPD detectives assigned to guard Justice Snyder and her family around the clock and guard Teresa Matushaj to and from work. Everybody's anxiety rose measurably when police learned that the elusive hit man Freddy Krueger had the contracts. Tebbens and Dugan pressed the Sepulveda brothers for more information about Krueger, and in fall 1994 they finally learned his real name: Francisco Medina. Both Lenny and Nelson said that Freddy was a wild man, ready to do anything on the street. With grudging admiration, Pasqualito allowed that Freddy Krueger already had 25 bodies on him.

Other witnesses found themselves also in danger after the September 1993 takedown. Corky Rios, for one, received many threats. The day after Lourdes Bonilla aka Lulu talked to investigators about the assault on her when she was pregnant, three men armed with shotguns showed up at her apartment to warn her not to testify.

Some witnesses carelessly heightened their own danger, drawing others into the line of fire. On February 25, 1994, authorities arrested Jude Ann and Steven Bohan for threats to Sarap Majid, then Corky's girlfriend. Sarap had grown up on West 171st Street and was thoroughly familiar with the whole Sepulveda operation. When she became a witness, Dugan and Tebbens relocated her into an Upper East Side apartment, carrying furniture up six flights of stairs to get her settled. The detectives pressed Sarap to promise that under no circumstances would she go back to Washington Heights. But return she did, even giving her new telephone and beeper numbers to her old pals. When a crew from Washington Heights followed her back to her new apartment one night, Sarap beeped Mark Tebbens, imperiously demanding that he meet her at a gas station at 155th Street and Broadway, where she arrived in a taxi filled with all her personal belongings, tailed by a car packed with young Dominican men. Tebbens had to shake them before depositing Sarap in a hotel for the night. A few days later, Garry Dugan relocated Sarap and her mother to an apartment in New Jersey. On the way, Sarap harangued Dugan about the food he had bought her and about his choice of music on the car radio. An unrecognized part of detective work is the care and feeding of truculent, often unpleasant, witnesses.

The trial's main drama consisted of the Cowboys' constant assertion of the ethos of the street against the Court's administration of our thoroughly rationalized system of law. Nearly every day, the courtroom was packed with defendants' girlfriends and the occasional uncomprehending mother. Along with this audience, the jury panel of 18 men and women watched with fascination as the nine defendants taunted Mark Tebbens with obscene hand gestures as he provided the main frame of the state's case. The obscenities escalated with former comrade Freddy Sendra's testimony and changed to menacing glares when the civilian witnesses, such as Fat Iris Cruz, Alejandrina Cruz, and Joey Morales, testified. When Frankie Robles, Zero Rodriguez, and George Santiago each took the witness stand, they received constant warnings in the secret hand language of the Latin Kings, a self-described nation for Latinos that emerged from and flourishes in prisons. Tensions reached a bristling crescendo of puffed-chest, hand-chopping-air hostility with Nelson Sepulveda's week-long testimony; the courtroom was jammed with armed court officers, and the narrow corridors to the holding pens were filled with beefy policemen with hats and bats, ready, indeed eager, to rush into the courtroom should Nelson's public betrayal of his former underlings provoke bravado demonstrations. Sometimes, defense attorneys publicly embraced their clients' ethos, as when one attorney denounced cooperators in open court as "snitches," or when another at sidebar allowed that Pasqualito had done "a yeoman-like job" in killing Franklin Cuevas. One day at sidebar, when one of the defense lawyers became as chesty with Justice Snyder as his client was on the street, she grabbed his regimental tie and pulled his tall frame down to her eye level, warning him never to bump her again.

There also were comedic episodes that parodied the main

drama. One day, Defense Attorney Valerie Van Leer-Greenberg suggested that Fat Danny had actually committed one of the crimes with which her client, Pasqualito, had been charged. When she returned to the defense table, Fat Danny leaned over and said to her, quite audibly: "I'm gonna kill you, bitch." Justice Snyder immediately cleared the courtroom of the jury and of all the defendants except Fat Danny, whom she up-braided about the serious breach of decorum. With massive outstretched palms, Fat Danny shrugged, asking with seeming innocence: "What'd I do?" prompting hands-over-mouths guf-faws on all sides.

Some of the defendants quickly learned that they could nettle officials and amuse themselves by turning the Court's necessary proceduralism against itself. Stanley Tukes and Pasqualito became Muslims, thwarting any court proceedings involving them on Fridays and requiring the Court to make an *imam* available for prayer sessions on other Muslim feast days. Several of the defendants, at one time or another, claimed to have developed serious health problems that, they argued, re-quired recesses, often forcing the bureaucratic magician, Hillel Bodek, to work around the clock arranging medical examina-tions to check out the claims and keep the trial moving. The most famous of these episodes became known as The Great Back Problem. The van transporting Fat Danny to trial on April 27th had a feather-touch fender-bender with a car on Second Avenue which stopped traffic. Thinking that the event might be part of a long-threatened escape plan, Correction officers armed with machine guns leapt out of the van and surrounded the motorist, who turned out to be only a hapless civilian now trembling like a caged gerbil. The next day Fat Danny claimed nearly complete paralysis because of the accident, requiring the Court to have Bodek put on record his observa-tions of Fat Danny putting on his trousers that very morning. This prompted Fat Danny to declare in court: "You a rat, Bodek! You a rat!"

Despite early, unsuccessful attempts to argue that police had targeted their clients because of ethnicity, defense attorneys challenged prosecutors in key areas throughout the trial. The defense attorneys' first line of defense was to ridicule the People's accusation that their clients had been engaged in a "conspiracy." The attorneys admitted that their clients were drug dealers. They argued, however, that the notion of conspiracy was a wholly implausible framework for describing the extremely decentralized, always contentious social structure of drug gangs on the street. In the Beekman Avenue area alone, they argued, there were several other crack operations besides Red Top or Orange Top. These included Pink Top, Black Top, and Green Top, in addition to the ill-fated Yellow Top. The sheer proliferation of crack spots in the area belied the People's image of a "conspiracy," with its suggestions of rigid hierarchy and monopoly. More specifically, the defense attorneys argued that events on the street belied the prosecutors' assertion that Orange Top was part and parcel of Red Top. What kind of conspiracy was it that had Nelson taking out a contract on Victor, and Lenny arranging to have Fat Danny shot, both instances of Red Top bosses going after Orange Top bosses?

Instead of a conspiracy, defense attorneys argued, this was a coterie of admittedly aggressive young men who were plying their own individual entrepreneurial futures. If they occasionally came together to do business, they did so because they were boyhood friends; if they quarreled, they did so because of rivalries that stemmed from that common boyhood. To construe such associations as evidence of an enveloping criminal enterprise strained all rules of consistency, credulity, and admissibility. The weakness of the prosecution's conspiracy theory was perfectly illustrated, some defense attorneys argued, by the inclusion of The Double as an overt act furthering the conspiracy. Clearly, whoever committed these murders was avenging the death of Miguelito Castillo, a much-beloved boyhood friend. However lamentable its result, revenge emerges from the red-hot coals of human passion, not from the cool, dead, banked ashes of economic calculation.

The second line of defense was to attack continually and sharply the credibility of the prosecution's witnesses. Although the prosecution had recorded narcotics buys and surveillance tapes as a frame for its main case, the case itself, as do the overwhelming number of cases in our system of justice, depended entirely on sworn testimony. In such a system, everything depends on how worthy of belief the jury perceives the testifier to be. Reputation, social standing, articulateness, demeanor, sex, race, age, as well as educational, occupational, and experiential "credentials" all matter in assessing a witness's credibility. None of the Beekman Avenue witnesses had lived particularly stable or exemplary lives; by mainstream measures of our society, they were what one might call sullied witnesses. Several had been addicted to crack cocaine, or alcohol, or both. Some had severe, documented psychological problems; indeed, one key witness to The Quad, Martha Molina, not only suffered from addiction and delusions but had been severely pistol-whipped by Mickey Tex in April 1992 (in an episode known as Martha's Head), putting her into a month-long coma and making her even more unstable than before. Some witnesses had been prostitutes. Several had children who were hardened violent criminals. Some, like Louise McBride and Loretta and Floretta Baker, were criminally involved in the lower levels of the Cowboys' operation. Most were on welfare, perceiving it as a permanent entitlement.

Some witnesses, of course, like Chubby Green of Yellow Top and gang members Frankie Robles, George Santiago, Zero Rodriguez, and Nelson Sepulveda, were themselves deeply involved in narcotics trafficking and in its associated violence. All had received considerable favors from the district attorney's office, where they had thoroughly rehearsed their statements before appearing in court. How, the defense attorneys asked, could anyone believe anything that such witnesses said?

Even the prosecution's centerpiece civilian witnesses—Little Iris, Joey Morales, and Michael Cruz—were all, youthfully innocent appearances to the contrary, thoroughly corrupted by the world of Beekman Avenue. Moreover, Joey Morales's mis-identification of Dominican Chino in the St. Mary's Park Stab-bing, plus his four different statements about The Quad to Tebbens, the Bronx district attorney, and two grand juries re-vealed inconsistencies in important details from one telling to the next. How can one trust so-called eyewitness accounts from suspect witnesses who can't get their own stories straight?

The defense also asked: Why wasn't Fat Iris Cruz, the state's other main civilian witness from Beekman, herself on trial, since she had allowed her apartment to be a drug stash? More-over, her choice of mates—first, English Clemente, a manager at The Hole, and then, after English's murder, one Maximo, a boss of another local crack operation—suggested Fat Iris's true moral character. Here indeed is the nub of the issue, the de-fense argued. The moral character of witnesses determines one's confidence in their veracity. Why was the state unable to produce a single morally upright civilian witness to testify in this case? How, the defense argued, could any juror vote to convict on the basis of such evidence? How can one do justice on the basis of testimony from witnesses so seriously tainted? If one cannot know the truth of what happened on the streets, how can one presume to fix responsibility? If one rushes to judgment without reliable knowledge, what happens to the entire scaffolding of procedural safeguards that is, in effect, our system of justice? Defense attorneys' claims, particularly the appeal to epistemological ambiguity and the consequent in-ability to make people accountable for their actions, are in-creasingly familiar ones in our civic and moral order, marked at every turn by doubt, self-doubt, and moral ambivalence.

The third line of defense was to argue that aspects of the prosecution's case simply made no sense. Robert Dunn, lawyer for Linwood Collins, argued that the prosecution's theory of The Rooftop Murder was absurd. Why would Linwood Collins, upstanding young man that he is, kill Oscar Alvarez if he were really angry at Shrimpo, Oscar's friend, for stealing crack? Since Oscar had neither the crack nor the cash from its sale, such an action would have been, for Linwood, wholly devoid of useful, reasonable purpose, beyond the ken of any normal person. Similarly, Donald Tucker, lawyer for Fat Danny Rincon, reminded jurors that Benjamin Green himself had seen his client on Cypress Avenue just after The Quad. It was Danny who had told Benjamin the terrible news about his brother Amp Green and offered to embrace and comfort their mother while Benjamin went to his brother. Such a human gesture utterly belied the prosecutors' image of Fat Danny as a cold-blooded murderer. In short, many of the prosecution's theories defied "common sense."

In their final line of defense, all the lawyers attacked prosecutors for making deals with Lenny and Nelson Sepulveda. How could the state rely on Nelson's testimony at trial? It was unseemly, indeed downright ugly, for the state to sponsor a turncoat boss's betrayal of his former underlings. And how could anybody believe Nelson's story that he had not been one of the shooters in The Quad? Even if one accepted his incredible story at face value, why was Nelson not being prosecuted for organizing The Quad, something he openly admitted? How could the state justify allowing him to take a guilty plea in return for 22 years to life? What kind of a deal had Lenny, clearly a more violent man than any of the defendants on trial, as demonstrated by his wanton murder of David Cargill, been able to wrangle out of prosecutors? When defense attorneys insisted on this issue, they learned to their chagrin that Lenny had accepted a plea for 25 years to life.

For their own part, prosecutors argued that their conspiracy theory mirrored the social realities of the street. To bolster their claim, they elicited from witness after witness similar perceptions of the hierarchically layered social structure of the gang and of the dependence of Orange Top on Red Top, specifically that all the crack sold at The Hole and at the Orange Top spots on East 141st and 138th Streets came from the same kitchens, was simply bottled with the different colored caps, and was identically bundled in long distinctive skeins of tape. Prosecutors also documented regularly performed actions that knit the defendants into a criminal enterprise. Privately, all the HIU investigators acknowledged that the actual social structure of the gang, while roughly coherent over time, depended greatly on the presence at given moments of different powerful personalities. When, say, Lenny or Pasqualito was in jail, or when Nelson fled to the Dominican Republic, or when Platano got shot and then arrested, the structure of the group shifted, sometimes dramatically. Moreover, in the early stages of the struggle with the Cuevas faction of the gang, personal loyalties among gang members shifted day by day until outright war broke out.

But the argument over the actual social structure of the gang was, in any event, legally irrelevant. Both sides understood clearly that the law is first and foremost an instrument of social control, not a framework for social analysis, though it can sometimes serve both purposes at once. The law rationalizes the complexities of social reality to impose a particular kind of order on it, one that is brokered, often bungled, and always mutable. The law often narrows issues severely through procedural refinement precisely to achieve a desired order. Indeed, the proliferation of procedures often takes on a life of its own; when this happens, substantive justice can fall victim to the law itself. New York's conspiracy laws, as with the federal RICO laws, enable prosecutors to escape the narrowing effects of the law, even as those laws require only a minimalist sketch of social reality.

Prosecutors faced the issue of sullied witnesses by providing, wherever possible, parallel accounts of all the key crimes in the indictment. Here, they followed the three-skell rule that applies in most criminal cases: one must produce credible testimony from three street people in order to equal testimony from one upstanding citizen. Moreover, under New York State law, one must corroborate the testimony of any active accomplice in the particular crime at issue, sometimes many times over. For The Quad, the cornerstone crime of the indictment, prosecutors brought forward sometimes partially overlapping, sometimes wholly congruent accounts from the following eyewitnesses to some or all of the murders: Janice Bruington, Benjamin Green, Fat Iris Cruz, Little Iris Cruz, Joey Morales, Michael Cruz, Ramon Jimenez, and Martha Molina. Added to these were: the account of Nelson Sepulveda, who described planning the crime; the account of Frankie Robles, who saw Nelson on the street that night giving orders; and that of George Santiago, who testified to the long-standing tension between Red Top and Yellow Top. In addition, prosecutors had Elizabeth Gesualdo and Timothy Leary testify as the first police officers on the scene, and of course Detective Mark Tebbens was called to the stand to describe his exhaustive investigation. Specialists from the NYPD's Crime Scene Unit and Ballistics Unit also testified, as did the medical examiner who posted the bodies.

What emerges from all of these stories, prosecutors argued, is a grainy but still clear picture that captures Stanley, Platano, Shorty, Fat Danny, and Renny as shooters at The Quad. There were, to be sure, other shooters, but their images are lost in the shadows. Here, by producing multiple, relatively consistent accounts of the same event, prosecutors tried to obviate defense attorneys' argument that a person's testimony is only as good as a juror's evaluation of the witness's moral worth. In effect, prosecutors argued that the rules for verifying events in the world differ from the rules for morally assessing those who tell us about those events. One mixes the two kinds of analyses only at the risk of extreme confusion.

Prosecutors followed exactly the same tactics for The Brighton Beach Murder, The Double, and the Fat Frankie Homicide, each of which had multiple witnesses. Brownell had flipped Ramon Madrigal aka Battata, who provided the whole background to The Brighton Beach Murder. In addition, Brownell had two witnesses from Papito's crew, Neil Valcarcel and Pirri Rodriguez, who eyewitnessed the shooting, plus Cynthia Williams, a pitcher not only for Papito but for Tezo, who was on the set the night of the murder. Tebbens had finally tracked down the missing witnesses to The Double, even finding Clifford Halsey in Oklahoma by establishing a rapport with Halsey's sister. And the three witnesses to Cuevas's murder were firmly in place.

But in a couple of cases prosecutors could not present multiple, reinforcing accounts of the same crime. For example, at the other extreme from The Quad was the accusation against Fat Danny for The Telephone Murder. Rob Base Lopez had pleaded guilty to being the shooter but refused to testify against Fat Danny for arranging the killing. In addition to the first police officer on the scene, the medical examiner, and the ballistics specialist, prosecutors relied only on the testimonies of Zero Rodriguez, who was in the back seat of the car driven by Fat Danny to the crime scene, of Frankie Robles, to whom Lopez had told the whole story, and of Corky Rios, who described the origins of the crime as revenge for the shooting of El Feo, the Cowboys' cocaine supplier.

The Rooftop Murder was the middle case. There, in addition to officials' testimony, prosecutors had testimony from Martha Molina, who had been on the rooftop with Oscar Alvarez when Linwood Collins came looking for Oscar's friend Shrimpo; from Zero Rodriguez, who accompanied Linwood Collins to the rooftop and saw him shoot Oscar; from Frankie Robles, who overheard Linwood admit the killing to Fat Danny; and from George Santiago, who had a direct admission from Linwood about the murder. In response to the defense argument that the People's version of the murder—that Linwood killed Oscar because Oscar's friend, Shrimpo, who was nowhere to be found, owed Linwood money—defied common sense, prosecutors pointed out that they didn't need to show motive, only specific intentional actions. Moreover, they pointed out that drug gangs create worlds with their own peculiar rules and taken-for-granted assumptions; what makes no sense at all in the middle-class world makes perfect sense in the underworld.

The eight-month trial staggered to a conclusion in late April with lengthy closing arguments from all nine defense attorneys and a dazzling two-day summary of the prosecution's evidence, complete with graphs and charts, by Dan Brownell that had even the defense attorneys shaking their heads in admiration at his remarkable mastery of detail. It took Justice Snyder almost four hours just to read the charge. The jury deliberated for 15 days. In addition to normal inquiries for clarification about elements of the judge's charge, the jury sent back a series of queries that everyone found unsettling. Among these was the following:

> If the children under 16, Little Iris, Joey Morales, *et cetera*, were used in any capacity in the drug organization and their parents knew what they were doing and did not object, call the police, protest, *et cetera*, can the defendants be held accountable under conspiracy one?

The inquiry prompted stern admonitions from Justice Snyder about the legal irrelevance of the question and about the necessity for the jurors to separate their own moral judgments about parental irresponsibility from the defendants' legal accountability for their actions.

Finally, on May 15, 1995, the jury returned its verdicts. It found all the defendants guilty on all counts of the indictment, except for Linwood Collins on The Rooftop Murder and

Pasqualito for the Brooklyn shooting of Michael Cruz. In both of these cases, the jury deadlocked at eleven to one for conviction.

On June 27, 1995, all the participants in the drama, except the jury, gathered once again in Part 88 of the Manhattan branch of the New York State Supreme Court. The convicted defendants, now shackled hand and foot, were brought from the holding cells, through corridors once again lined with cops in full riot gear, to their familiar seats. Behind them stood rows of white-shirted unarmed court officers and, behind those officers outside the rail that splits the court proper from the spectators' pews, yet another row of officers, all fully armed. In the jury box sat Mark Tebbens, Garry Dugan, Terry Quinn, Walter Arsenault, and other investigators and attorneys from the Homicide Investigation Unit, as well as members of both the print and broadcast media. The spectator section of the courtroom was jammed with the mothers, wives, children, and girlfriends of the defendants, as well as the usual array of court observers.

The sentencing proceeding, a secular ritual steeped in religious themes of guilt and retribution, was as acrimonious as the trial itself. Speaking for their clients, the defense lawyers petitioned the Court to set aside the verdicts against their clients for want of adequate evidence either of an integrated conspiracy or of specific acts of violence. After Justice Snyder denied all of these motions, Dan Brownell prefaced the proceeding by characterizing the long reign of Red Top and Orange Top crack. He noted the human misery that the defendants had helped bring to tens of thousands of crack users between 1986 and 1993. He stressed the remarkable level of violence routinely used by the gang against its rivals, its own workers, and witnesses to its crimes. He closed by noting that, on the defendants' sentencing day, it was the community's turn to speak against them and their violence. He announced that the People wanted sentences to remove the defendants permanently from our society since they had amply demonstrated their unfitness for civil life.

The defendants were then arraigned individually, with the court clerk, Rocco DeSantis, reading aloud the crimes of which they stood convicted. After each arraignment, the three prosecutors took turns portraying the moral character of each defendant by recounting his crimes, dropping all semblance of dispassion. They openly voiced outrage and righteous indignation about the defendants' depredations, both criminal and moral. In particular, Don Hill castigated Fat Danny not only for his murders but for his manipulativeness in trying to blame others for his own crimes and for his attempts to "get over" on the system by intimidating witnesses. Dan Brownell pointed out Pasqualito's penchant for extreme violence and his wanton disregard for human life, as evidenced in The Double and The Fat Frankie Homicide, where bystanders could easily have been killed. Lori Grifa focused on Platano's crucial roles as enforcer and especially as the corrupter of children in the Mott Haven neighborhood by recruiting them to carry bundles of crack in their bookbags. Hill dwelt on Stanley's viciousness, demonstrated by his murder of Amp Green and attempted murder of Janice Bruington, people he had known all his life. Grifa pointed out Tezo's hard-working striving to be a hit man, noting that his ambitiousness had led him into a wilderness of violence, greed, and corruption of youngsters.

Hill pointed out Renny's deep involvement in the narcotics-trafficking conspiracy from its earliest days, although he was clearly a middle-level manager who did what he was told. Although Renny was present at The Quad and was guilty of acting in concert, Hill suggested that the judge might consider mitigating Renny's sentence because no witness had seen him actually shoot a specific victim. Brownell charged Victor with distinguishing himself not only by his violence but by his cruelty, citing specifically how he disciplined pitchers by smashing their hands with a brick or a board. Brownell argued that one could discern Shorty's whole character by remembering the image of him, only one day after he got out of jail for a drug arrest, racing from East 141st Street and Beekman to the alley at 320 Beekman, gun in hand, to shoot Cynthia Casado in the neck. Grifa pointed out that Linwood Collins had been arrested for narcotics possession and sale when he was sixteen years old. Only 60 days after receiving Youthful Offender status from a Bronx judge in exchange for a promise to lead a law-abiding life, he was arrested again for the same crime. Even by that point, he was already a manager at The Hole, a position he held until his arrest on February 17, 1992, for witness intimidation. Linwood was a drug dealer, plain and simple.

After each statement by prosecutors, defense attorneys spoke on behalf of their clients, with a few defendants speaking for themselves. The attorneys for Fat Danny, Victor, and Linwood simply protested their clients' innocence once again. But Robert Soloway stated that his client, Platano, believed that he did not receive a fair trial and did not accept the judgment of the Court. Steven Kaiser said that his client, Stanley Tukes, had no remorse for crimes he didn't commit and that he hoped the Court could separate fact from the so-called overwhelming proof constructed by prosecutors with lying and well-coached witnesses. Tukes himself then said:

> I know when I first got locked up that they was going to find me guilty, you know what I'm saying, I got wisdom here, you know what I'm saying, I know they was going to find me guilty. When Tebbens locked me up, he told me they was going to find me guilty. He is the one who made this case. He told me he knows who did it. I know you're prejudice against me. You, the DA, the police are prejudice against me. That is all I got to say.

David Tougher expressed amazement at the inequity that threatened to send his client, Tezo, to prison for life while

Lenny or Nelson could be out on the streets before they were fifty years old, rich with ill-gotten gains, hidden away in the Dominican Republic, that the state had not seized as part of their plea agreements. Richard Wojszwillo argued that everything he had learned in two years from decent, hard-working people in Mott Haven about his client, Renny, indicated that Harris was a "gentle," "nonviolent," "nice" young man who was incapable of the brutality and violence presented at trial. If he was at The Quad, he was there only because he was told to be there, not because it was in his nature to commit the barbaric act of killing four people. Harris himself, with voice choked, said: "I would like to say I feel bad for what happened to the people that died, that was murdered, and I would like to let Miz Green and Mr. Green know that I did not kill their son or anyone else."

After his lawyer, Robert Katz, reaffirmed his innocence, Shorty spoke for himself in Spanish, translated by the court interpreter. He said:

> Yes, I am here because I have done something, but here there hasn't been any justice at all. I am a man, yes, I can pay for what I was doing on the street and what I was doing on the street it was selling drugs. I can't hide from that. Yes, I was doing that, but I have never killed anybody and that is the major charge here and if in that day December 16, 1991, I was there killing people as they say here, let God take my life right now because I wasn't there and what they have done here is an injustice.
>
> There are two or three innocent people here about those four killings that we are charged with. We only want justice and we hope in God that he will give justice because waiting for this court, there will never be justice, first, with the Hispanics and [then] with the Blacks. That's it.

Finally, Valerie Van Leer-Greenberg provided fireworks for the occasion in speaking for her client, Pasqualito. After praising Pasqualito's gentlemanly behavior toward her in the course of her representation of him, she excoriated the prosecution for relying on the testimony of Nelson Sepulveda, an out-and-out liar, she argued, who was the principal shooter in both The Double and The Quad and the sole shooter of Anthony Villerbe in which Nelson had implicated Stanley Tukes. She cited large portions of Nelson's testimony on cross examination by Robert Soloway in which Nelson forthrightly argued the necessity in the drug trade of murder, intimidation, and mayhem in order to gain and maintain respect on the streets. Lenny, the heartless slayer of David Cargill, and Nelson were, she said, "animals, lying animals." She denied that Pasqualito had ever killed anyone; he had only dealt Orange Top crack at 600 East 141st Street. Van Leer-Greenberg raised the jurisdictional issue, implicitly suggesting the unfairness of trying Pasqualito in Manhattan for The Double, a Bronx crime. Justice Snyder promptly responded: "Just to make something clear. Some of these defendants have been arrested in some of these charges in the Bronx and Brooklyn. They were let out and proceeded to commit further crimes before they were brought to justice in this courtroom in which they have always been remanded."

Then, the courtroom became electric when Van Leer-Greenberg accused Justice Snyder of a conflict of interest.

Van Leer-Greenberg: My client is not the animal that has been painted by the People. When I opened, I said that he is boisterous. He is just pleasant, easy-going. Your Honor feels that he is a murderer. Your Honor had gotten on television and said my client has plotted with others to put her life in jeopardy. I say this, Judge.

The Court: Do not misspeak. I never said that.

The Defendant Llaca: Yes, you did.

The Court: You will speak when you are spoken to or you will be removed from the courtroom. Proceed.

Van Leer-Greenberg: Judge, it concerns me because you were the person who feels you were in danger from my client and you're sentencing my client.

The Court: No, I never felt I was in danger from any indi-

vidual defendant. Yes, threats have been made. They
will not affect me in the slightest.

Justice Snyder went on to say that threats were part and
parcel of the defendants' whole mode of operation. Yet, she said
the system will work in spite of threats to witnesses, district
attorneys, police, and judges. Van Leer-Greenberg rejoined, her
voice rising to a shriek: "Our constitution of the United States
of America is based on neutral magistrates, people that are free
and have untrammeled thoughts and that is my concern for
my client, that he be treated fairly, that his rights be protected." Van Leer-Greenberg's argument stirred looks of righteous indignation from the defendants and guffaws from the
police and investigators in the jury box.

Finally, after all the arraignments and responses were concluded, Justice Snyder addressed her courtroom. She said:

> This gang represents the worst fear and dread to society to-
> day. Guns, drugs, incredible violence. I don't intend to de-
> tail the brutality and the viciousness of the violence that
> came out during this trial. I will rest on the record as to
> the overwhelming evidence presented in this case.
>
> But the extent of the violence, the tragedy of the vio-
> lence . . . I have never presided over a trial or been in-
> volved in a case where I saw whole families destroyed in
> the way we all saw here. When the Morales-Cruz children
> took the witness stand, I really almost wanted to cry to
> see their lives virtually destroyed, destroyed by this gang
> and their drugs and their seduction of many people in a
> community where it is difficult for any fine citizen to sur-
> vive when they are brutalized and virtually raped by a
> gang such as this.

At this point in Justice Snyder's remarks, there were horse-
laughs from the defendants' table. Justice Snyder continued:

> These children have a chance at a second life because
> they have been relocated thanks to the threats made to
> them and their entire family. But as to many other fami-

lies about whom we heard throughout this case who were
sucked into this gang's drug operation in every capacity,
children eight years old and younger, they have had no
chance. It is one of the most tragic things I have seen in
any case: an entire neighborhood almost destroyed by this
group.

Typically, during any sentence, most defendants accept
no responsibility for their actions. Some of these defendants sit here smirking and laughing. It's a joke. Nothing
affects them. They accept no responsibility. Let's examine
whom they blame. They blame the police. They were totally unfair. Prejudice. They blame the prosecutors. They
were totally unfair and prejudiced. They blame the witnesses because after they tried to shoot and kill them they
still came forward. So they blame the witnesses. They
blame the judge. Yes, general threats were made to me. I
was never allowed to know about them, thanks to the
New York City Police Department and the District Attorney's office. But let's get all these people off the case. Let's
threaten them. Let's make sure there is no case. No witnesses. No prosecutors. No judge. What these defendants
cannot accept is that the criminal justice system applies
to them and it will work in spite of their best efforts to
threaten everybody in it.

I have some general remarks to say to all of these defendants. You have no values. You have no morality. You
have no respect for the law. Your lives were simple. You
had only one law. If someone got in your way, kill them.
Well, I intend to make the rest of your lives very simple.
A tired neighborhood almost brought to its knees in fear
and hopelessness thanks to your reign of terror and we
can only count the visible victims. Who knows how many
others exist? You thought you were above the law. You
think you're above the law. No wonder. You were let out
on bail all the time in the past and you committed more
crimes and you were still let out on bail. You scared the
witnesses off. You laughed in the faces of the police and
the criminal justice system. No one could touch you. You
could get away with virtually everything.

But now, we know this: you are not above the law. Because the witnesses in this case did their job. They came forward and spoke truthfully despite threats, intimidation, and shootings. The police did their job, especially Detective Mark Tebbens, bravely and courageously and with absolute perseverance because it took years. The District Attorney's offices of New York County, the Bronx, and Brooklyn came together to their job. And the men and women on the jury did their job.

Now I have to do my job. Let this sentence be a message to every other vicious and violent drug gang terrorizing our streets. You will be brought to justice and you will be removed from society forever. That is my job and that is what I am going to do here.

That very afternoon, a sign on the blackboard of HIU's fifteenth-story offices at 100 Centre Street noted the sentences of each trial defendant: Fat Danny, 158 1/3 years; Shorty, 141 2/3 years; Stanley Tukes, 133 1/3 years; Platano, 133 1/3 years; Pasqualito, 116 2/3 years; Victor Mercedes, 66 2/3 years; Tezo, 50 years; Renny Harris, 48 1/3 years; Linwood Collins, 20 years—for a total of 868 1/3 years. But the postscript told the whole story. It read simply: "Adios Vaqueros!"

urban
badlands

Downtown justice had triumphed. But everyo perhaps especially the Wild Cowboys, understood that only the nearly herculean efforts of relentlessly persistent investigators, determined and articulate prosecutors, and a clear-minded, fearless judge made the system work at all. In public, of course, all the forces of order echoed the claims made by Justice Snyder in her sentencing statement. Taking the Wild Cowboys off the streets had indeed given Mott Haven a respite in the urban wars and a chance, if seized, for city-wide and local community groups to reconstruct some kind of viable commercial and social structures there. Moreover, the children of the Morales-Cruz family had been given a rare second chance to make something of their lives.

But even in the midst of the raucous post-trial celebrations at Forlini's Restaurant, the downtown watering hole for the whole criminal justice community, no one among the forces of order had any illusions about the larger significance of the victory. Everyone knew that right around the corner was another group of wild cowboys, masked in multiple identities, from other urban badlands. In fact, preliminary hearings on the 48-member Young Talented Children crack crew from 107th Street between Amsterdam and Central Park West in Manhattan's Two-Four precinct had begun in Justice Snyder's courtroom even before the Cowboys' trial was completely finished. Then, on October 27, 1995, less than six months after the jury verdict in the Cowboys' trial, the Bronx District Attorney announced the arrest and indictment of seven major crack and heroin dealers who had begun to operate out of 328 Beekman

Avenue, trying to seize the market vacated by the Wild Cowboys. Those arrested included Eladio Padilla aka Caco, Chi Chi's brother, who finally got off Rikers Island and was trying to keep his vow to take Beekman Avenue back from the Dominicans. Then, some fourteen months after those arrests, on December 17, 1996, federal, state, and city authorities arrested 61 more drug dealers and dismantled twelve gangs that had established lucrative crack and heroin operations in the Diego-Beekman Houses in Mott Haven. The federal Department of Housing and Urban Development financed the raids to the tune of $107,000 to protect the government's huge subsidy of the housing project.

Prosecutors' optimism about the futures of Morales-Cruz family members was dampened when the family took with them $10,000 worth of furniture belonging to the DANY safehouse in Middletown when they moved to the distant state where Mark Tebbens relocated them. And then in the no-good-deed-goes-unpunished wisdom of the police department's bureaucracy, Tebbens himself was suddenly transferred out of HIU because, he was told, he had spent enough time working for the District Attorney. Although he was expected to be a desk jockey at One Police Plaza, he promptly went back to the Bronx to clear some old homicides connected to the Cowboys case.

Tebbens discovered that Chris Collins, Linwood's brother, had eyewitnessed the murder of Kennedy Earl Thomas by Boogie Frazier on March 16, 1992. Collins was in federal prison for robbing a bank. When Tebbens went to see him in prison, Collins greeted him by saying: "Yo, Tebbens. What you doin' here? You homicide. I'm a bank robber." But Collins refused to testify, and Boogie's trial ended in a hung jury. Tebbens also learned that Collins's sister, Iwana, had teamed up with Zia, the girl whose information had led to Pasqualito's apprehension, to deal heroin at Manor and Watson Avenues. But in December 1996 two young men from Atlantic City, who had been dating Iwana and Zia, robbed them of $7,000 and heroin. The robbers shot both girls square in the chest at point-blank range, leaving Zia a quadriplegic. Iwana, however, got out of bed the very next day to show detectives autographed photographs that the robbers had presented the girls in a more romantic moment.

Finally, prosecutors and detectives alike continue to face the problem of witness intimidation in other cases because judges, refusing to use their judicial discretion, still give bail to dangerous men so that they can "assist their lawyers in preparing their defenses."

Everyone who pursues downtown justice knows that the criminal justice system is simply our society's end-of-the-line bureaucracy to address the consequences of the collapse of social authority, self-discipline, and self-control, particularly but by no means solely in the underclass. The process is marked by the coincidence of several main trends: the catastrophic failures of families; the decline of standards in the public educational system that demands little and offers little; the disappearance of well-paid, physically risky, nonfeminized industrial work that aggressive young men consider worthy employment; and the institutionalization of occupations that reward and celebrate the pursuit of avarice, lust, pride, envy, and wrath for their own sakes.

The trial victory coincided with the widely publicized sharp decline in New York City's violent crime from the highs of 1990, 1991, and 1992 if one uses murder as the yardstick. In each of these years there were over 2,000 murders in the city; in 1996 there were 984—the first time since 1968 that the number had dropped below 1,000. That drop stirred considerable credit-claiming debate, although one must attribute it to a combination of factors: aggressive policing instituted by Police Commissioner William Bratton with the backing of Mayor Rudolph Giuliani, a former federal prosecutor, that has made New York City inhospitable to crime for the time being; lock-

ing up gangs like the Wild Cowboys who commit a disproportionate amount of violence; hitting a demographic trough in
the supply of young men, always the heavy infantry of street
wars; and the death or disablement of many of the most violent
street warriors. One must also allow for the hidden, as yet
undocumented, ravages of the AIDS epidemic in debilitating
criminals and reducing violence.

Yet, despite the current quiet on the streets, police and
prosecutors know that eventually the drug trade will enter a
new cycle, bringing, in all likelihood, a re-escalation of its
associated violence. The drug trade continues to flourish because of the seemingly insatiable demand in our society for
Lotus-Land-like oblivion. Drug dealers enter the occupation
fully prepared to do whatever violence is required. They know
that uptown killings are difficult to solve. And, if they are
Dominican nationals, they know they can commit violence
and then flee to the Caribbean with impunity.

When Leonel Fernández Reyna was elected president of the
Dominican Republic in 1996, Police Commissioner Howard
Safir had great hopes that Fernández would reform the DR's
extradition policy because Fernández had grown up in Washington Heights and had, it was said, a real understanding of
how drug-related violence had ravaged the Heights' streets.
But after a Dominican say-yes, act-no dance, complete with
extensive media coverage, Safir was left dancing alone. And
Fernández's Dominican Republic, like Balaguer's before him,
whose economy benefits greatly from narcotics trafficking,
still provides safe refuge to over two hundred of its nationals
who, according to the NYPD, have committed murder in New
York City and who now live in comfortable freedom on the
island. When murder regularly goes unpunished, not only does
law seem arbitrary and capricious to the general public but,
sooner or later, some decide that crime pays.

The Cowboys' cocaine supplier, Jose Reyes aka El Feo, was
prosecuted in spring and summer 1996 by AUSAs Bruce Ohr

and Thomas Arena. The result was Reyes's conviction for racketeering under federal RICO laws and conspiring to kill seven people in furtherance of his drug-trafficking enterprise. On January 30, 1997, he was sentenced to life with no possibility of parole. The 1997 federal trial and conviction of Raymond Polanco (prosecuted by AUSAs Paul Weinstein and Kelly Moore) for narcotics and firearms trafficking, for two murders furthering the enterprise, and for the murder of David Cargill, along with the retrial conviction of Linwood Collins for The Rooftop Murder (prosecuted by ADA Greg Carro), pretty much closed the circle eleven years after Nelson Sepulveda opened 1H on Beech Terrace.

Of the major players in the whole case, only Freddy Krueger remained at large. Based on a variety of sources, including testimony at El Feo's trial that answered some of the remaining riddles in the Wild Cowboys case, investigators sketched a bold-relief image of Freddy Krueger. Francisco Medina aka Freddy stowed away on an American-bound freighter from the Dominican Republic in 1988, jumped into the sea before the ship reached Miami, and swam ashore. He made his way to New York, where he sought out El Feo. In late 1986 or early 1987, El Feo had taken over the heroin spot of his much older friend and father figure, Rogelio Emilio Pérez Almodovar aka Chocolate, at 167th Street and Amsterdam, when Chocolate went to prison. Sometime in 1987, Manuel de la Rosa aka Vive Bien, Chocolate's first cousin, came to New York and began working for El Feo, first as a lookout and then as a manager. Freddy Medina hailed from the same island village as Vive Bien, and Freddy's half brother, Henry Dia Guzman, was already working for El Feo. These connections helped Freddy get a job with El Feo, and he began selling heroin at 167th and Amsterdam. When El Feo expanded his operations, he asked Freddy to manage the new spot at 183rd and Audubon. But Freddy was still very much an outsider; he was seen as a bumpkin, a hick from the sticks, slow company for guys in the fast lane. At least one of El Feo's trusted "table crew," namely Hippolito Polanco, made no bones about his antipathy toward Freddy.

One of El Feo's main men in the Bronx was Miguelito Castillo, who supplied Chico and Tito at Marcy Place. Chico then resold El Feo's heroin to Edwin Ortiz, who had a spot at East 141st and St. Ann's. This arrangement worked well enough until Ortiz tried to bypass Chico and deal directly with Miguelito. When Miguelito indicated his receptivity to the idea, Chico killed him. Ortiz told Lenny and Nelson Sepulveda what happened; the result was The Double. El Feo was deeply saddened by Miguelito's death and seemed to go through a fitful conversion. He encouraged people in his Manhattan neighborhood to seek drug counseling, and he took his own brother and sister, both addicts, into a clinic. But there was simply too much money to be made, especially in the Bronx. So, when Chocolate got out of jail in 1990, El Feo set him and Freddy Medina up at 1770 Andrews Avenue, Daniel Mirambeaux's old haunt, a long-time drug building where the pair were bosses over a large crew that sold crack, coke, and heroin. They took in money hand over fist from the multidrug operation; even after El Feo got his own cut, Chocolate took home $15,000 a week, and Freddy took $10,000.

Despite his great success as a manager, however, Freddy Medina longed to be an insider, and he repeatedly expressed his willingness to do anything El Feo needed done. His first opportunity came in late October 1990. James Tolson, a pitcher for El Feo's crew, got arrested for holding drugs but was quickly released on bail. The very next day, the cops raided Vive Bien's spot and found drugs, guns, and money. Vive Bien complained to El Feo that Tolson must have snitched. So El Feo offered $3,000 to anyone in his crew willing to dispatch Tolson. Freddy jumped at the chance, found Tolson in his apartment, and shot him several times. Tolson's body remained undiscovered for several days, and the resulting unpleasantness for the cops and medical examiner was cause for great merriment among the crew, as was Freddy's new self-assertion: "I'm a smoker; I ain't no joke."

Freddy got a chance to prove himself again a few months later. Beginning in late 1990, El Feo tried to expand to 166th Street near Amsterdam, only a block from his main headquarters. Victor Battista aka Paelo and his brother Angel Santana aka Morenito controlled the heroin trade on 166th Street. Paelo and Morenito had never liked Chocolate, even though they had coexisted peacefully with him before he went to prison. They resented the attempt of his protégé, El Feo, to intrude on their territory; they saw Chocolate's hand at work. On March 10, 1991, Johnny Richards, a local heroin addict, ran into El Feo and Freddy on Amsterdam near 167th Street. Richards told El Feo that Paelo and Morenito had given him a $25,000 contract to kill El Feo. Richards told El Feo that he would reverse the contract if El Feo doubled the fee. When El Feo told Richards to get lost, he pulled a gun and shot El Feo in the leg. Freddy intervened in the struggle, getting shot in the arm, a bullet that he later gouged out with a knife. Freddy grabbed El Feo's gun and shot Johnny Richards three times, following him as he staggered into the middle of Amsterdam Avenue and finishing the job there. Freddy had saved El Feo's life and shown himself to be fearless under fire.

El Feo knew a great resource when he saw it. Every man of authority needs a hammer, and El Feo began taking Freddy with him on his rounds. Together, on April 10, 1991, they schooled the crew's young Raul Vargas in how to kill, demonstrating with Ronnie Gedders, a hapless interloper into the business of one of El Feo's bulk customers. A short time later, on June 2, 1991, El Feo heard that Alberto Ortiz aka Pescao or Encarnacion Arismendi was hanging around 174th Street and Audubon, the Sepulvedas' stomping ground. El Feo had a score to settle with Pescao. He had paid Pescao and Pescao's colleague, Leonardo Carpio Rosario aka Mingolo, good money to vacate yet another Bronx spot that El Feo had opened, near East 167th Street. Pescao and Mingolo took El Feo's money but then went down the block and took their customers with them, not only a serious breach of business ethics but a nose thumbing that could have incalculable consequences if left unrequited.

El Feo took a ride with Freddy and Raul Vargas over to West 174th Street, where he spotted Lenny and Nelson on the street. The Sepulveda brothers asked El Feo not to bring heat to their street, so El Feo and his crew waited until Pescao wandered over to 175th Street between Audubon and St. Nicholas Avenue, following him in their car. From the rear window, Freddy shot Pescao with a 9-millimeter pistol, dropping him in the middle of the street. Freddy then got out of the car and made his way to Pescao, who was trying to crawl to cover, and shot him several more times at close range, paralyzing him from head to toe. Pescao died in Columbia Presbyterian Hospital on September 7th.

The country bumpkin was becoming an urban hit man. Only two days after shooting Pescao, Freddy teamed up with Platano to blow away Smiley at Manor and Watson. Freddy and Platano liked each other and enjoyed working together; each admired the other's nerve. When he went out on a job, Freddy often disguised himself as a Jamaican, complete with a hat and a shirt in Jamaica's flag colors of red, gold, and green; Platano sometimes dressed similarly. On July 20, 1991, Platano asked Freddy to shoot someone for him, Ivan Lugo, by any measure small fry on East 141st Street, who was nonetheless disrupting local market equilibrium. With Meow Meow driving, and Platano pointing out the victim, Freddy cut Lugo down in a drive-by. Freddy Medina's reputation was growing quickly. He became known as Freddy Krueger after the psychotic killer of cinematic fame.

On September 23, 1991, El Feo went to prison for a shooting incident involving his whole table crew at the Marisco del

Caribe Restaurant on February 5, 1990. He had pleaded guilty to criminal possession of a weapon. But with good lieutenants, prison is just an office at some remove from daily operations. Freddy Krueger and Chocolate held down the fort at 1770 Andrews Avenue; Alexis Garcia aka Mono ran the show at 167th Street. Freddy had some brushes with the law, but nothing serious enough to keep him in jail.

For example, on October 3, 1991, police collared one Miguel Perez in the Five-Two precinct for pointing a .357 Magnum, with serial number defaced, at another man. Police charged Miguel Perez not only with weapons possession and menacing but also with an attempt to bribe the arresting officer. Since it was Miguel Perez's first arrest, and since he pleaded not guilty, he was released on his own recognizance. He made required court appearances on both November 6th and December 3rd, 1991. Only after another gun collar in spring 1992 under his actual name, and his subsequent avoidance of court, did the system finally "drop a warrant" on Francisco Medina on June 11, 1992.

On December 16, 1991, according to Nelson Sepulveda, Freddy Krueger participated in The Quad. Then four days later, accompanied by Chocolate, Freddy tracked down Walter Ortiz near 1705 Andrews Avenue and shot him to death. Ortiz had accused the two of stealing customers, and, it was thought, had put out a contract on Chocolate. A month later, on January 20, 1992, Freddy and Maximo Almodovar, Chocolate's cousin, fatally shot Nelson Garcia aka Collita in the Bronx, and on February 24th Freddy participated in the murder of Porfirio Reyes in Manhattan for underselling El Feo's brand of heroin.

El Feo and Vive Bien had a falling out just before El Feo went to do his eight-months' time. El Feo told Vive Bien that his services were no longer needed. After a while Vive Bien got restless. He went down the block and began selling for Paelo, who saw a way of exploiting Vive Bien's first-cousin-kinship with Chocolate to enrage El Feo. And enrage him it did. How dare Vive Bien work for and consort with Paelo, who had hired Johnny Richards to kill him? Vive Bien had to go, and Paelo with him. But nobody wanted the job; Vive Bien had been part of the gang all the way back to the island. Even Freddy, the hit man on the make, balked at killing a fellow homeboy from the Dominican sticks. So El Feo asked Lenny and Nelson to loan him Platano to hit Vive Bien. Platano accepted the contract, but then passed it along to a man called Elia.

On March 12, 1992, Elia burst into the auto parts store at 166th Street and Amsterdam where Vive Bien hung out and blasted him five times. Late that same night Freddy and Platano found Paelo on the northeast corner of 166th Street and Amsterdam and shredded him with eleven bullets from an AK-47 assault rifle and a 9-millimeter Glock. By the time Detective Angel Morales of the Three-Four squad reached the scene at 0000 hours, the official story on the street was that Paelo had shot Vive Bien and had been killed in retaliation. But there were two loose ends. Miraculously, Vive Bien wasn't dead, confirming once again detectives' view of the inverse relationship between social worth and invulnerability. And Elia was bragging all over town about how he had shot up the famous Vive Bien. According to street legend, Freddy Krueger, Platano, and Tezo took Elia for a ride over to Hunts Point. No one has ever heard of Elia again.

Only a few days later, on March 16th, as a favor to Platano, Freddy went with Pasqualito to ambush Frankie Cuevas and Manny Garcia at 185th Street and Audubon, wounding Cuevas in the arm and leaving Garcia a paraplegic for life.

Then Freddy, working again with Platano, finally caught up with Mingolo. Mingolo had been laying low after a little trouble in Manhattan. On May 25, 1991, at 2330 hours, just a few days before Pescao got gunned down, Mingolo was driving up Amsterdam Avenue and got into an accident at 172nd Street. A crowd gathered on the street and began chastising Mingolo for his recklessness. He left the scene, saying that he would return immediately; after running uptown to 174th Street, he did indeed come back, with gun in hand, blazing wildly at the crowd. He killed two civilians and seriously wounded three others. He then fled on foot. Detective Pete Moro of the Three-Four squad, a man who went straight from the jungles of Vietnam to those of the South Bronx and later the Three-Four with never a trace of self-dramatization, identified Mingolo as the shooter only three days later, tracked him to Washington, D.C., but couldn't nab him.

Three-Four detectives knew that Mingolo had a wild streak. Detective Austin Francis "Tim" Muldoon III, lover of books, poetry, and, to his colleagues' dismay, John Cage's music, had had a previous case with Mingolo. While in a titty bar, Mingolo started arguing with another patron about the relative charms of one of the dancers. To settle the dispute, he pulled out his gun and began shooting at the other patron, who escaped unharmed. Nobody talked to the police on this case. Detective Muldoon tried to interview one of the barmaids, and word of his attempt got back to Mingolo. So Mingolo went to the home of the barmaid's sister and broke both of her arms with a baseball bat as a warning to the barmaid.

No one dared give Mingolo up, and the police were never able to catch up with him until, finally, Lenny Sepulveda, while he was still incarcerated at Ogdensburg, heard that Mingolo was back in town, staying at 159th Street and Riverside Drive. Lenny tipped El Feo, who was at the neighboring Cape Vincent state facility. So on April 4, 1992, Freddy Krueger and Platano in a gray Celebrity, and Raul Vargas and Maximo in another car, waited outside Mingolo's hideout. They watched as he came downstairs to a waiting gypsy cab, and followed closely as the cab went down to 155th Street and started heading over to the Bronx across the Macombs Dam Bridge. Just as Mingolo's cab reached the usual pile-up at the traffic light on the Manhattan side of the bridge, Raul and Maximo swung their car out into the westbound lane, completely blocking the line of traffic coming from the Bronx into Manhattan. Freddy Krueger jumped out of the gray Celebrity and raced up behind Mingolo's cab, his AK-47 blazing in one hand and his 9-millimeter pistol in the other, strewing Mingolo's brains all over the cab and pumping twenty-one bullets into his body. Freddy then ran back and dove into the Celebrity, just as Platano made a sharp U-turn and fled in the cleared westbound lane.

Freddy had a busy spring. Less than a week later, on April 10, 1992, he participated in the shooting of Carlos Rodriguez Santana in the Bronx. On May 11th he took $15,000 from a good customer of El Feo named Cholene to bump off Angel Suarez at West 141st Street and Hamilton Place. Suarez had robbed Cholene. When El Feo got out of prison on May 22nd, he sharply chided Freddy for taking money for this particular job: "Cholene is good people." One gives services freely to good customers and friends. Then, late on June 21st, detectives think that Pasqualito and Freddy shot up Manor and Watson, killing Kevin Nazario and wounding five other people as one of the skirmishes in the war with Frankie Cuevas.

All the while, 1770 Andrews was booming, drawing droves of customers from the entire Tremont area of the Bronx, as well as predators always looking to scoop the honey of others' hard work. Christopher Livingston aka Dred led the Macombs crew, Jamaican drug dealers who hung out on Macombs Road near Andrews and Tremont. Dred had watched the fantastic growth of business at 1770 Andrews Avenue and wanted part of that action. So he had his boys begin selling in the vicinity. On June 23, 1992, Dred went to 1770 Andrews, ostensibly to make a buy but actually to test his opposition's mettle. He pulled a gun on the crew working that day and then left, laughing. The workers phoned Freddy Krueger and told him about the encounter.

With Maximo and Gilberto Rivera aka Puto, one of El Feo's best friends, Freddy immediately headed over to the Bronx. Freddy had his AK-47; Maximo had a street sweeper; and Puto carried a 9-millimeter pistol. They found the Macombs crew around 1751 University Avenue, just around the corner from their Andrews Avenue spot. A pitched battle ensued, with each side firing hundreds of rounds. Finally, the Macombs crew fled to safety down Macombs Road, leaving a fallen comrade, 15-year-old Craig Prentice, behind them on the battlefield.

Maximo was seriously wounded. Freddy helped him to the car. But Puto was lying dead, his body riddled with bullets. Freddy said: "We can't leave Puto here." He went out into the middle of the battlefield, picked up Puto's body, and carried it back to his car. On the way, Freddy spotted Craig Prentice moving, badly wounded but still alive. Freddy put Puto's body in the rear seat of his car. Then he walked back across the battlefield and stood over Prentice, watching as the boy feebly tried to inch away on his back. With wailing police sirens drawing near, Freddy shot Craig Prentice right between the eyes. Then Freddy dumped Puto's body in the Four-Three precinct and burned the blood-soaked car. On July 10th, with Pasqualito driving his motorcycle and Freddy riding behind him, the pair shot Dred on Tremont Avenue, ending the Jamaicans' bid for Andrews Avenue once and for all.

Back in Manhattan, El Feo was worried about Morenito coming after him to avenge Paelo's death. Street rumor had Morenito putting out big contracts on both El Feo and Chocolate. El Feo was constantly vigilant, always cautious. But right after midnight on July 12, 1992, an assailant slipped past his defenses. El Feo and Raul Vargas had gone to a party for the baptism of El Feo's nephew. Afterwards, they picked up the daily receipts from the Bronx at the bodega at 2172 Amsterdam, where Maximo regularly dropped them off. Vargas stood guard outside; El Feo was on the phone inside the bodega. A man with his head down walked by the bodega. Suddenly he pulled a gun and pointed it at Vargas, who froze on the spot. Then the gunman burst just inside the bodega, shot El Feo three times, and fled, leaving El Feo paralyzed for life.

Vargas found himself out of a job, unsure of his future and growing more nervous by the day. No one knew who shot El Feo, although the word on the street was that Morenito had hired a hit man. But everybody blamed Vargas for losing his nerve when his boss's life depended on it, something that never happened to Freddy Krueger. Krueger began keeping El Feo steady company when he went out in his dark van, which had been specially equipped for his wheelchair. The precaution was warranted. On August 25, 1992, Chocolate's cousin Maximo was found lying naked in his own bed, his penis stuffed in his mouth, five bullets in his body. Chocolate had been deported to the Dominican Republic in early summer 1992; on February 4, 1994, in Santo Domingo he was assassinated by five Dominican military and police officers said to be in Morenito's pay. When Special Agent Laurie Horne of Alcohol, Tobacco, and Firearms, accompanied by Terry Quinn and Jose Flores, finally arrested El Feo on December 2, 1994, in Miami's Hilton Hotel, she also seized a copy of a book on how to hone oneself into a hit man, said to belong to Freddy Krueger. But the book contained little that Freddy hadn't already perfected on the streets. He no longer had to announce his ferocity to the world. Now everybody paid him the accolade reserved for those street warriors whose very name provokes dread: "Nobody fucks with Freddy Krueger."

After Reyes's arrest, Freddy sold heroin in Charleston, South Carolina, for Reyes's organization, which flourished even though its boss was in prison. Horne nearly nabbed Freddy there. But he escaped to the Dominican Republic in mid-1995 and, with bodyguards funded by Reyes, supported himself by robbing banks. Freddy also devoted himself to the magic known as *brujería*. Indeed, it is said that he was a *brujo*, a witch of great powers, within *santería*, the Afro-Caribbean religion that mingles West African gods and Roman Catholic saints. Horne—working with DEA Agents Efrain de Jesus and Kevin O'Brien in Santo Domingo and U.S. Marshal Joseph

LoBue in New York—learned that Freddy frequented a house in the Santiago barrio of La Joya for ritual baths to ward off evil spirits and to guard against apprehension.

Meanwhile, U.S. government officials pressed President Leonel Fernández to alter the DR's stance on extraditing its nationals, making a formal request on February 26th for Medina's provisional arrest. His egregious crimes, they argued, presented a who-could-possibly-oppose-it opportunity to change the policy and allow killers to be brought to justice. The U.S. Information Service gave an exclusive story on Medina to *La Nación*, a new daily, for its February 27th inaugural issue. *Listín Diario*, the Dominican newspaper of record, picked up the story and ran articles on extradition through the prism of Medina's case. *Sucesos*, a blood-and-guts island tabloid, then published three front-page profiles of Medina as Freddy Krueger, complete with vivid crime-scene photos of his alleged New York handiwork. All the papers suggested that Freddy was a menace on the island, prompting a firestorm of public debate.

At that point, de Jesus and O'Brien provided the Dirección Nacional de Control de Drogas with the location of Freddy's religious hideaway, and the spot was put under round-the-clock surveillance. At 0200 hours on April 3, 1997, more than fifteen DNCD officers stormed the site and took Freddy into custody. Now ballooned to well over 300 pounds, exhausted, and tearful, he acknowledged to de Jesus and O'Brien that he was at the end of the road. But he strongly protested the media's portrayal of him as a monster, arguing that he had never killed an innocent person. In the end Freddy refused to return voluntarily to the United States to face trial, leaving President Fernández between the Scylla of caving in to Yankee imperialism and the Charybdis of confirming the Dominican Republic's reputation as a haven for murderers.

There are, of course, tried-and-true passages through such straits. On April 23rd Santiago prosecutors notified the U.S. Embassy that they were indicting Medina for two island homicides, charges that will obviate extradition proceedings for a few years, perhaps for good. Meanwhile, Freddy Krueger was handed over to the custody of the Dominican National Police in Santo Domingo, the same agency that, on June 29, 1989, was escorting Daniel Mirambeaux to U.S. Marshals for extradition for the murder of PO Michael Buczek, when the securely cuffed and chained prisoner, regrettably, "leapt to his death."

The 1996 federal trial of El Feo, like the Cowboys' trial earlier, prompted the New York mass media to feature titillating stories of brutality and violence, coupled with ain't-it-awful handwringing written or broadcast for middle-class audiences. *The New York Times*, which, despite tributes to Tebbens and Brownell, had made the Morales-Cruz family the real heroes of the Cowboys' tale, romanticized El Feo as a sensitive, intellectual lad seduced by the lure of the streets. The media's fascination with crime and criminals, coupled with marked ambivalence toward the work of police and prosecutors, reflects a central paradox in our society. Key elites, who are the principal beneficiaries of whatever domestic tranquillity the forces of order achieve and who are typically insulated from the ugly consequences of the ethos of the streets, regularly sympathize and side with forces of disorder whose actions threaten the very groundwork of the elites' prosperity. These elites include some members of the forces of order. Such profound social, cultural, and moral confusion, highly irrational on its face, gets played out against the backdrop of—and sometimes through the peculiar, and often perverse, institutional logics of—law and bureaucracy, the rational foundations of modern social order.

Police and prosecutors, themselves sometimes united, often at odds, end up fighting battles on several fronts: against criminals; against intellectuals who champion those criminals by romanticizing them, or by providing them with excuses and justifications for their depredations, or by disbelieving, almost instinctively, the forces of order; against the media, which circulate whatever stories present themselves, the more dramatic and compelling the better, regardless of the sources and with little concern for veracity, since lies and false allegations make stories just as good as, sometimes much better than, truth; and against bureaucratic and legal exigencies as interpreted by their bosses and the courts.

In addition, our society's extraordinarily developed apparatus of advocacy stands at the ready for any group strong and wily enough to commandeer it. With the help of technicians in moral outrage, specialists in transforming particular incidents into symbols of larger social conditions, always with rhetorics of accusation and blame, one can quickly whip up maelstroms of fervor to serve a cause.

July 3, 1992, was sultry, stifling, and rainy in upper Manhattan. The Democratic National Convention, a lucrative bonanza for the economically depressed New York region, was due to hit town in ten days, so the police had already begun dispersing the working girls from midtown to the outer precincts. As a result, many of the prostitutes from Washington Heights were plying their trade where they lived that night. The Dinkins administration had also scooped up from the midtown area most of the growing army of relatively able-bodied, drifting young men who, as the "homeless," exemplify our society's current penchant for manufactured social identities. They had been temporarily relocated in hostels and low-rent hotels in the lower end of the Three-Four precinct in order to spare delegates from Idaho the endless parade of derelicts, down-and-outers, and con-men that most New Yorkers take for granted.

The Three-Four precinct was in its usual 1992 Friday night turmoil, presaged by the wild violence of the previous spring. In the late afternoon, a gunman on the lam from the police for a double homicide in the Bronx had managed to get inside an apartment in the Inwood section, where he held an entire family hostage, threatening to kill everybody unless the cops outside the apartment door went away and let bygones be bygones. But the gunman eventually seemed to weary of the soothing sweet talk from the police hostage negotiation team and "did the right thing," that is, blew his own head off.

On that same Friday night, Local Motion, the anticrime cops from the Three-Four precinct, tooled southbound on St. Nicholas Avenue in their unmarked blue Chevrolet. PO Tommy McPartland drove the car with PO Michael O'Keefe sitting next to him and PO Matteo Brattesani in the rear. When the car stopped for a red light at the corner of 162nd Street, one of the most notorious drug blocks in Washington Heights, O'Keefe spotted a young man in his mid-twenties standing on the sidewalk. Despite the extremely muggy weather, he was wearing a black sports jacket that he constantly tugged across the center of his waistband. The man showed all the street signs of having a gun, and the officers decided to approach him.

O'Keefe's two partners made a U-turn and dropped him off at 163rd Street and St. Nicholas and then circled the block. The plan was for the car to drive east on 162nd Street, from Broadway toward St. Nicholas. If the man was in fact armed, he would almost certainly identify the unmarked police car and bolt toward St. Nicholas, where O'Keefe was waiting. O'Keefe's partners radioed him that they were just entering 162nd Street, driving east; O'Keefe walked down St. Nicholas to 162nd and headed toward the young man. Just then cries of "Bajando! Bajando!" (Coming down! Coming down!) were heard from the other young Dominican men who worked the block. The young man darted toward 505 West 162nd, where O'Keefe caught up with him just as he tried to enter the building.

In the meantime, O'Keefe's partners had given chase to another man carrying a weapon in full view and had disarmed him of a .357 Magnum when they heard O'Keefe calling out a 10–13 code (police officer in distress) on his radio. But they were unable to locate him, since he had not broadcast his exact location. A few minutes later, two other police officers arrived at 505 West 162nd Street to find the young man, later revealed to be Jose Garcia aka Kiko, shot twice by O'Keefe. When the officers arrived, they found O'Keefe, covered with blood, holding his own police revolver in one hand and another fully loaded .38-caliber Smith and Wesson in the other, standing over Garcia in the vestibule of 505 West 162nd Street.

The following day, July 4th, Washington Heights exploded into a full-scale riot. At the southern end of the precinct, roving bands of young men smashed store windows, focusing particularly on banks, and barricaded streets with overturned cars and garbage dumpsters, setting the vehicles and debris on fire, thereby blocking police and ambulance vehicles from responding to scenes of destruction. When firemen, guarded by police officers, found their way through the obstacles to put out the hundreds of fires on the streets, mobs hurled bottles, rocks, bricks, metal fragments, and trash from rooftops at both firemen and police, and fired weapons randomly at the police.

The news media went berserk. Juana Madera, an occupant of Apartment 110 of the building at 505 West 162nd Street, gave several interviews to the print and broadcast media saying that she knew Garcia well. He was the hardworking father of two sons, aged seven and eight, who supported himself by working part-time jobs, in a bodega and in an electronics store. She claimed that she had eyewitnessed the entire encounter between Garcia and O'Keefe from the stairwell of the building and that another eyewitness would come forward later. On July 6th, the *Daily News* ran a banner headline: "He Begged for Life." Madera claimed that O'Keefe had beaten Garcia unconscious with his police radio, then turned him on his stomach and shot him in the back. She said that Garcia had begged her to save him, saying: "Rubia, Rubia. He's killing me. Don't let him kill me." But O'Keefe executed Garcia in cold blood.

The same day, the *Daily News* further reported that friends of the slain man dipped their fingers in his blood and wrote on the wall: "Kiko, We Love You." Other media reported similarly lurid stories as well as pictures of the makeshift shrine erected outside the building where Garcia died, complete with a photograph of the "martyred" young man and loads of flowers accompanied by handscrawled personal sentiments from local residents. On July 14th Ana Rodriguez, Madera's sister, came forward with Madera to DANY with a more elaborate version of this same story. Both sisters claimed that they were returning from a local grocery store when they saw Officer O'Keefe confront Garcia, curse him, and begin to beat him with his police radio. According to the sisters, O'Keefe then dragged Garcia into their building, continuing to beat him savagely. The sisters followed the pair into the building, they said, and went up to the landing between the ground and second floors. Although Garcia was a husky 6'1" and O'Keefe was 5'8", Garcia did not, according to the sisters, resist the beating. When Garcia was unconscious, O'Keefe pulled out his pistol. Madera claims to have fled to her apartment at that point, although she says she heard three shots; Rodriguez said that she witnessed the shooting, peering through the landing's railing, on her hands and knees with her head touching the ground.

Immediately after receiving word of the shooting, Mayor David Dinkins rushed to the Garcia family residence on West 162nd Street, where he was televised comforting the family and pledging an unrelenting search for justice. Dinkins invited the family members to visit him at Gracie Mansion. He then persuaded American Airlines to fly Garcia's body to the Dominican Republic for burial, accompanied by his relatives, all free of charge. New York City paid for the funeral from the Human Resources Administration's burial fund for poor families. A large crowd mourned Garcia in his home town of San Francisco de Macoris, mingling chants for justice with the declaration that "New York cops are a band of assassins" (*New York Newsday*, July 10, 1992). John Beckman, a mayoral spokesman, said: "Irrespective of any individual's background, there are instances where there are questions of whether an appropriate level of force was used by a police officer. That's the case here. Beyond that, the sins of a son should not be visited on a mother or her family. The mayor is in a position to offer comfort and consolation to that family" (*New York Post*, July 10, 1993).

Dinkins's re-election chances in 1993 depended heavily on his capturing the 70 percent of the city's swelling Spanish-speaking vote that he had received in 1989. Guillermo Linares, the first Dominican elected to the City Council and the key to the Dominican vote, was at the Mayor's side at the Garcia residence and later throughout the crisis, as were other key players in the core clique of politicians around Dinkins: City Councilman Stanley Michels, State Senator Franz Leichter, and Assemblyman Herman "Denny" Farrell, who, together, have exerted great influence over Washington Heights. Linares, who made his political career as an advocate for bilingual education for the city's growing Latino population, reportedly had been urging the then-Police Commissioner, Lee Patrick Brown, to pay more attention to community complaints about the police in Washington Heights. Officer O'Keefe himself, it turns out, had previously been the subject of more than one civilian complaint for aggressiveness and roughness in arresting drug suspects. Moreover, a judge had sharply reprimanded O'Keefe for being evasive in his responses about his conduct when on the witness stand in an earlier case.

Echoing a widely voiced clamor in Washington Heights that Garcia's death typified "racist" police harassment of hard-working immigrants that only more police jobs for Dominicans could remedy, Guillermo Linares urged Commissioner Brown to deploy more Latino cops in the area, arguing that a Latino police presence was vital to maintaining the peace. In this view, only Latino cops could be "sensitive" to the needs of the complex Spanish-speaking community. Some residents of Washington Heights saw the matter differently, arguing that Latino cops were needed because they typically have fewer inhibitions about the regrettable exigencies necessary to restore and maintain order. But Linares's main point was crystal clear. Like every other immigrant group, the Dominicans want their own place at the groaning table that the police bureaucracy has been for other groups. In fact, about 15 percent of New York police officers are Latino, but only a handful are Dominican. Most Latino police officers are Puerto Ricans born in the United States. And many Puerto Ricans have a very dim view of the growing and aggressive Dominican presence in the city that signals the eclipse of Puerto Rican dominance over New York Latino political affairs.

On July 7th Linares led a massive and angry march down Broadway toward the Three-Four station house at 183rd Street. Police barricades stopped the march at Broadway and 181st Street, but eventually the police yielded to the most vociferous demonstrators, who streamed down the hill to take up places in front of the ugly, squat precinct building, corralled by more police barricades there. Within minutes, the street in front of the station house was packed with a surging, frenzied mob shouting: "Policia assesino! Policia assesino!" The crowd consisted almost entirely of young Dominican men, with a few young women in their midst. There was a white face here and there, members of vestigial radical groups such as Socialist Workers Party or quickly formed "community organizations" like the International Committee against Racism or the Washington Heights Committee of the Movement for a People's Assembly. In the crowd were also several politicians and, of course, representatives of the media. Some of the demonstrators wore bandannas as masks, perhaps to conceal their faces from police, though most did not.

Speakers mounted the blue police barricades to address the demonstration, with the crowd's chants rhythmically punctuating their harangues. Linares spoke first while the crowd burned an American flag and then raised a Dominican national flag and burst into a rendition of the Dominican national anthem. Ruth "Elbows" Messinger, the elected Manhattan Borough President and a strong supporter of Mayor Dinkins, spoke next, demanding a "full and fair investigation," telling the crowd, as she did later in a written flyer, that "Jose Gonzalez Garcia could have been your son—or even you." Following

Ms. Messinger, the Reverend Al Sharpton, his never-to-be-cut-until-James-Brown-dies coiffure glistening with pomade, was hoisted onto the barricades as the crowd changed its chant to "No Justice, No Peace!"—the slogan, and threat, that the Reverend Sharpton made famous in his advocacy for Tawana Brawley (the upstate girl who, with her mother's connivance, as established later by a gubernatorial commission, falsely accused cops of raping and brutalizing her), for the young men who were convicted of raping and nearly killing the Central Park Jogger, and for many other blacks and Hispanics whom he celebrates as victims and resisters of an oppressive system.

In the meantime, detectives, who were looking out on the scene directly below them from the second-floor window of the squad's lunchroom, began to pick out familiar faces among the demonstrators who did not wear masks: Jose, the main coke dealer on 165th Street and Audubon; Ramon, the kingpin heroin dealer from 159th Street and Broadway; Jorge, one of the leaders of a crack gang from 160th Street, a group that sidelines in robbing other dope dealers; and Flaco, crack dealer from 162nd Street. From the detectives' standpoint, local drug dealers, tired of being continually harassed by Local Motion, were orchestrating the demonstration, as well as much of the ongoing riotous violence on the streets. The politicians and "rabble rousers" were, as usual, pandering to the most vocal, and in this case the very worst, elements of the community.

The detectives had specific evidence for their version of events. Whenever police discharge their weapons in New York, even in open-and-shut cases, a massive inquiry takes place. Since police shootings always draw attacks from some quarter, police, the most beleaguered occupational group in our society, aid one another whenever possible in constructing public defenses. Immediately after the Garcia shooting, the Three-Four squad put out its lines to all the police agencies for any information that might contextualize the shooting. Among the many leads that the squad received, including unusual offers from some police units to allow Three-Four squad detectives to speak to these units' confidential informants, was word from Manhattan North Narcotics that it had something that might interest detectives.

As it happened, on March 25, 1992, Narcotics had done a warranted search of a safe house, Apartment 110, 505 West 162nd Street, the same building where the Garcia shooting took place, indeed the very apartment of Juana Madera and Ana Rodriguez. The search had yielded not only cocaine, marijuana, drug paraphernalia, a loaded .38-caliber revolver, and 42 rounds of ammunition but also photographs and a videotape. Both the photographs and videotape showed a midlevel drug dealer, Jose Rodriguez, with several companions. In the videotape, Rodriguez juggled bags of cocaine in broad daylight on the street, and a man, presumably a drug customer, was led into the building. With Rodriguez in the still pictures and on the videotape were Kiko Garcia and the two women who claim to have eyewitnessed Kiko's death, Juana Madera and Ana Rodriguez—the mother of Jose Rodriguez. The overvoice on the tape referred to narcotics as "food" and said: "It's legal here on these blocks; it's liberated."

Kiko Garcia, it turned out, worked in Rodriguez's drug organization as a street steerer; it seems that he took his wages in kind, since his autopsy revealed a perforated septum as well as other indications of chronic, heavy cocaine abuse. When his criminal record was finally tracked down through his fingerprints, detectives discovered that he had pleaded guilty to a charge of criminal sale of cocaine to an undercover police officer in 1989, identifying himself as Jose Gonzalez; he was sentenced to probation, which he quickly violated. At the time of his death, there was a warrant out for his arrest. According to the later report from the Manhattan District Attorney, his gravestone in the Dominican Republic reads Jose Luis Hidalgo.

Detectives talked about leaking the tape to the media or, better, splicing some of the videotape's footage together with shots of Mayor Dinkins's visit to Garcia's family. Instead, the police handed the tape over to the District Attorney's office. Although the tape became crucial to the DA's investigation of the shooting, it was not shown publicly.

Up and down the police hierarchy, officers privately excoriated the Mayor for his actions. In the public arena, police union officials attacked the Mayor in print. At one point, Ted Buczek, the father of slain police officer Michael Buczek, released a letter that he had written to Mayor Dinkins on July 14th, after Dinkins's visit to Garcia's family. In his letter, Ted Buczek recalls that, though Dinkins had been Manhattan Borough President at the time of his son's murder, Dinkins did not come to Michael Buczek's wake, nor did he visit or comfort the Buczek family in any way.

Occupational solidarity played a much greater role in the police assessment of these events than did skin color or ethnicity. Mayor Dinkins consistently played the morally freighted race card during his tenure in office, sometimes by acting directly, sometimes by not acting at all when action was direly needed, always allowing the police to be the lightning rod for diffuse racial conflicts. One can cite many examples. After a black woman trumped up an accusation against a Korean grocer of assaulting her while she was shopping on January 18, 1990, black activists boycotted the grocer's Church Street store in the Flatbush section of Brooklyn, immediately expanding the protest to another Korean-owned store across the street. For months, demonstrators obstructed the groceries' trade, all the while threatening anyone daring to break the boycott, urinating in the streets, assaulting passers-by and local residents alike, and playing raucous music. The police acted gingerly, arresting only those boycotters engaged in outright assault. Throughout the six-month protest, boycotters distributed literature exhorting blacks not to buy from "people who don't look like us" and calling the police "pigs." The Mayor's office never commented on the boycotters' sentiments. When a court issued orders on May 7th and 10th requiring boycotters to keep their distance from the stores, the Mayor's office argued that it was the police department's responsibility to enforce the court order and curb protesters' increasingly aggressive behavior.

Eventually, the police did cordon off boycotters with a minimum of disturbance and the Mayor did visit one of the Korean stores. Dinkins appointed a mayoral commission, studded with his own allies and clients, to study the boycott. The commission's report blamed everyone—grocers, police, and the mass media—but not the boycotters themselves nor the Mayor's office; moreover, the report declared that the boycott was not racially motivated. Later, the City Council excoriated the mayoral commission report, arguing the opposite case. The Korean grocer was acquitted at trial, but both grocers lost their businesses.

There were other incidents as well. When two black youngsters in the Bronx claimed to have had their faces spray-painted white, the Mayor offered a $10,000 reward for the apprehension and conviction of the culprits in this "truly heinous, horrific attack." After hundreds of hours of police overtime investigating the incident, the police determined that it was a complete hoax. No charges were pressed, and the Mayor's office made no further mention of the incident. When, following the traffic death of a young boy, blacks in the Crown Heights section of Brooklyn rioted, killing two white men, Yankel Rosenbaum and Anthony Graziozi, and injuring many others, the Mayor's inaction paralyzed the police department, until the Mayor himself was assaulted during a visit to the Brooklyn neighborhood on the third night of rioting. From its inception in 1854, of course, the New York City Police Department has been run by City Hall simply because the Mayor appoints the Police Commissioner. No one in Mayor Dinkins's office gave an order to the police not to act when the Crown Heights rioting broke out, but neither did Mayor Dinkins nor anyone on his staff give an order to the police *to act*. With the police convinced that Mayor Dinkins was hostage to his primary constituencies, that is, blacks and Latinos, bureaucratic caution did the rest. By the time directives reached the street, first-line officers were being told by their sergeants simply to contain the violence, not to quell it.

Although black police brass, along with judges in the criminal courts and top and middle-range officials in every city agency, were the beneficiaries of Dinkins's old-time New York political cronynism, except of course with colors changed, and although the NYPD, in all a remarkably integrated work organization, has had its full share of racial animosities, black cops did not stand with the Mayor on his handling of the Kiko Garcia affair. Black policemen of both high and humble rank privately referred to Mayor Dinkins in extremely derogatory terms.

The most telling episode occurred several weeks after Garcia's shooting, when the Mayor tried to repair the breach with the police department by visiting the Three-Four precinct station house with his own and the police department's top brass. To make sure that there were no confrontations, the captain of the precinct had sent all the aggressive cops out to the far ends of the precinct, leaving for the most part only the house mouses and Dinkins's and his Commissioner's favored Community Policing cops to greet the Mayor. The police who remained stood in the muster room in starched blues complete with white gloves, a true rainbow coalition of officers, black, white, Hispanic, Asian, male, and female.

While the television cameras rolled, Dinkins harangued the officers, reminding them that he was an ex-Marine and that his support for the police was unwavering. He told them how deeply he resented the accusations of the police union, which had excoriated him in full-page press ads. He said that he understood just how tough the streets were and that the police were all that stood between most hard-working citizens and the lawlessness of the streets. In the background, the detec-

tives listened impassively, with only occasional asides revealing their sardonic appraisal of the scene. After the media representatives had finished and were hustled out of the muster
room, Dinkins lingered a bit with some of his aides and asked
if the cops had anything to say.

Tommy Barnett said that he did. A young white police officer, there because he was the union representative for the
precinct, Barnett had been newly assigned to the anticrime
force because of his and his partner's spectacular apprehension
of five armed robbers in 1989. The robbers had taken 25 hos-
tages at a beer distributor's warehouse just around the corner
from the home of then-Manhattan Borough President Dinkins.
Later, with two partners, Barnett gained local fame by hauling
in a drug dealer who had offered the policemen $256,000 in
brown-bagged cash to look the other way.

Barnett, looking the Mayor straight in the eye, said: "Mr.
Mayor, sir, in choosing to visit Garcia's family, you betrayed
those of us who are out on the streets day after day. It's as
simple as that." After stammering back a version of his earlier
statement, Dinkins left the room, sweating and trembling vis-
ibly. Chief David Scott, the highest ranking uniformed officer
in the department at the time, a black man of imposing military bearing, universally revered by the force both for his re-
nowned physical courage and his reputation for always being
a fair boss, walked over to Barnett and stared at him for a long
moment while the room became absolutely still. Then Scott
removed his hat, bowed his head to Barnett, turned, and
walked out of the room.

During the weeks that followed, the Dinkins administration cranked out several more justifications for the
Mayor's actions after the shooting. The Mayor's principal ob-
ligation, his office argued, was to "keep the peace." The city
therefore paid for Garcia's funeral in the Dominican Republic
in order to get the funeral out of the city and prevent it from

becoming a symbolic flashpoint for emotional displays of grief in the Latino tradition that might trigger more violence.

The administration also promised that the notorious Three-Four precinct would be divided into north and south sectors in order to allow for better community policing, the centerpiece idea of Dinkins's thinking about police. As it happens, the implementation of CPoP varied dramatically from precinct to precinct, depending on commanding officers' responsiveness to community clamor, itself a function of these bosses' ambitions for promotion beyond the highest civil-service rank of captain. In the Three-Four precinct, those police assigned to CPoP units received considerable advantages over their peers in choosing work hours; they were given collars actually made by other officers both to beef up CPoP statistics and to provide CPoP units with overtime work that produces extra pay. All of this produced a sharp division between the CPoP units and those units committed to aggressive anticrime efforts, such as Local Motion. And some community groups, and especially some defense attorneys, aware of the new premium in the department on community policing and the splits it produced, targeted those police units that remained overtly aggressive for organized choruses of civilian complaints that inevitably led to extensive internal investigations. Aggressive cops came to be considered liabilities to their bosses.

For the rest of the summer, an army of nearly 3,000 police occupied Washington Heights to prevent further outbreaks of civic violence. The police were so omnipresent that a great deal of the normal crime in the Three-Four migrated across the river to the Bronx's Four-Four, Four-Six, or Four-O precincts, or south to Manhattan's Three-O precinct. In all of those precincts, murder rates soared. On September 10, 1992, the Manhattan District Attorney made public a comprehensive report, including many forensic details, that it had presented to the grand jury. The report completely exonerated Officer O'Keefe, arguing that the evidence clearly showed that O'Keefe had killed Garcia in the midst of a fierce struggle for control of

Garcia's gun. The report also exonerated Lieutenant Roger Parrino, who had been falsely accused in the death of another
Dominican man, Dagberto Pichardo, at the height of the riots.
PO O'Keefe, who after the shooting of Garcia had been immediately removed from the precinct and transferred to a remote
corner of another borough, eventually received the detectives'
gold shield.

The New York Post ran the headline: "Lying Drug Dealers!"
But the District Attorney declined to prosecute Juana Madera
and Ana Rodriguez for clearly demonstrated perjury, despite
the enormous harm and mistrust that their lies had caused the
city. Although many thousands of police were mobilized to
contain another outbreak of violence, the streets remained
strangely calm. Informants told detectives that the drug dealers thought that further violence was bad for business.

In mid-September, the police themselves held a raucous
demonstration in front of City Hall, what the media termed a
"police riot," during which police officers and their union
officials made disparaging remarks about Mayor Dinkins. A
few weeks later, the standing army of police was dispersed
from upper Manhattan, and the normal violence associated
with the drug trade resumed. By year's end, the precinct vied
once again to lead the city in homicides. However, the massive
police presence certainly had a long-term disruptive effect; the
number of homicides in the precinct dropped significantly in
1993 down to 76 murders (a 24 percent drop), while the city-
wide decrease was 9.6 percent.

DANY's report exonerating Officer O'Keefe was roundly
condemned by Dominican community activists and their several allies, including Dominican intellectuals, because it and
the grand jury were used to "exercise control over the just
demands of a community." In this view, "justice" demanded
conviction of the police officer, regardless of what actually
happened in the lobby of 505 West 162nd Street on July 3,
1992. And each day for more than a year, fresh flowers and
new community tributes to the hard-working father martyred

by an oppressive system appeared at the makeshift shrine and wall mural put up in memory of Kiko Garcia. Even today, powerful Dominican community leaders speak of Garcia's death as an "assassination."

Meanwhile, several social commentators looked back at the riots as a "popular uprising," one that demonstrated anew that poverty causes crime, that the systemic blocking of legitimate aspirations leads ambitious young people to employ illegitimate means to obtain culturally sanctioned rewards.

Police officers respond with some skepticism to this tidy, often-heard, we're-all-in-this-together-we-just-do-things-differently explanation for crime. One day in the middle of the riots in Washington Heights, with officers under siege everywhere on the streets and in the newspapers, a mock fight erupted in the Three-Four squad room. Detectives of different colors and ethnic groups began to argue vociferously with one another, each detective adopting the appropriate strident, moralistic, essentialist rhetoric that echoed exactly the cacophony of the streets, of the academy, and of the dailies. Then, suddenly, Detective Angel Morales, famous for his satirical cartoons as well as for his detailed knowledge of the Washington Heights drug scene, fell to one knee and, with his hands upraised, folded in prayer, pleaded with his colleagues: "Can't——can't——can't we all get along?" He then jumped up and, joined by several other detectives, black, Puerto Rican, Italian, Irish, male, and female, began to dance in a circle, right hands held together high above heads, lumbering bodies moving now with grace, while everyone sang: "We Are the World."

Perhaps more than any other occupational group, police officers believe that our society rests on irreconcilable differences that neither mawkish sentimentality nor recycled social policies can resolve; only the strong assertion of legitimate authority, backed by force, secures the public order that makes the civil quest for tolerable compromises possible.

troubled
order

But the problem is always: Whose order? When common visions o order collapse, people fight about the rules that keep wills in check and established order in place; they fight especially about the rulekeepers. Public debate shifts away from the profound social, political, and moral issues that crime and criminals pose. Instead, police officers, and the procedures governing their conduct, become the problem.

New York City has a long history of rogue cops and of public figures who have made careers crusading against them. But the sea of drugs flooding the city since the late 1960s has changed the very nature of police corruption. Gone are the days when officers merely clipped meals on the arm, or got comped a hotel suite measured by how long it takes to chase a bimbo from one end to the other, or raised a family on the pad, or looked the other way while Mafia stiffs unloaded hijacked trucks. The Mollen Commission, initiated by Mayor Dinkins, discovered cops who were out-and-out violent thugs, who under color of authority would shake down and rob drug dealers and then cover their misdeeds with systematic perjury. This occurred in several precincts, including the Three-O just south of the Three-Four.

When brought to light, such official criminality poses catastrophic legal problems for district attorneys, who must review all cases involving the corrupt officers and often release from prison criminals who, even though they confessed to crimes, now claim they were framed. Moreover, New York City itself immediately becomes the object of enormously costly civil law suits. And the gleeful, though ostensibly solemn, media accounts of such events provide yet more materials for defense attorneys to tar all police, especially aggressive officers in communities like Washington Heights, awash in drugs and guns.

The July 1992 riots were followed by an avalanche of civilian complaints against Local Motion, many brought by defense lawyers for drug dealers and many by local advocacy groups. By spring 1993 the police department responded to the complaints by taking all members of the Local Motion anticrime unit off the streets, except for PO Johnny Moynihan, who was never placed on restricted duty. Everyone else was placed under "house arrest," either at police headquarters or in one of the station houses, while federal authorities and the NYPD's Internal Affairs Bureau investigated allegations about the unit's violation of search and seizure laws, sometimes accompanied by perjury, in two federal cases and five state cases.

The case of Jorge Almonte became the focal point of the investigation. According to Local Motion officer Matteo Brattesani, he, Tommy McPartland, and Paddy Regan were riding in their unmarked blue Chevrolet on West 187th Street on August 14, 1992, when they spotted a man on the sidewalk who, the officers thought, had a gun on his person. The officers began to get out of their car when the man, Jorge Almonte, made them for cops. Almonte ditched a paper bag he was carrying and rushed into the basement of 534 West 187th Street. Brattesani and McPartland followed him into the basement where, according to Brattesani's later sworn statement, the man threw a loaded .38-caliber revolver to the ground right before the officers grabbed him. Brattesani said that the officers never went above the basement. Meanwhile, Regan retrieved the paper bag on the sidewalk; it contained three little bags: one of crack, one of coke, and one containing little baggies of marijuana. Regan remained outside the building to make sure that the police car's tires were not slashed, a common practice in the precinct since the riots.

The police took the case to federal prosecutors, as they did with many of their gun and drug cases, because federal law allows accomplice testimony without corroboration and provides stiffer sentences than New York State law. David Goldstein of Goldstein, Weinstein & Fuld represented Almonte. Goldstein immediately alleged to the federal prosecutor, Assistant U.S. Attorney Chauncey Parker, that the Local Motion officers had done an illegal search and then had concocted the story of Almonte's dropping the bag of drugs and the gun to justify the search; in short, Goldstein alleged that the cops had "flaked" Almonte.

Goldstein argued that there were several witnesses to the cops' deception. Parker interviewed four of these. Brigido Hidalgo and Carmen Nunez-Cartaya, who had been on West 187th Street that day, claimed that Almonte was not on the street but in the building. The cops arrived, went into the building, and came out with Almonte cuffed. Anilda Martinez said that she was upstairs in her third-floor apartment and had asked Almonte, her next-door neighbor, to go to the basement and fix the circuit breaker. Cops came to her apartment, pushed in, and searched it, asking her if there was a way to get into Almonte's apartment from hers. An unnamed cable installer present in her apartment interpreted her conversation with the police. After Parker was able to track him down, the cable installer said that there had been four policemen involved; three, he said, went upstairs and a fourth kept watch over Almonte, who was cuffed to a railing on the first floor. The cable installer knew this, he said, because he had to get an additional piece of equipment from his truck. AUSA Parker never spoke to Almonte.

All three women were friends with Almonte, and therefore Parker was skeptical about their accounts. Though Parker argued later that the cable installer was an independent witness and had no reason to lie to authorities, the cable installer never testified in court; moreover, he completely disappeared, and all later efforts to find him failed. Indeed, his name was never revealed to the police officers who subsequently came under investigation on the strength of his account.

Parker also went out to West 187th Street with PO Paddy Regan, since the arresting officer Brattesani was out of the country. But at the scene, Regan's recollection of the arrest was extremely shaky, Parker thought; Regan said that Brattesani and McPartland had chased Almonte up a flight of steps to the front door and had arrested him outside the building. Later, Regan phoned Parker to say that he had mixed up the Almonte case with another arrest and that Almonte had actually been arrested in the building's basement.

Since all of the witnesses' accounts varied dramatically from those of the police officers, Parker met with his boss, who then handed the case over to the corruption unit, where AUSAs Matthew Fishbein and Deborah Landis, in conjunction with IAB, began a formal investigation of Local Motion for search and seizure civil rights violations as well as perjury.

The six other state and federal cases exhibited similar patterns to the Almonte case. Local Motion made arrests and produced hard evidence of wrongdoing, namely illegal guns, sometimes accompanied by drugs. Defendants, aided by defense attorneys, and witnesses, often defendants' friends or relatives, alleged that the police had done illegal searches, thus violating defendants' civil rights, and then had lied about the circumstances of the arrests.

In the one other federal case at issue, some of the circumstances did seem exceptionally suspicious. Police officers Artie Barragan, Matteo Brattesani, and Tommy McPartland had arrested Rafael Nieves and Jose Abreu at 2258 Wadsworth Avenue on July 22, 1992. The officers claimed that they had seen a man with a gun on the rear fire escape of the building and another man with a gun standing in a window. The officers said that the men barricaded themselves inside an apartment. After the Emergency Service Unit broke into the apartment and took the men into custody, the Local Motion officers did a security sweep, searching for more gunmen. During that security sweep—the search with the narrowest scope, confined to looking for a person—the officers claimed that they bumped into a table and that a secret compartment sprang open, revealing more weapons, ammunition, and several pounds of cocaine in plain view. But later, when the table was in police custody, no amount of bumping into it could make the compartment spring open. In that case, prosecutors claimed independent corroboration for their suspicions from the ESU officers, who, prosecutors said, told the story differently, although these officers are unnamed in court records.

In one state case, the NYPD had filed administrative charges in late spring 1994 against POs Johnny Moynihan and Paddy Regan and Sergeant Patrick Duffy for allegedly conducting an illegal search on September 17, 1992, at 209 Dyckman Street. The team of Local Motion officers was cruising the lower end of the precinct near 160th Street and Broadway when (according to Incident Record x10494 for September 17th, received at 2042 hours) they heard a radio run about an incident on Dyckman Street near Broadway. A female caller had reported that two males were after a woman and her baby in a third- or fourth-floor back apartment in the building next to the pharmacy with a dental office. It sounded like a push-in or home-invasion robbery, common in the Three-Four precinct.

Patrol officers, responding at 2047 hours, went first into 207 and then 209 Dyckman, and, after looking around, judged the report unfounded. The Local Motion officers decided, however, to take a ride up to Dyckman; frequently, home-invasion robbers hide in a building or on its roof until uniformed police leave the scene. When they arrived on the block, they sat in their unmarked car, with blacked-out windows, for about a quarter of an hour watching for anyone plausibly connected to the robbery report. The street was filled with people, several with pit bulls on leashes, clusters of men here and there playing cards or dominoes.

At about 2115 hours, the officers saw two men leaving 209 Dyckman, one carrying a large black plastic garbage bag and the other wearing a bulging windbreaker, though the night was warm. Sergeant Duffy put a 10-85 call over the radio for assistance. When the officers got out of their car to challenge the men, the crowd began yelling: "Local Motion, Local Motion!" Both of the men bolted back inside 209 Dyckman; the officers followed them into the building. Regan and Duffy caught the man in the bulging windbreaker on the landing between the fourth and fifth floors. He turned out to be Russell Castillo, and he had a MAC-11 under his jacket loaded with 20 live rounds; he went the hard way, flailing his arms to avoid being handcuffed.

Moynihan flew past Duffy and Regan, chasing the other man to the fifth floor and finally catching him just as he was opening the door to Apartment #52 with his keys. Moynihan tackled and arrested the man, Rafael Nunez, and disarmed him of a TEC-9 Luger, loaded with 18 live rounds; Nunez also went the hard way. Then Moynihan, hearing noise in the opened apartment, entered it and did a security sweep to see whether the woman and her baby—the supposed victims reported earlier—might be there. The apartment was a typical drug-sale apartment, complete with table and scales but devoid of furniture except for a couch and a chair or two. A window leading to the fire escape was open. Moynihan locked the apartment on his way out.

By this time, the building was sheer bedlam, with Castillo's family, which lived on the third floor, screaming at the Local Motion officers and at the other cops who had responded to Sergeant Duffy's call. Duffy had recovered the black plastic bag dropped by Nunez: it contained one kilo of cocaine and two pounds of marijuana. In a subsequent interview with investigators, Castillo admitted that he used marijuana and cocaine himself and that he dealt drugs for an organization that sold about a kilo of cocaine a day in small quantities out of 209 Dyckman.

By 2117 hours (according to Incident Record x10945 for September 17th) the two men with guns were under arrest. The following day, the assistant district attorney at DANY wrote up felony complaints for the guns and narcotics but decided not to write up the search warrant Moynihan requested, arguing that by the time the police could return the apartment would surely be stripped of any evidence of drug activity.

At the evidence suppression hearings, Castillo and Nunez argued that Local Motion had searched them illegally. The pair were backed up by a chorus of other residents of 209 Dyckman, all but one of whom were acquaintances or relatives of Castillo. Castillo later told investigators the following story. On September 17th, he said, he and Nunez had been playing dominoes on the street with some friends, including two Dominican NYPD police officers, whom he refused to name. During the game, he went to the local bodega, where he ran into a "white guy" who wanted to buy three and a half grams of coke. With Nunez, Castillo then went to 209 Dyckman to get the cocaine for the customer; Nunez went to his own first-floor apartment while Castillo went upstairs. According to Castillo, when he left the building to meet his customer at the nearby McDonald's, a tin-foil packet of coke in his pocket, a Local Motion officer, with others nearby in the car, stopped him in the street, took his keys out of his pocket, and demanded to know where his apartment was. The officers then took Castillo back into the building, where they met and detained Nunez.

Taking both men up to Castillo's third-floor apartment, Castillo continued, the officers returned his keys and had him open the apartment, and then went inside. Several of his relatives were inside the apartment. One officer had Castillo empty his pockets. Altogether, according to Castillo, they were inside the third-floor apartment for 20 minutes. Then the officers took both Castillo and Nunez upstairs to Apartment #52, their tee-shirts pulled over their heads, appropriated the keys from Nunez, and went inside, forcing Castillo and Nunez to lie on the floor; one officer, Castillo said, periodically kept their heads to the floor with his foot. The officers rampaged around the apartment for 30 minutes, breaking things and pushing the refrigerator around. Then the officers made a call on their radio, and several uniformed officers arrived and took the two men to the station house. The Local Motion officers left with black garbage bags in their hands. Castillo said that $20,000 and a kilo of cocaine were missing from Apartment #52.

Assistant district attorneys continually hear stories from drug dealers about cops seizing their keys, entering their apartments, and stealing their drugs and money. And some cops do engage in "booming," that is, entering apartments illegally either to make arrests or to steal drugs and money, or both; these were the allegations against Local Motion, already under constant fire in the aftermath of the July riots. But in this arrest, the officers recovered and vouchered two hand-submachine guns plus felony weight of both cocaine and marijuana. Moreover, Castillo's story simply didn't fit the time sequence established by the radio-call records, and, when police searched his person back at the station house, they found no trace of the three-and-a-half-gram packet he claimed to be delivering. Eventually Castillo retracted the allegation that the officers had stolen money and drugs.

DANY decided that the allegations against Local Motion in the 209 Dyckman case were unfounded, and it filed gun and narcotics charges against Castillo and Nunez. But DANY also did not press the case. In the end, both Castillo and Nunez ended up walking for want of a speedy trial. Castillo was represented by David Goldstein of Goldstein, Weinstein &

Fuld. Once the larger federal investigation into Local Motion went into high gear, DANY passed the case on to the United States Attorney's office for further probing.

Despite its nearly two years of exhaustive investigation into all the allegations made against Local Motion in all seven state and federal cases, including the Almonte case, the United States Attorney's office came up completely empty on all officers in the unit and was unable to proceed legally against them. It is said that top NYPD brass and the United States Attorney's office made a deal sometime in spring 1994 to end the matter by having the police department file administrative charges against the Local Motion officers involved in the 209 Dyckman case.

Then in May 1994 federal prosecutors and IAB received an allegation against Paddy Regan, accusing him of threatening to plant drugs on Jorge Almonte. It came from one Jose Rodriguez (a different Jose Rodriguez from the man involved in the Kiko Garcia affair). Rodriguez told authorities that in December 1992 he was introduced to Regan by his brother, Ramon Rodriguez—the former DEA informant who only a couple of years earlier had worked undercover for Staten Island Borough President Guy Molinari on behalf of Joseph Occhipinti. Ramon had had a long-standing, though deeply ambiguous, relationship with Paddy Regan. Sometime after June 1991, when the DEA ceased employing him as an informant, Ramon approached Regan in the street one day, telling him that he knew where a lot of narcotics were located. Regan rebuffed the offer, saying that Local Motion focused on guns. Ramon insisted that he knew about guns as well. Regan gave Ramon the phone number of Manhattan North Narcotics for any information about drugs, and his own beeper number for information about guns. A few days later, Ramon called Regan with information about a large shipment of guns from Virginia to West 171st Street and Audubon. Regan took Ramon to see Dan Rather, then prosecuting gun-trafficking cases. But Rather didn't offer the money for each gun seized that Ramon wanted.

Because he felt slighted, Ramon never called Rather back and never became formally registered as an informant. The police department has long required that its officers, whether in uniform or plainclothes, register confidential informants if they use information from the informants more than once. Registration has important administrative purposes: it helps monitor the flow of money paid to informants, and it certifies the informants as sources of reliable information, thus circumventing the usual requirement for officers to produce informants before a magistrate to obtain search warrants. But many police officers feel that one of registration's unacknowledged purposes is to protect their bosses at blame-time if cases fall apart because of faulty information. Since the procedure involves photographing and fingerprinting, the best confidential informants—criminals who play both sides of the street—refuse to be registered.

But Ramon latched onto Regan, becoming the kind of person police consider a "buff," calling Regan regularly, always claiming to know something important but never giving substantive information that led to gun arrests. Then, in 1992, during an epidemic of car-jacking of high-priced foreign cars from the Silk Stocking district in the Nineteenth precinct, Ramon led Regan to a garage on Nagle Avenue that coordinated the robberies and altered the identification numbers on the stolen vehicles. But when the Nineteenth's Robbery Identification Program stole the case, with approval from downtown, once again Ramon Rodriguez was left out in the cold, with no reward for the information that broke the case.

In December 1992, however, Ramon Rodriguez called Regan once again, telling him that he had information on the November 30th slaying of Jose Cuevas, a sports columnist for a local Spanish newspaper who was shot in the lobby of 620 West

172nd Street during a botched drug robbery. The killing of Cuevas—an innocent bystander—generated a great deal of publicity and consequent pressure on the police department. Regan called Gennaro "Jerry" Giorgio, a legendary senior detective in the Three-Four squad who has broken scores of famous cases over a distinguished 36-year police career and who was working the journalist's case. Regan characterized Ramon Rodriguez's mixed record and asked Giorgio if he wished to interview Ramon. Giorgio told Regan to handle it himself and keep him informed.

Regan met Ramon at Ramon's mother's house at 135th Street near Broadway. It turned out that Ramon had no reliable information about the journalist's homicide, saying only that the killer hung out on Dyckman Street. At that point, Ramon introduced Regan to his brother, Jose. Jose told Regan that he was a confidential informant for federal authorities, working off his guilty plea to crimes that could have brought him life imprisonment. He had pleaded guilty in federal court to smuggling 12 kilos of heroin into the United States and to hiring a hit man to murder a rival. While testifying in another trial, Jose also admitted under cross examination that he had smuggled more than 200 kilos each of heroin and cocaine into the United States over a five-year period. For his crimes, Rodriguez spent two and a half months in the Metropolitan Correctional Center in Manhattan in fall 1992.

Almost a year and a half later, on May 6, 1994, Jose alleged to federal investigators and to Detective Sergeant Thomas McGuigan, who was supervising IAB's investigation into Local Motion, that Regan had then asked Jose if he knew Jorge Almonte when he was at MCC. When Jose answered yes, Regan told him that Almonte was responsible for the investigation into Local Motion. Then, according to Jose, Regan produced Almonte's photograph and asked Jose to go to West 187th Street and find him. When Jose asked Ramon in Spanish why Local Motion was looking for Almonte, Ramon replied that

Local Motion wanted to plant drugs on Almonte. Jose also told McGuigan that Regan admitted to him that his partners had indeed gone upstairs on the day Almonte was arrested, but that the officers intended to deny this.

McGuigan arranged for Jose to make a taped phone call to Regan on June 2, 1994, to test the veracity of the allegations. In that very brief conversation, Jose told Regan that he had discovered the whereabouts of "the guy from 187th Street" (Jorge Almonte) and asked if Regan still wanted the address. Regan said: "We're inside now and . . . we're not going to get involved in anything . . . We're just going to play it, play it by the book." Although IAB and federal authorities later argued that Regan's response clearly indicated recognition of what Rodriguez meant, they had not expected it, since they had already set up a sting operation in the Bronx where Almonte was supposedly hiding. The sting, called Operation Bagpipes, because most officers in Local Motion were Irish, consisted of an ostensible drug apartment manned by police officers posing as drug dealers. Video and audio equipment was on hand to catch Local Motion storming into the apartment to arrest Almonte or, even better, to rob the supposed drug apartment. Maintaining the set-up around the clock for a few weeks cost hundreds of thousands of dollars. Local Motion never went near the place.

Later, McGuigan interviewed Ramon, who told him that he had been an informant for Local Motion on several cases. If this were true, IAB and federal authorities reasoned, Local Motion's unauthorized, regular use of an unregistered inform- ant might be reason enough for the officers to lie. Ramon went on to tell McGuigan that he had spoken with Regan just the evening before and Regan had told him to lie to federal authori- ties about his past relationship with Local Motion, telling Ramon to say falsely that he passed on any information he obtained about guns to ADA Dan Rather, who then relayed it to Local Motion.

McGuigan had Ramon phone Regan five times in the following few months, with a cluster of three calls coming in the
late summer of 1994. In these recorded conversations, Ramon
told Regan that he had been interviewed by IAB and the FBI
about Local Motion and about Regan in particular and that, as
Regan had instructed him, he had told investigators that Dan
Rather was the go-between for information. Regan responded:
"Right." Regan went on to ask Rodriguez whether he had been
questioned about other arrests made by Local Motion, including the Nieves-Abreu arrest. Ramon said that he had been
queried about that and one other arrest. Regan said: "They're
full of shit. They have nothing." Later in the same conversation, Regan insisted to Ramon: "[There's] nothing to hide here.
We never did nothing wrong."

In a subsequent recorded phone conversation on August
29th, Ramon referred to the picture of Almonte and said: "I'm
glad we didn't do nothing with this guy, man." Regan did not
acknowledge giving Ramon or Jose the picture, but he went on
to insist: "You don't know that guy. I don't know what you're
talking about . . . I don't know what you're talking about, you
understand?" And later, Regan said: "I have no idea. I forget
about that guy." He also told Ramon: "[We've] nothing to hide,
tell the truth." But he also told Ramon: "You didn't call me,
you didn't talk to me, you didn't whatever, okay?" Federal
authorities then served Ramon with a subpoena to produce the
photograph of Almonte; Ramon was never able to do so. When
Ramon spoke again to Regan on September 8th and told him
about the subpoena, Regan insisted that he had never given a
picture of Almonte to anyone.

Ramon's comments and questions were delivered in the
classic patterns of street talk: sporadic bursts of words strung
together, a kind of talking in circles punctuated by expletives
and continual demands for reassurance and self-validation,
such as "Ya know whaddim sayin'?" "You undastan' me,
man?" All the phone calls from Ramon to Regan, as well as
the single phone call from Jose to Regan, produced only ex-

tremely ambiguous information about the relationship between the Rodriguez brothers and Patrick Regan and certainly
no incriminating evidence against either Regan or other Local
Motion officers. Indeed, at that point, Detective Sergeant
McGuigan determined that the case had little, if any, merit.

But once a case is opened, the logic of bureaucracy dictates that, one way or another, it must be closed.
On October 13 and 18, 1994, Assistant U.S. Attorneys Deborah
Landis and Paul Gardephe called Regan into the grand jury
under a court-ordered grant of immunity, presumably to testify
about the investigation into the Almonte and Nieves-Abreu
cases, among others. At that point, prosecutors had insufficient evidence to charge any of the Local Motion officers,
including Paddy Regan, with wrongdoing. But instead of inquiring about the seven cases under investigation, the prosecutors focused entirely on Regan's recollections of his own
phone conversations with the Rodriguez brothers, without
telling Regan that they were working from tapes of those calls.

Regan had encountered Landis before. She had once summoned him to her office early on in the investigation, and told
him that she was examining all of Local Motion's arrests of
drug dealers in the Three-Four. But then she asked Regan questions such as: Did you take any drugs from these guys? Any
money? Given the way she looked at him and the questions
she asked, Regan began to think that he, not the drug dealers,
was her quarry.

Then two days after that interview, Regan came home from
work late one afternoon to find two investigators from the
United States Attorney's office outside his house in a car. They
asked him to take a ride with them. Regan phoned his partners
to tell them where he was and to give them the plate number
of the car; he refused to ride in the front seat as requested. The
investigators drove to a nearby Waldbaum's parking lot, where
they sat and talked for an hour. The investigators' basic mes-

sage was: "You're a married man with a family that needs you. The other guys in Local Motion aren't married, or don't have children, and don't really have the cares you do. Forget about your friends. Save yourself. Tell us about Local Motion."

Regan saw his future narrowing to two stark choices: being the fall guy so that federal prosecutors could close their cases, itself a bureaucratic imperative, or betraying his brother officers by trying to explain to prosecutors that in order to take guns off the street from wild cowboys, one sometimes has to act like a cowboy.

Regan is from the old country, a welder and carpenter by trade. He came to the United States in 1986 and joined the police force in time to help put the blood-drenched, dying PO Michael Buczek into the ambulance the night of October 18, 1988. He shares with other men who take guns off the streets a unique brotherhood of death, the knowledge that one's death in the line of duty, should it come, has meaning, that one dies to make the city safer for its citizens even if, in our times, such a sacrifice might be honored only by brother officers.

In front of the grand jury, AUSA Landis took the lead, spelled occasionally by Gardephe. Landis asked if the Local Motion officers used informants. The issue of unregistered informants was dangerous ground for Regan, given the NYPD rules; Regan denied that his unit used informants. Landis asked if Local Motion had ever utilized information from Ramon Rodriguez. Regan conceded that Local Motion received information from someone named Rodriguez in cases worked with ADA Dan Rather. Landis then pressed Regan about every aspect of his conversations with the Rodriguez brothers.

Since Regan had expected to be grilled once again on the seven Local Motion cases, the prosecutors' queries about his conversations with the Rodriguez brothers threw him off stride. As Regan's discomfort increased, Landis continued to pepper him with questions about details of those phone calls, inquiring whether he had ever discussed the federal investigation of Local Motion with Ramon Rodriguez, whether Ramon had told Regan that he had been subpoenaed by the government to testify about Local Motion, and whether Regan had given Ramon advice about what to do in such inquiries.

Regan became defensive; then he became evasive. To almost every question, he answered: "Not that I'm aware of"; "Not that I can recall"; "I don't really recall"; "I'm not aware"; or "I don't remember." Regan stressed that he had told Ramon simply to tell the truth, something amply demonstrated in phone-conversation transcripts. But he also denied that Ramon had told him of the subpoena for Almonte's photograph, insisting that, if he had had conversations with Ramon Rodriguez, he didn't recall them because they were of no significance to him.

> **Landis:** Isn't it a fact, Officer Regan, that during August and September of 1994, you had a series of telephone conversations with Ramon Rodriguez in which he discussed with you at length the fact that he had been downtown to speak to Federal authorities, including the FBI and the Internal Affairs Bureau, concerning you and other members of the Anti-Crime Unit?
> **Regan:** He possibly was.
> **Landis:** I'm not asking you whether he was or wasn't, Officer.
> **Regan:** Conversations. He called me all the time. He always calls.
> **Landis:** You have no recollection of these particular conversations that I am talking about; is that your testimony?
> **Regan:** Right.

As Regan dug in his heels, Landis became more and more impatient. Toward the end of the second day of inquiry, she asked:

> **Landis:** Officer, do you care at all whether the investigation into the Anti-Crime Unit is resolved favorably or resolved at all?
> **Regan:** Well . . . I have been under investigation for approximately two years and I did nothing wrong. I was a good police officer. And I have been taken off the street

and put behind a desk where I don't belong and I have a lot of animosity toward the U.S. Attorney's office for doing this and I think it's terrible and . . . I want this investigation to be over with as soon as possible. But when it's going to be over with, it's going to be over with. I don't have any control over that, but I do not like what's going on.

Regan was in full dress regalia that day, October 18th, since he had come to court directly from the emotionally wrenching annual Buczek memorial mass at St. Elizabeth's Church in the Three-Four precinct, where hundreds of Dominican schoolchildren, dressed in uniforms of blackwatch plaid, sang accompaniment to police bagpipes wailing "Amazing Grace." Over his heart Regan displayed his many decorations, including his Combat Cross, a coveted award that only 300 New York City police officers have ever received. The Combat Cross is awarded for courage under fire to an officer "who, while engaged in personal combat with an armed opponent in line of police duty, successfully performs an act of extraordinary heroism at risk of life."

On May 1, 1992, Regan had been with Tommy McPartland at 505 West 158th Street at around 1700 hours. As they drove past the building, they saw a man showing a gun to two other men in the vestibule of the lobby. The officers drove on past, parked their car, and then walked back down the block toward the building. When they reached the building, they displayed their shields and identified themselves. The man with the gun bolted and ran downstairs to a basement apartment, with the officers following. The culprit tried to slam the door to the apartment as the officers tried to force their way in, Regan blocking the door with his foot. When the officers forced the door open, the gunman backed up, then started firing at Regan and McPartland. Suddenly, Regan felt a shot near his face. He couldn't see. He dove to his left, knocking McPartland down to the floor to keep him out of the line of fire. Then, in the small apartment reeking now with cordite from the shots and from dust shaken off the walls, both officers, with Regan still temporarily blinded, plunged forward and grabbed the gunman, and after a hard, slow-motion struggle, subdued him.

Landis began to query Regan about his service medals, focusing on yet another decoration for valor in yet another gunfight. Acting on a tip relayed by radio from PO Joe Romano, Regan and PO Brattesani had grabbed three culprits, all with guns, in front of a McDonald's at 170th Street and Broadway, where children in party garb were framed in the restaurant's window. Brattesani had fired his weapon in the scuffle. Since, however, Ramon Rodriguez claimed that *he* had given Local Motion the information that led to those arrests, Landis pressed Regan for an account of the circumstances of the incident. Regan claimed not to remember. Landis asked if Rodriguez had been with the officers immediately before the arrests. Regan said: "I don't have any memory of that or recall if he was with them or not." Landis questioned the validity of Regan's decoration, suggesting that Regan had really been in danger from friendly fire, rather than from the criminals he was arresting. Regan brushed aside her query.

Landis pressed ahead. She asked Regan what, briefly, he remembered about that incident. Regan, the man of action becoming more laconic as the interrogation proceeded, said: "Briefly, that we arrested a couple of guys with guns." With sarcasm evident even on the transcript's dry page, Landis, the woman of words, asked: "Did you swoop down on them from the sky and arrest them or did something happen before you arrested them?" Regan paused and then said: "Well, I'm not saying I'm Superman or anything like that. *But I know how to make a gun arrest on the street.*"

Local Motion officers took more than 600 illegal guns off the streets of Washington Heights between 1990 and 1993, risking their lives every day to make a turbulent city safer. During that period, Patrick Regan personally arrested more than 50 gunmen. From the perspective of men of action, one cannot take guns off the streets without walking very close to the edge of the controverted and continually changing prohibitions of search and seizure laws. One relies on one's sixth sense, developed only over long experience. One watches for the man wearing a heavy jacket in summertime; for the man running or walking quickly, one arm swinging free, the other held close to his body; for the men running five or six blocks away from the site of a reported shooting. One listens to neighborhood complaints about shells on a block and one sits there for hours, waiting to see men pull whole arsenals out of car trunks. One learns the cars likely to have *clavos*—the Ford Taurus with generous spaces in the doors and the trunk, the Chevy Lumina big under the dashboard and small shock absorber, the Chevy Caprice capacious under the dash. One listens carefully to street people, trying to pick one's way through the always garbled, often dead-wrong, sometimes right-on-the-money information that leads to armed criminals.

Most important, if public safety is at issue, one is willing to act on borderline information and especially on one's instinct, and to roust and confront men whom one suspects. But in the worldview of guardians of formalistic procedures, who have no experience whatsoever of the savagery of uptown streets, packing illegal weapons or selling drugs becomes marginally important. Instead, skirting rules, or breaking procedures, or acting without covering one's posterior, even if circumstances are exigent, or, especially, refusing under any circumstances to betray the comrades with whom one has risked one's life becomes the real crime.

The United States Attorneys obtained an indictment against Patrick Regan for two counts of perjury with 32 specifications arising from his grand jury testimony on October 13, 1994, and with 18 specifications from his testimony on October 18th, all relating to his evasiveness in answering questions about his conversations with the Rodriguez brothers.

In the trial that followed, beginning on August 10, 1995, the Assistant U.S. Attorneys, with the acquiescence of Judge. Denny Chin, who was hearing his first criminal trial, were able to exclude from consideration every substantive issue, despite repeated efforts by Regan's lawyer, David Greenfield, to broaden the inquiry. This included all questions about the truthfulness of allegations made against Local Motion and Patrick Regan by Jose and Ramon Rodriguez and Jorge Almonte and his lawyer, as well as those of other drug dealers whose charges precipitated the investigation of Local Motion in the first place.

The federal prosecutors decided not to call Jose Rodriguez as a witness and therefore dropped four specifications of perjury that required his testimony. The government also did not call Ramon Rodriguez. Still, the government offered "the allegations made by the Rodriguez brothers, not for the truth of those statements, but in order to establish the scope and subject matter of the investigation." The government thus precluded Regan from extracting evidence on cross examination to impeach the credibility of the Rodriguez brothers on direct testimony. Moreover, the court prohibited Regan from calling the Rodriguez brothers specifically for the purpose of impeaching them.

Had Regan been able to call Ramon Rodriguez, he could have posed an interesting problem to the jury: Why did federal authorities rely on Ramon Rodriguez at all in Paddy Regan's case, since they had completely discounted Ramon's reliability in the Occhipinti case a few years earlier, when he provided evidence that would have helped to exonerate Occhipinti? Not only was Regan unable to confront his accusers, but the court did not allow the trial jury to be informed about the disposition of the cases involving them—namely, that the government had dismissed all charges against Jorge Almonte on December 15, 1992, and that on July 20, 1995, Jose Rodriguez received time served of two and a half months for smuggling 12 kilos of heroin and hiring for murder. Nor did the court allow Regan to call any witnesses, such as Detective Giorgio, who could have confirmed the reason for Regan's meeting with Ramon and Jose Rodriguez at their mother's house in December 1992 and indeed contextualized the entire case for the jury.

On August 17, 1995, in a case tried on the head of a pin, in a complete triumph of formalism, where the only consideration allowed was a textual comparison of the taped conversations between Regan and the Rodriguez brothers and the transcripts of Regan's testimony to the grand jury, a jury convicted Regan on 27 specifications of perjury, acquitting him on 19 specifications. Detective Sergeant McGuigan, a stalwart of the prosecution's case, who later submitted a declaration to the court completely backing the government's position, nevertheless wept openly in court at the verdict.

Then, on December 8, 1995, anticrime officers in the Three-Four precinct arrested Ramon Rodriguez for passing a forged check for $2,500. The officers handed Ramon over to the detective squad, which conducted two taped interviews in which Ramon confessed that his brother's allegations against Regan were complete fabrications. But in what the police see as completely typical behavior, federal prosecutors seized the tapes and began probing not the substance of Ramon's confession but whether anticrime officers in the Three-Four precinct, in collaboration with detectives, had deliberately arrested Ramon Rodriguez in order to help Paddy Regan.

In the course of investigating that question, federal prosecutors—in front of a new grand jury—interrogated every anticrime officer and every member of the Three-Four detective squad. Under questioning by AUSA Deborah Landis, PO Johnny Moynihan, mindful of Paddy Regan's experience, invoked the Fifth Amendment several times. Detectives also discovered that federal authorities had placed "dumps" on the home phones of all the detectives in the squad.

Police officers in every corner of the city saw direct parallels between Regan's case and the Occhipinti case. They wondered what strange kind of order and justice federal prosecutors thought they were pursuing. Were the prosecutors just engaged in "big game hunting," nailing a cop as a trophy to display nerve and prowess to peers? Of course, this might be reason enough. But Regan's case lacked all sense of proportion, let alone of equity.

Garry Dugan and Mark Tebbens, for instance, could not understand why, despite their constant urging, prosecutors showed no interest whatsoever in going after Roberto Lazar (a pseudonym), the former cop in the Four-O precinct who not only used to pass along to the Red Top crew the names of witnesses to crimes, obviously placing the witnesses in grave jeopardy, but who, while still a cop, used to shake down the Beekman Avenue dealers for their guns, drugs, and cash. Why, the detectives wondered, is Roberto Lazar still out there selling drugs on the corner of Watson and Manor, the former stomping grounds of his old boyhood pal Frankie Cuevas, while Paddy Regan is heading to prison? Why, other cops wondered, should Paddy Regan be prosecuted for perjury when Juana Madera and Ana Rodriguez, whose sworn false accusations against PO Michael O'Keefe plunged the entire city into chaos, got a free walk?

Some of the top brass of the NYPD were, it was said, outraged by the federal prosecutors' actions. Sergeant Patrick Duffy was allowed to resign from the force with a three-quarters pension (three quarters of his annual salary), the white unicorn of every cop's dreams, despite the 1994 administrative charges still pending against him for the arrests at 209 Dyckman Street on September 17, 1992. Then, just before Thanksgiving 1996, the department gave gold shields to Regan's Local Motion partners, Johnny Moynihan, Matteo Brattesani, and Tommy McPartland. But key figures at the United States Attorney's office were enraged when they heard about the promotions of their office's long-pursued quarries. With

Regan already convicted and Duffy now out of reach, they insisted that the NYPD press the administrative charges emerging out of the 209 Dyckman Street case against Moynihan. In early January 1997 the department buckled. It amended Moynihan's charges to include specifications of perjury and ordered him to face departmental trial on March 31, later changed to the summer of 1997. Moynihan was told privately that the department wanted his job.

To many officers, the Regan case, indeed the entire Local Motion affair, symbolized a much larger problem: What kind of leaders are they that send officers into mortal danger, ask them to clean up ugly uptown messes created or perpetuated by those of far higher social station, and then pillory them, or allow them to be pilloried, when they come out of the wreckage with dirty hands? What kind of cultural ambivalence, indeed profound self-doubt, so afflicts our social order that educated and well-placed elites need to demonstrate their moral probity to the world by paying heed to the claims and assertions of the worst elements of our society and their advocates?

On March 19, 1996, Judge Chin's federal district courtroom at 500 Pearl Street was jammed with police officers from precincts all across the city who had come downtown to be with Paddy Regan on his day of sentencing. Indeed, so many officers, some in uniform, some in plainclothes, crowded into Judge Chin's courtroom that he ordered all who could not sit down to stand outside in the corridor. As they waited for the proceedings to begin, crowded into the yellow oak pews, the officers were silent and somber; the federal prosecutors chattered amiably at the government's table.

When the courtroom came to order, and the court clerk had arraigned Patrick Regan on two counts of perjury, the prosecutors urged the judge to follow federal sentencing guidelines and to impose the maximum sentence of a year and a half to two years in federal prison. Regan's lawyer, David Greenfield, reminded the court that the extraordinarily narrow scope of the government's case had not only prevented Regan from confronting his original accusers but had kept the jury completely in the dark about Local Motion's documented seizure of hundreds of guns from uptown streets; legal casuistry is a world unto itself, but words cannot keep a city safe. Then Regan spoke briefly, expressing his confidence that a higher court would vindicate him.

Once all the statements were finished, Judge Chin addressed the courtroom. He acknowledged the difficult work of police officers, but said that their work was not the issue before his court. He said that Regan's perjury had resulted in a "substantial interference with the administration of justice," a finding that could enhance Regan's sentence. Nevertheless, he announced his intention to depart from the federal guidelines. He then told Patrick Regan to stand for sentencing. And every police officer in the room stood up, as one man, to face the bench.

Paddy Regan was ordered to federal prison for a year and a day. His appeal to the U.S. Court of Appeals, Second Circuit, was rejected, and his petition to remain free until the U.S. Supreme Court finally ruled on his case was denied. On April 18, 1997, he entered federal prison in Manchester, Kentucky, to begin serving his time.

epilogue

On March 18, 1992, at the height of the drug war between Lenny Sepulveda and Frankie Cuevas, PO Patrick Regan was assigned to shepherd Sergeant Kevin McMahon on night tour. McMahon, who was substituting for Local Motion's regular sergeant, Patrick Duffy, was on his last tour of duty in the Three-Four before taking a promotion to lieutenant in the Bronx's sleepy Five-O precinct. Well aware of Local Motion's aggressive reputation, McMahon stressed to Regan that, above all else, he wanted to take it easy that night. The officers bought tea and coffee and, with Regan sitting in the driver's seat, parked their unmarked police car in the left-hand lane of Haven Avenue at West 177th Street, facing the George Washington Bridge and New Jersey beyond it.

The officers were just settling in to enjoy their drinks when, at about 1740 hours, a four-door blue and gray 1988 Chrysler with three men in it suddenly drove past, heading southbound on one-way Haven Avenue. To Regan, the car looked suspicious, and so did its occupants. He decided to follow the Chrysler, and tailed it slowly for two blocks. The Chrysler double-parked at Haven and West 175th Street. While the driver stayed in the car, a dark-skinned Dominican man of medium height stepped out of the back seat. Out of the front passenger seat emerged a husky, dark-skinned Dominican man about six feet tall, 240 pounds, with a moonlike face and broad, flat features. With an almost instinctive judgment forged over years of hard experience—so uncannily accurate that it had earned him the reputation of being able to "smell a gun"—Regan made this man for being armed.

Regan told the sergeant to get rid of his coffee; he was going to make a gun arrest on the street. With his own weapon drawn and Sergeant McMahon behind him, Regan left his vehicle and approached the two men outside the Chrysler. Regan ordered both men to raise their hands. He frisked the larger man and found a semiautomatic 9-millimeter Smith and Wesson in his waistband, discovered later to have its serial number defaced. Regan took the gun, put the man face down on the ground, and told the sergeant to cover him with gun to head. Suddenly, the smaller man bolted, running south on Haven Avenue toward Fort Washington; Regan holstered his weapon and gave chase.

Then he heard rubber screaming as the Chrysler also took off down Haven. Regan raced back to the police car, leapt into the driver's seat, and "put it over" for backup for the sergeant, all the while ripping down the street after the Chrysler, which had stopped briefly to pick up the culprit who had fled on foot. The fleeing vehicle turned left on West 172nd Street and then right on Fort Washington, with Regan close behind. As he made the right turn, Regan nearly smashed into a bus, swerved, and hit the brakes, sending his car careening into the other lane. Both cars flew down Fort Washington to West 165th Street, where they whipped around another bus. As the Chrysler tried to make the sharp turn at West 165th Street and Fort Washington to go over to Riverside Drive, it crashed into another car at the corner but still managed to make the turn. Regan stayed with the fleeing car, though by now he was driving from the passenger's seat. As the Chrysler cut right on Riverside Drive, Regan saw a gun being thrown out of the window; the weapon turned out to be a fully loaded .45-caliber Smith and Wesson revolver.

The Chrysler sped northbound on Riverside Drive toward the Henry Hudson Parkway, reaching 130 miles per hour with Regan right behind. By this time, police cars were out all over the precinct, but the Chrysler slipped through the net. It raced off the Henry Hudson Parkway at the Dyckman Street exit at high speed, still followed closely by Regan, tearing down the exit route through Inwood Plaza, then suddenly cutting right, back to Thayer Street. The Chrysler then ripped east on Thayer against one-way westbound traffic, scattering startled drivers left and right. But Regan couldn't follow in his vehicle without risking a serious accident; he jumped out of his car, gun in one hand, radio in the other, and started running east on Thayer.

At the intersection of Thayer Street and Sherman Avenue, Regan found the culprits' car abandoned, doors wide open, a major traffic jam in the making. Regan radioed for help and, after recovering his own vehicle, went back to scene, to Haven Avenue and West 175th Street. Backup arrived just as Regan did. There, Sergeant McMahon, who had one last tale about the wild and woolly Three-Four to tell his friends and family, was still holding the first culprit prone on the ground at gunpoint.

Regan placed the man under arrest and took him to the Three-Four station house. The man was calm and collected; Regan noticed that the whites of his eyes were often visible. When he was put briefly into the tiny holding cell in the detectives' squad room, he promptly dozed off into what policemen everywhere call the sleep of the guilty.

Later that night, when Regan took him downtown for booking, the man evinced complete indifference to his situation throughout the grueling 14-hour process. He identified himself as Francisco Medina. There were no prior arrests listed under that name. Although the assistant district attorney on duty that morning asked the court for $3,000 bail, Paddy Regan's collar was released on his own recognizance.

At 0800 hours on the morning of March 19th, Freddy Krueger walked out of 100 Centre Street a free man.

cast of characters

New York City Police Department

UNIFORMED AND ANTICRIME OFFICERS

PO Joseph Barbato, 34th precinct
PO Tommy Barnett, 34th precinct
PO Artie Barragan, 34th precinct
PO Matteo Brattesani, 34th precinct
PO Michael Buczek, 34th precinct
PO Tim Burke, 40th precinct
PO Michael Callahan, 34th precinct
PO Kermit Collins, 34th precinct
Sgt. Patrick Duffy, 34th precinct
PO Elizabeth Gesualdo, 40th precinct
PO Harold Hernandez, 34th precinct
PO Chris Hoban, Manhattan North Narcotics
PO Roberto Lazar [pseudonym], 40th precinct
PO Timothy Leary, 40th precinct
Sgt. Kevin McMahon, 34th precinct
PO Tommy McPartland, 34th precinct
PO Johnny Moynihan, 34th precinct
PO Michael O'Keefe, 34th precinct
Lt. Roger Parrino, 34th precinct
PO Paddy Regan, 34th precinct
PO Joe Romano, 34th precinct
Chief David Scott, Chief of Patrol
PO Mark Traumer, 28th precinct
PO Vasquez, 34th precinct

DETECTIVES

Bobby Addolorato, 40th squad
Ray Aguilar, HIDTA
Louie Bauza, 34th squad; later sergeant in 30th squad
Eddie Benitez, HIDTA
Maria Bertini, MNHS
Captain Salvador Blando
John Bourges, 34th squad
Lieutenant Mike Bramble, 40th squad
Kevin Bryant, HIDTA
Thomas Burke, New York City Transit Police
Miguel Calderon, 40th squad
Jerry Dimuro, 30th squad
Edwin Driscoll, JALTF
Garry Dugan, MNHS; later Senior Rackets Investigator,
    HIU, DANY
Gennaro Giorgio, 34th squad
Ruben Gonzalez, 40th squad
Sam Gribben, 34th squad
Richard Gwillym, 60th squad
John Hickey, MNHS
Ron Hoering, Bronx Homicide Task Force
Tony Imperato, 34th squad
Mike Lopuzzo, 40th squad
Jeremiah Lyons, New York City Transit Police
Tommy McCabe, MNHS
Sergeant Thomas McGuigan, IAB, NYPD
Greg Modica, Manhattan Robbery squad
Joe Montuori, 34th squad
Angel Morales, 34th squad
Pete Moro, 34th squad
Austin Francis "Tim" Muldoon III, 34th squad
Al Nieves, HIDTA
Pete Odiot, 40th squad
Cesar Ortiz, HIDTA
Gil Ortiz, 34th squad
Annie Peters, 34th squad
Joel Potter, MNHS
Hank Primus, 34th squad
Marta Rosario, 34th squad

John Saccia, HIDTA
George Slater, Major Case Squad
James Slattery, 40th squad
Bobby Small, 34th squad
Mark Tebbens, 40th squad, Bronx DA squad, Major Case squad
    [HIU, DANY]
Clarence Williams, 40th squad

District Attorneys and Federal Prosecutors

Thomas Arena, AUSA, Southern District, NY
Walter Arsenault, Chief, HIU, DANY
David Blaxill, ADA, Brooklyn DA's Office
Dan Brownell, ADA, HIU, DANY
Fernando Camacho, ADA, HIU, DANY
Greg Carro, ADA, HIU, DANY
Richard Chin, ADA, DANY
Matthew Fishbein, AUSA, Southern District, NY
Paul Gardephe, AUSA, Southern District, NY
Lori Grifa, ADA, Brooklyn DA's Office
Don Hill, ADA, Bronx DA's Office
Eric Hirsch, ADA, Bronx DA's Office
Charles J. Hynes, DA, Kings County
Jeh Johnson, AUSA, Southern District, NY
Robert J. Johnson, DA, Bronx County
Deborah Landis, AUSA, Southern District, NY
Kelly Moore, AUSA, Eastern District, NY
Robert M. Morgenthau, DA, New York County
Bruce Ohr, AUSA, Southern District, NY
Chauncey Parker, AUSA, Southern District, NY
Dan M. Rather, ADA, HIU; later Chief of Firearms
    Trafficking Unit, DANY
Nancy Ryan, Chief, Trial Division, DANY
Robert H. Silbering, Special Narcotics Prosecutor, Manhattan
Paul Weinstein, AUSA, Eastern District, NY

Defense Attorneys

Robert Beecher
Robert Dunn

Steven Frankel
Elliot Fuld
David Goldstein
David Greenfield
Steven Kaiser
Robert Katz
Michael Nedick
Howard Ripps
Robert Rosenberg
Sol Schwartzberg
Robert Soloway
David Tougher
Donald Tucker
Valerie Van Leer-Greenberg
Barry Weinstein
Richard Wojszwillo

Other Law Enforcement

General Julio César Ventura Bayonet, Dirección Nacional
    de Control de Drogas, DR
Mary Ellen Beekman, FBI
Harold Bickmore, FBI
Julian Blanco, ATF
William Bratton, Police Commissioner, New York
Lee Patrick Brown, Police Commissioner, New York
Jamie Cedeno, FBI
Efrain de Jesus, DEA, US Embassy, DR
Jose Flores, Senior Rackets Investigator, HIU, DANY
Angel Garcia, Senior Rackets Investigator, HIU, DANY
Laurie Horne, ATF
Raymond W. Kelly, Police Commissioner, New York
Patrick Lafferty, HIU, DANY
Joseph LoBue, US Marshal
Trooper Brian Long, Totowa Barracks, New Jersey State Police
Kevin O'Brien, DEA, US Embassy, DR
Joseph Occhipinti, Immigration and Naturalization Service
Sergeant Francisco Ortíz, Dirección Nacional de Control
    de Drogas, DR
Terry Quinn, Senior Rackets Investigator, HIU, DANY

Howard Safir, Police Commissioner, New York
Bobby Tarwacki, Senior Rackets Investigator, HIU, DANY

Judges and Court Personnel

Hillel Bodek, consultant to New York State Supreme Court,
    Manhattan
Alex Calabrese, Court Attorney, Part 88, New York State Supreme
    Court, Manhattan
Judge Denny Chin, Federal District Court, Manhattan
Rocco DeSantis, Clerk, Part 88, New York State Supreme Court,
    Manhattan
Judge Laura Safer Espinosa, New York Criminal Court
Justice Ira Globerman, New York State Supreme Court, Bronx
Judge Sterling Johnson, Jr., Federal District Court, Brooklyn
Teresa Matushaj, Court Attorney, Part 88, New York State
    Supreme Court, Manhattan
Judge Constance Baker Motley, Federal District Court, Manhattan
Judge Shira A. Scheindlin, Federal District Court, Manhattan
Justice Leslie Crocker Snyder, New York State Supreme Court,
    Manhattan
Judge Angelo Tona, Brooklyn Criminal Court

Politicians and Community Activists

Joaquín Balaguer, President, Dominican Republic
William Barr, Acting US Attorney General
John Beckman, spokesman for Mayor Dinkins
George Bush, President of the United States
Altagracia Crucey, member of the Federation of Dominican
    Merchants and Industrialists
Jose Cuevas, journalist
Mario Cuomo, Governor, State of New York
Dennis deLeon, Human Rights Commissioner, New York City
David Dinkins, Mayor, New York City
Manuel de Dios Unanue, journalist
Herman "Denny" Farrell, State Assemblyman
Leonel Fernández Reyna, President, DR
Rudolph Giuliani, Mayor, New York City

Ray Hagemann, Investigator, Staten Island Borough President's
   Office
Edward Koch, Mayor, New York City
Franz Leichter, State Senator
Jose Liberato, member of the Federation of Dominican Merchants
   and Industrialists
Rhadames Liberato, member of the Federation of Dominican
   Merchants and Industrialists
Leonides Liberator, member of the Federation of Dominican
   Merchants and Industrialists
Guillermo Linares, City Councilman
Ruth Messinger, Manhattan Borough President
Stanley Michels, City Councilman
Guy Molinari, Staten Island Borough President
Congresswoman Susan Molinari, (R) New York
Milton Mollen, former judge, head of the Mollen Commission
Jose Prado, member of the Federation of Dominican Merchants and
   Industrialists
Congressman Charles Rangel, (D) New York
Hector Rodriguez, undercover investigator
Luis Rodriguez, undercover investigator
The Reverend Al Sharpton, community activist
Michael Stanton, Press Attaché, US Embassy, DR
Percy Sutton, former Manhattan Borough President
Jose Elias Taveras, member of the Federation of Dominican
   Merchants and Industrialists
Congressman James Traficant, Jr., (R) Ohio

Victims

Maximo Almodovar, killed, assailants unknown
Rogelio Emilio Perez Almodovar aka **Chocolate**, killed by police
   and military officers in Dominican Republic
Oscar Alvarez, killed in The Rooftop Murder
Rodney Baines aka **G**, assaulted in The Double
Edwin Battista aka **Fresh**, wounded in killing of Andres Carela
Victor Battista aka **Paelo**, killed by Freddy Krueger
Orlando Berrios aka **Tito**, killed in The Double
Lourdes Bonilla aka **Lulu**, shot by Nelson; later by Fat Danny
Renee Brown aka **Nee-Nee**, assaulted by Stanley
Janice Bruington, wounded in The Quad

PO Michael Buczek, killed by Daniel Mirambeaux
Gilbert Campusano, assaulted, later killed by Cuevas crew
Andres Carela aka **Smiley**, killed by Freddy Krueger and Platano
David Cargill, killed by Lenny Sepulveda
Cynthia Casado, killed in The Quad
Miguel Castillo aka **Miguelito**, killed by Luis Rivera
Esteban Clemente aka **English**, killed by Boogie Frazier
Iwana Collins, shot and wounded in drug robbery
Marilyn Colon, killed by Dominican Chino on Vyse Avenue
Angel Cruz aka **Tito**, pistol-whipped by Pasqualito and Frankie
    Robles
Elvis Cruz, drug dealer killed during robbery in 34th precinct
Michael Cruz, shot in the face by Pasqualito and Lenny
Leonida Cuella, killed by Ralphie Suarez
Franklin Cuevas aka **Fat Frankie**, killed by Pasqualito
Jose Cuevas, journalist bystander killed in botched drug robbery
Manuel de Dios Unanue, journalist killed by Colombian drug cartel
Manuel de la Rosa aka **Vive Bien**, wounded in assault by Elia
Wilfredo de los Angeles aka **Platano**, wounded in assault
Rafael Delvalle, killed by Red Top crew; Lenny prime suspect
John Doe, killed in The Quad
Delasanto Ferreria aka **Chepe**, killed in Newburgh by Anibal
    Rivera Hernandez
Juan Francisco aka **Papito**, killed in The Brighton Beach Murder
Guy Gaines, former Correction officer, killed on Beekman;
    Pasqualito acquitted at trial
Jose Garcia aka **Kiko**, killed by PO Michael O'Keefe
Manny Garcia, paralyzed in assault
Nelson Garcia aka **Collita**, killed by Freddy Krueger
Ronnie Gedders, killed by Raul Vargas
Frankie Gonzalez, shot by unknown assailant
Anthony Green aka **Amp**, killed in The Quad
Manny Guerrero, assaulted in the Fat Frankie Homicide
Miguel Guzman, assaulted by Red Top crew; Lenny prime suspect
Clifford Halsey, assaulted in The Double
Ramon Jimenez, slashed in The Witness Slashing
Randall Johnson aka **Fats**, killed by Eric Murell
Kevin Kryzeminski, friend assaulted with David Cargill
Quentin Lee, shot by Stanley at party
Christopher Livingston aka **Dred**, killed by Freddy Krueger and
    Pasqualito

Anthony Lopez, assaulted in The Double
Ivan Lugo, killed by Freddy Krueger
Darlene Pearce McPherson, assaulted by Rob Base
Edgar Maldonado aka **Eddie**, killed in St. Mary's Park Stabbing
Elvis Matos, killed by Rob Base in The Telephone Murder
Meow Meow, shot by Bogototo
Taj Meyers, robber killed in 34th precinct during drug robbery
Linda Miner, assaulted in Las Vegas Nightclub
Mono [last name unknown], assaulted by Victor
Danny Montilla aka **Madonna**, killed in 34th precinct
Michael Mobley, shot and paralyzed by Rasheed Rice and Pachulo
Stanley Mobley, killed by Rasheed Rice and Pachulo
Martha Molina, pistol-whipped by Mickey Tex
Johnny Morillo, killed by Alex Sime
Kevin Nazario, killed in drive-by shooting at Manor and Watson
Quincy Norwood, killed by Red Top crew
Alberto Ortiz aka **Pescao,** killed by Freddy Krueger
Walter Ortiz, killed by Freddy Krueger
Giordano Pagan, killed in robbery in 30th precinct
Roberto Peralta, wounded in wild shootout in 34th precinct
Dagberto Pichardo, killed accidentally during July 1992 riots in
     34th precinct
Jenny Platero, assaulted on Beekman Avenue
Craig Prentice, killed by Freddy Krueger
George Quinones, killed; Cuevas crew prime suspects
Rafael Ramirez aka **Spec**, killed by Johnny Handsome
Jose Reyes, aka **El Feo**, shot and paralyzed by unknown assailant
Porfirio Reyes, killed by El Feo's crew
Johnny Richards, killed by Freddy Krueger
John Riguzzi, friend assaulted with David Cargill
Fat Danny Rincon, assaulted by Smiley
Corky Rios, assaulted by Pasqualito
Eduardo Rivera, assaulted by Fat Danny
Gilberto Rivera aka **Puto**, killed in battle with Macombs Road crew
Leideza Rivera, killed on Jerome Avenue by Platano
Luis Rivera aka **Chico**, killed in The Double
Rey Alejandro Rivera, killed by Nester Salaam
Jose Alberto Rodriguez aka **El Gordo**, killed in The Halloween
     Murder
Rafael Rodriguez, assaulted in Las Vegas Nightclub by Platano
Lexington Rojas aka **Mask**, killed; Cuevas crew prime suspects

Leonardo Carpio Rosario aka **Mingolo**, killed by Freddy Krueger
Carlos Rodriguez Santana, killed by El Feo's crew
James Singleton, assaulted by Stanley and Plutano, later by Linwood
John Soldi, killed in drive-by shooting at Manor and Watson
Pedro Sotomayor, killed by Red Top crew; Lenny prime suspect
Pedro Stevens, shot by Victor
Glen Stretching, beaten in prison by Fat Danny and others
Angel Suarez, killed by Freddy Krueger
Daniel Suarez aka **Francisco**, killed by Leonida Cuella
Jovanny Suarez, killed by unknown assailants
Kennedy Earl Thomas, killed on Beekman Avenue
Harold Thornton aka **Hippy**, killed by Kasheem Guiden
James Tolson, killed by Freddy Krueger
Michael Turner, shot by Victor
Carlos Ventura, killed by Dominican Chino on Vyse Avenue
Manuel Vera, killed in The Quad
Anthony Villerbe, killed by Nelson and Stanley
Norman Wade, killed by Nester Salaam
Charles Walker, robbed and killed on Cypress Avenue by Cory Jackson
Watusi [last name unknown], killed by Platano
Nathan Wilder, shot and blinded by Stanley
Zia [pseudonym], shot and paralyzed in drug robbery

The Cargill Murder

D. Innis Cargill
David Cargill
Kevin Kryzeminski
Anne Love (Mrs. Cargill)
John Riguzzi
[The names of all other civilians connected to the Cargill case are pseudonyms.]

The Red Top Crew [*trial defendants]

Juan Abarca aka **Charlie**
Oscar Alvarez
Floretta Baker aka **Baldie**
Loretta Baker aka **Winkie**

Brenda Blair
Frank Blair
Jude Ann Bohan
Nicholas Bohan
Stephen Bohan
William Caceras
Felipe Capellan aka **Max**
Miguel Castillo aka **Miguelito** (also with El Feo's crew)
Esteban Clemente aka **English**
Allen Checo
Linwood Collins aka **Cool Water***
Manuel Crespo aka **Manny**
Angel Cruz aka **Tito**
Iris Cruz aka **Fat Iris**
Miguel Cruz aka **Michael**
Wilfredo de los Angeles aka **Platano** or **Darkman** or **Paul Santiago***
Dominican Mickey Mouse, real name unknown
Rafael Fernandez aka **Kiko**
Daniel Gonzalez aka **Shorty***
Juan Gonzalez aka **Lace**
Miguel Gonzalez aka **Mickey Tex**
Russell Harris aka **Renny***
Jose Llaca aka **Pasqualito***
Robert Lopez aka **Rob Base**
Ramon Madrigal aka **Battata**
Sarap Majid
Louise McBride aka **Smokie**
Darlene Pearce McPherson
Enrique Mejias aka **Ricky**
Ulysses Mena aka **Dominican Chino**
Victor Mercedes*
Martha Molina aka **Martita**
Mono [last name unknown]
Jimmy Montalvo aka **Heavy D**
Myra [last name unknown]
Marilyn Perez aka **Smiley**
Nyxida Perez aka **Nikki**
Rafael Perez aka **Tezo** or **Flaco***
David Polanco aka **Dominican David**
George Quinones
Marcos Reyes aka **Rocky**

Daniel Rincon aka **Fat Danny***
Israel Rios aka **Junior**
Jose Rios aka **Corky**
Francisco Robles aka **Frankie**
Siro Rodriguez aka **Zero**
Teddy Rodriguez
Lexington Rojas aka **Mask**
Carmen Saez
Hector Saez
Jasmine Saez
Lisette Saez
Myra Saez
Nester Salaam aka **Funi**
Edd Sanchez aka **Eddie OD**
Elizabeth Santiago aka **Yvette**
George Santiago aka **Seller**
George Santos aka **Scarface Chino**
Freddy Sendra
Jose Sepulveda
Lenny Sepulveda aka **Lenny Rodriguez**
Nelson Sepulveda aka **Wack**
Robert Sepulveda
Shrimpo [last name unknown]
Glen Stretching
Lamar Taylor aka **L**
Stanley Tukes aka **Trigger*** or **Stanley Black**
Luis Villanueva aka **Little Louie**

Beekman/Cypress Avenues Area Locals

Edwin Agusto, half-brother to Michael Cruz
Mireya Betancourt, operator of informal social club at 354 Cypress
Brenda Blair, resident of 352 Beekman
Chris Collins, bank robber
Alejandrina Cruz aka **Ita**, Elizabeth Morales's daughter
Elizabeth Cruz, Elizabeth Morales's daughter
"Little Iris" Cruz, Elizabeth Morales's daughter
Marion Frazier aka **Boogie**, Louise McBride's son, sometime robber
Cory Jackson, robber
Ramon Jimenez, sometime robber
Yolanda Jordan, resident of 352 Beekman

Quentin Lee

Edgar Maldonado aka **White Boy**, son-in-law to Elizabeth Morales

Jesus Maysonnet, Cypress Avenue resident caught up in The Double

Mono [last name unknown], sometime pitcher

Joey Morales, Elizabeth Morales's son

Elizabeth Morales-Cruz

Angel Quinones aka **Pachulo**, sometime robber

Rhasta [last name unknown]

Rasheed Rice, robber and sometime hit man

Eduardo Rivera, sometime pitcher and errand boy for Fat Danny

Nester Salaam aka **Funi**, sometime robber (also with Red Top crew)

Satan [last name unknown], brother of Ulysses Mena

Stacey Scroggins, wife of Pasqualito

Shrimpo [last name unknown], sometime pitcher, friend of Oscar Alvarez

James Singleton, sometime robber

Clifford Skinner

Smooch, Louise McBride's son, sometime robber

Zia [pseudonym], informant who led police to Pasqualito

Franklin Cuevas's Crew

Edwin Battista aka **Fresh**

Emilio Bera aka **Nicholas**

Gilbert Campusano

Andres Carela aka **Smiley**

Jose Castillo aka **Cubita** or **Little Cuba**

Franklin Cuevas aka **Fat Frankie** or **Gus**

Miguel Cuevas

Francisco [last name unknown]

Manny Garcia

Frankie Gonzalez

Manny Guerrero

Benjy Herrera

Edward Herrera

Jackson [last name unknown]

Jose [last name unknown]

Jose Menor aka **Papo**

Danny Montilla aka **Bumblebee** or **Madonna**

Roberto Peralta

Rafael [last name unknown]
Jose Vizcaino aka **Big Cuba**

El Feo's Crew

Maximo Almodovar
Rogelio Emilio Perez Almodovar aka **Chocolate**
Miguel Castillo aka **Miguelito** or **Heater** or **Dice**
Manuel de la Rosa aka **Vive Bien**
Alexis Garcia aka **Mono**
Henry Dia Guzman
Francisco Medina aka **Freddy Krueger** or **Miguel Perez**
Hippolito Polanco
Jose Reyes aka **El Feo** or **Moncheche**
Gilberto Rivera aka **Puto**
James Tolson
Raul Vargas aka **Rugs**

Assorted Drug-Trade Players

MANHATTAN

Victor Battista aka **Paelo**
Bogototo [real name unknown]
Charro [pseudonym], former worker for Yayo, sometime informant
Cholene [real name unknown]
Dominican King
Elia [last name unknown], hit man
Hector Feliz, marijuana dealer
Jose Garcia aka **Kiko** or **Jose Gonzalez** or **Jose Luis Hidalgo**
Kasheem Guiden aka **K**
Benjy Herrera
Jacinto [last name unknown]
Joaquin [last name unknown], hit man
Joe [last name unknown], marijuana dealer
Randall Johnson aka **Fats**
Juana Madera
Martinez Brothers, heads of the Gerry Curls gang
Jose Roberto Mejia-Nunez aka **Capo**
Meow Meow [last name unknown], Carlito Peña's brother, getaway
    driver

Eric Murell aka **E**
Otis [last name unknown]
Lenny Ovalles aka **RT**
Papito [last name unknown], drug supplier to Frankie Cuevas
Ruben Perez, marijuana dealer, Lenny's associate and partner
Juan Carlos Peña aka Carlito, associate of Ruben Perez
Santiago Antonio Ysrael Polanco-Polanco aka **Chi Chi**
Santiago Luis Polanco-Rodriguez aka **Yayo**
Porfirio Reyes
Johnny Richards
Ana Rodriguez
Jose Rodriguez, head of drug operation at 505 West 162nd Street
Julio Cesar Romero aka **Ace**
Angel Santana aka **Morenito**
Taco [pseudonym], sometime informant
Freddy Then
Harold Thornton aka **Hippy**
Ramon Tijada, former worker for Yayo
Francisco Ulerio

BRONX

Juan Astwood aka **Johnny Handsome**
Rodney Baines aka **G**
Victor Battista aka **Paelo**
Orlando Berrios aka Tito
George Calderon
Iwana Collins
Benjamin Green aka **Chubby,** Amp Green's brother, Yellow Top
  crack
Clifford Halsey, driver
Gerard Heard, owner, Yellow Top crack
Christopher Livingston aka **Dred**, leader of Macombs crew
Anthony Lopez
Manuel Lugo aka **Supra,** employee of Lenny on Vyse Avenue
Maximo [last name unknown], husband of Fat Iris Cruz
Edwin Ortiz
Lenny Ovalles aka **RT**
Eladio Padilla aka **Caco**
Jose Padilla aka **Chi Chi,** pitcher for Yellow Top crack

Craig Prentice, Macombs crew
Luis Rivera aka **Chico**
Wilfredo Roman, employee of Supra on Vyse Avenue
Carlos Ventura, drug dealer on Vyse Avenue
X-Man [real name unknown], hit man

BROOKLYN

Juan Francisco aka **Papito**
Raymond Polanco, gun dealer
Pirri Rodriguez, witness to The Brighton Beach Murder
Neil Valcarcel, witness to The Brighton Beach Murder
Cynthia Williams, witness to The Brighton Beach Murder

Robber Crews

MIRAMBEAUX CREW

Pablo Almonte aka **Emilio**
Juan Jose Alvarez-Salazar aka **Rhadames Matos**
Jose Fernandez-Peralta aka **Freddy Parra**
Marcos Jaquez
Daniel Mirambeaux

GARAGE ROBBERY CREW

Elvis Aduan aka **Macho**
Miguel Amador [pseudonym]
Juan Flete aka **Baldie**
Juan Mejia aka **Terror** or **Suicide**
Anthony Miner aka **Lumpy**
Maximo Reyes
Anibal Rivera Hernandez aka **Al** or **Johnny**
Rafael Toribio aka **Clint**

Local Motion Cases

Jose Abreu
Jorge Almonte
Russell Castillo

Brigido Hidalgo
Anilda Martinez
Rafael Nieves
Carmen Nunez-Cartaya
Rafael Nunez
Jose Rodriguez, accuser of PO Patrick Regan
Ramon Rodriguez, sometime informant for DEA, Local Motion,
    and IAB

timeline

This timeline lists chronologically events described in detail in the text. Its sources include: investigative records and reports on individual crimes written by NYPD detectives in precincts throughout New York City and by HIU investigators; official HIU reports to DANY documenting the ongoing investigation of the Wild Cowboys; unsealed grand jury transcripts; and both state and federal trial proceedings. More details about sources may be found in the Notes on Sources.

February 1987	Lenny Sepulveda shoots a customer at 603–605 Beech Terrace in the 40th precinct. Nelson Sepulveda intervenes and is arrested after a chase.
Early 1988	The Red Top crew shoots up a rival drug gang at the Ten-Eighteen Club in Manhattan.
Early 1988	Contract drug homicide in the 25th precinct. Police suspect Platano, Benjy Herrera, and two others.
July 20, 1988	Guy Gaines is killed and an addict/witness is wounded. Jury acquits Pasqualito for the assaults in December 1988.
October 18, 1988	PO Michael Buczek is killed by Daniel Mirambeaux in the 34th precinct while interrupting a drug robbery.
Early 1989	INS Agent Joseph Occhipinti begins Project Bodega in 34th precinct.

May 11, 1989	Johnny Handsome kills Rafael Ramirez in the 40th precinct. Platano's name surfaces in the investigation.
May 31, 1989	Miguelito Castillo is murdered in the 44th precinct and his body is dumped in Eastchester, New York.
Late June 1989	Drive-by shooting at Marcy Place in the 44th precinct by Nelson and Lenny Sepulveda, Victor Mercedes, and Fat Danny Rincon (driver).
June 29, 1989	Daniel Mirambeaux dies while in the custody of the Dominican National Police.
September 3, 1989	Chico and Tito are murdered in **The Double** in the 40th precinct in retaliation for Miguelito's murder.
Mid-September 1989	Drive-by shooters at Marcy Place wound one victim in the leg.
September 28–29, 1989	Pasqualito and Victor are arrested for The Double and are held until August 13, 1991.
November 14, 1989	Frankie Cuevas is released from prison, where he was serving time for a 1981 burglary and assault.
Early 1990	Confrontation between Frankie Cuevas and El Feo in the 34th precinct.
Early 1990	Lenny and Frankie Cuevas shoot at two men in a car at the entrance to the West Side Highway in the 6th precinct.
February 5, 1990	Police arrest El Feo in a shooting incident at Marisco del Caribe Restaurant in the 46th precinct.
February 19, 1990	Norman Wade is killed in the 46th precinct. Police suspect Funi of doing shooting at Platano's request. Frankie Robles and Rob Base Lopez are in the car.

February 24, 1990	Nelson shoots Lulu—who is 17 weeks pregnant—for tapping vials and selling dummies in **The Lulu Shooting** in the 40th precinct.
February 27, 1990	Freddy Sendra is arrested for firing at police officers near The Hole in the 40th precinct in **Freddy's Shootout**.
March 1990	Nelson offers Freddy Sendra money to have Victor killed in prison in **The Contract on Victor**.
April 28, 1990	Fat Danny shoots at a customer on 141st Street in the 40th precinct and hits Lulu in the head by mistake.
July 14, 1990	Red Top pitcher Rafael Delvalle is murdered for stealing vials in the 40th precinct. Police suspect Lenny.
July 1990	Fat Danny abducts Eduardo Rivera in the 40th precinct and throws him off the 207th Street Bridge into the Harlem River.
Summer 1990	Smiley shoots Platano in the back of the head in the 43rd precinct.
October 21, 1990	Stanley Tukes and Platano cut James Singleton's face and threaten him with a gun in the 40th precinct.
October 23, 1990	Smiley shoots Fat Danny seven times in the 40th precinct.
October 25, 1990	Freddy Krueger kills James Tolson in the 34th precinct.
November 5, 1990	Giordano Pagan is murdered in a robbery in the 30th precinct. Five suspects arrested on the scene all name Clint as the organizer.
November 10, 1990	Platano shoots Smiley, wounding him slightly in the head, in the 43rd precinct.

December 21, 1990	Dominican Chino shoots Loretta Baker in **The Winkie Shooting** in the 40th precinct after Platano threatens her.
December 30, 1990	Dominican Chino, accompanied by Lenny, Lace, and Platano, kills Carlos Ventura and Marilyn Colon in the 48th precinct. Supra Lugo arranged the hit.
January 1, 1991	Stanley Tukes shoots Quentin Lee five times in New Year's Eve altercation in the 40th precinct.
January 10, 1991	Members of the Red Top crew abduct Quincy Norwood, who had robbed a Red Top pitcher, and set him on fire in St. Mary's Park in the 40th precinct, burning off half of his leg and killing him.
January 12, 1991	Anibal Rivera Hernandez kills Chepe in Newburgh, New York, and names Clint as the organizer.
January 18, 1991	Stanley Tukes shoots Nathan Wilder seven times, blinding him, in the 40th precinct.
February 18, 1991	Stanley Tukes throws Renee Brown off the terrace of 370 Cypress Avenue in the 40th precinct, seriously injuring her.
March 3, 1991	Platano, with Lenny Ovalles aka RT, shoots and kills 13-year-old Leideza Rivera by mistake in the 46th precinct.
March 4, 1991	An unknown assailant drops a metal barbell weight off the roof of 348 Beekman in the 40th precinct, striking deaf-mute crack-addict Jenny Platero in the head and leaving her in a vegetative state.
March 6, 1991	INS Agent Joseph Occhipinti is indicted in federal court for violating the civil rights of bodega owners in Washington Heights.

March 10, 1991	Freddy Krueger kills Johnny Richards in the 34th precinct after Richards shoots El Feo.
April 10, 1991	Raul Vargas, accompanied by Freddy Krueger and El Feo, who points out the victim, kills Ronnie Gedders in the 49th precinct.
April 27, 1991	Pedro Sotomayor is killed in the 40th precinct for selling drugs on Courtland Avenue. Police suspect Lenny of the shooting.
May 12, 1991	Linwood Collins kills Oscar Alvarez in **The Rooftop Murder** in the 40th precinct.
May 19, 1991	Lenny, with Raymond Polanco driving, kills David Cargill on the West Side Highway in the 30th precinct in **The Cargill Murder**.
May 22–June 28, 1991	Joseph Occhipinti is tried and convicted in federal court for civil rights violations of bodega owners in Washington Heights.
June 2, 1991	Freddy Krueger kills Pescao in the 34th precinct.
June 4, 1991	Smiley is killed in the 43rd precinct; Fresh is critically wounded. Police suspect Freddy Krueger and Platano, with Meow Meow driving.
July 20, 1991	Freddy Krueger kills Ivan Lugo at Platano's request in the 40th precinct, with Meow Meow driving.
August 13, 1991	Pasqualito and Victor are released from jail.
August 26, 1991	Rafael Rodriguez is shot and paralyzed at Las Vegas Nightclub in the 34th precinct. Police suspect Platano of the shooting, under contract.

Summer 1991	Watusi is killed in the 43rd precinct. Police suspect Platano, on a contract from Frankie Cuevas.
Summer 1991	Platano shoots at two men after a road dispute in the 52nd precinct.
September 13, 1991	Miguel Guzman is shot in the 40th precinct after a quarrel. Police suspect Lenny of the assault.
September 14, 1991	Wild melee in the 40th precinct, **The Great Calderon Shootout**, between George Calderon's outfit and the Red Top crew.
September 23, 1991	El Feo goes to prison at Cape Vincent near Canada to serve eight months for the February 5, 1990, shooting in Marisco del Caribe Restaurant.
October 7, 1991	Lenny goes to prison in Ogdensburg, New York, to serve eight months for a gun possession charge.
October 18, 1991	Victor, accompanied by Fat Danny, shoots at Michael Turner and his cousin Carolyn in the 40th precinct. Though wounded in his right leg, Turner refuses to press charges against Victor.
October 31, 1991	Tezo, accompanied by Platano, kills El Gordo in **The Halloween Murder** in the 34th precinct, under contract from Ruben Perez.
November 7, 1991	Edgar Maldonado is butchered in **The St. Mary's Park Stabbing** in the 40th precinct. Police suspect Platano, Stanley Tukes, and one other of the crime.
November 8, 1991	Victor is arrested on a gun warrant for shooting Pedro Stevens on Cypress Avenue in the 40th precinct.

December 5, 1991	Cory Jackson murders Charles Walker in the 40th precinct during robbery.
December 16, 1991	Platano, Stanley Tukes, Fat Danny, Renny Harris, and Shorty, along with several other unknown shooters, kill Manuel Vera, Cynthia Casado, Anthony Green, and John Doe, and wound Janice Bruington, in **The Quad** in the 40th precinct.
December 20, 1991	Freddy Krueger, accompanied by Chocolate, kills Walter Ortiz in the 46th precinct.
January 3, 1992	Nelson and Stanley Tukes kill Anthony Villerbe in the 40th precinct.
January 11, 1992	Police suspect Carlito of shooting up the Las Vegas Nightclub in the 34th precinct and wounding Linda Miner after a dispute with the owners.
January 17, 1992	Stanley Tukes is arrested for The Quad.
January 20, 1992	Nelson Garcia is murdered in the 46th precinct. Freddy Krueger is a co-conspirator and a passenger in the getaway car.
January 29–30, 1992	Platano is arrested on drug and weapon possession charges in New Jersey. He gives a statement about the Cargill murder and is released on bail.
January 30, 1992	Shorty is arrested for The Quad.
February 1, 1992	Madonna is found dead in the 34th precinct. Frankie Cuevas is suspected of ordering the murder.
February 7, 1992	Linwood Collins holds a gun to James Singleton's head and threatens to kill him if he testifies against Stanley Tukes.
February 17, 1992	Linwood Collins is arrested for witness tampering.

February 24, 1992	Porfirio Reyes is killed in the 34th precinct. Freddy Krueger is a co-conspirator and in the getaway car.
March 12, 1992	Vive Bien is shot five times in the 34th precinct. Police suspect Elia, subcontracted by Platano, of the assault. Elia disappears.
March 12, 1992	Freddy Krueger, accompanied by Platano, kills Paelo in the 34th precinct.
March 1992	Rob Base, wearing heavy military boots, punches and kicks Darlene Pearce McPherson, a Red Top pitcher short on the *cuenta*, in **Darlene's Beatdown**.
March 16, 1992	Freddy Krueger, possibly with Pasqualito, shoots Frankie Cuevas and Manny Garcia in the 34th precinct.
March 16, 1992	Kennedy Earl Thomas is killed in the 40th precinct, circumstances unclear. Boogie tried but jury deadlocks.
March 17, 1992	Platano, under the name of Paul Santiago, is arrested in the 34th precinct in the company of Gilbert Campusano.
March 17, 1992	Frankie Gonzalez, runner for Ruben Perez, friend of Frankie Cuevas, is shot in the 34th precinct. He is taken to a hospital by Mask.
March 18, 1992	Francisco Medina aka Freddy Krueger is arrested for gun possession in the 34th precinct by PO Patrick Regan. Released on his own recognizance.
March 19, 1992	Rasheed Rice and Pachulo kill Stanley Mobley and paralyze his brother Michael Mobley in the 40th precinct.
March 20, 1992	Boogie shoots and kills English, Fat Iris's husband, in the 40th precinct.

March 20, 1992	Pasqualito and Frankie Robles threaten Morales-Cruz family in the 40th precinct unless missing drugs are returned in **The Lost Packages**.
March 20, 1992	Gilbert Campusano is shot in the head in Frankie Cuevas's mother's apartment in the 34th precinct; he is later escorted to the hospital.
March 21, 1992	Pasqualito, accompanied by Frankie Robles, pistol-whips Tito Cruz in the 40th precinct.
Spring 1992	Mickey Tex pistol-whips Martha Molina in the 40th precinct for being short on the *cuenta* in **Martha's Head**.
April 4, 1992	Freddy Krueger kills Mingolo at 155th Street Macombs Dam Bridge in the 32nd precinct. Platano drives one car; Maximo Almodovar and Raul Vargas another.
April 7, 1992	Mask is killed in the 34th precinct. Police suspect Frankie Cuevas.
April 8, 1992	Frankie Cuevas and Big Cuba are stopped in a black Nissan with no license plates in the 30th precinct. Search at the 34th precinct garage reveals a *clavo* containing three guns but the case is dismissed on search issues.
April 10, 1992	Maximo Almodovar, accompanied by Freddy Krueger, kills Carlos Rodriguez Santana in the 46th precinct.
April 14, 1992	Platano is shot and critically wounded in the 34th precinct. Police suspect Cuevas crew.
April 20, 1992	Pasqualito is arrested for pistol-whipping Tito Cruz.
April 23, 1992	Frankie Robles is arrested for pistol-whipping Tito Cruz.

April 26, 1992	Roberto Peralta is shot in the 34th precinct in a wild shootout originating in the 43rd precinct. Police suspect Pasqualito, Freddy Krueger, and others.
April 29, 1992	Torching of 20 de Mayo Restaurant in the 34th precinct, with ten attempted murders.
May 3, 1992	Drive-by shooting of Frankie Cuevas's 43rd-precinct drug spot kills John Soldi and wounds seven others. Police suspect Pasqualito and Fat Danny.
May 11, 1992	Freddy Krueger kills Angel Suarez in the 30th precinct under a contract from Cholene.
May 13, 1992	Platano is arrested in Columbia Presbyterian Hospital in the 34th precinct for The Quad.
May 22, 1992	El Feo is released from Cape Vincent.
June 6, 1992	Fat Danny is arrested for The Quad.
June 21, 1992	Lenny is released from Ogdensburg.
June 21, 1992	Drive-by shooting of Frankie Cuevas's 43rd-precinct drug spot kills Kevin Nazario and wounds five others. Police suspect Pasqualito and Freddy Krueger, among others.
June 23, 1992	Freddy Krueger kills Craig Prentice in the 46th precinct after a shootout with the Jamaican Macombs crew.
July 3, 1992	PO Michael O'Keefe kills Kiko Garcia in a struggle. Riots engulf Washington Heights for several days.
July 10, 1992	Pasqualito, accompanied by Freddy Krueger, kills Dred, leader of the Macombs crew, in the 46th precinct.
July 12, 1992	El Feo is shot and paralyzed for life in the 34th precinct.

July 14, 1992	Pasqualito, accompanied by Tezo, who points out the victim, kills Papito in **The Brighton Beach Murder**.
July 21, 1992	Gilbert Campusano, shot six times, dies in the street in the 26th precinct. Police suspect Frankie Cuevas.
July 21, 1992	Tezo and Rafael Fernandez aka Kiko are arrested in the 34th precinct for possessing an AK-47 and several bundles of crack.
August 4, 1992	Lenny, Pasqualito, and Manny Crespo lead Local Motion officers on a wild car chase beginning in the 34th precinct, culminating in the 24th precinct; guns are later found in a *clavo*. DANY files a felony gun complaint; the trio make bail immediately.
August 6, 1992	El Feo is discharged from the hospital, paralyzed and in a wheelchair.
August 14, 1992	Pasqualito and Lenny shoot Michael Cruz, witness to The Quad, in the 73rd precinct in **The Witness Shooting**.
August 18, 1992	Lenny escapes an attempt to arrest him in the 40th precinct for The Witness Shooting.
August 22, 1992	Local Motion officers arrest Rafael Nieves and Jose Abreu at 2258 Wadsworth Avenue on gun and narcotics charges.
August 25, 1992	Maximo Almodovar is found dead, shot five times and decomposed, in his room in the 94th precinct.
August 25, 1992	Pasqualito is arrested in the 40th precinct for The Witness Shooting. He immediately makes bail in Brooklyn.

August 28, 1992	L slashes Ramon Jimenez, witness to The Quad, in the 46th precinct in **The Witness Slashing**.
Late Summer–Early Fall 1992	Shorty rapes and sodomizes a female pitcher and then robs her of her wages in the 40th precinct in **Shorty's Sex Attack and Robbery**.
September 5, 1992	Detective Mark Tebbens observes Lenny in a Cadillac on West 171th Street in the 34th precinct, follows him into the Bronx, but loses him in traffic.
September 9, 1992	Police officers stop a black Nissan Maxima because of heavily tinted windows in the 34th precinct. Search by Garry Dugan yields a ski mask from a *clavo*, thought to be used by Pasqualito in The Brighton Beach Murder.
September 11, 1992	Tezo is arrested for The Brighton Beach Murder.
Mid-September 1992	Fat Danny is released on $250,000 bail for The Quad.
September 17, 1992	Local Motion officers arrest Russell Castillo and Rafael Nunez at 209 Dyckman Street on gun and narcotics charges.
September 24, 1992	A warranted search of The Hole yields 500 vials of Red Top crack and two firearms. Louise McBride, Frank Blair, and David Polanco arrested.
November 9, 1992	Elizabeth Morales is warned not to testify in **The Middletown Attack.**
February 4, 1993	Lenny is arrested at 100 Centre Street while attending court on the gun charge emerging from the car chase of August 4, 1992.

February 4, 1993	A warranted search of 20 de Mayo Restaurant in the 34th precinct yields two firearms. Miguel Cuevas is arrested for gun possession.
May 13, 1993	Renny Harris is arrested for possession of 300 vials of crack in the 40th precinct, later charged with The Quad.
May 15, 1993	Rob Base kills Elvis Matos in the 40th precinct in **The Telephone Murder**. Fat Danny drives the car and points out the victim.
Late May 1993	Pasqualito beats Corky Rios for missing bundles in the 34th precinct in **Corky's Beatdown**.
June 4, 1993	A warranted search of 352 Beekman yields one pound of cocaine and two guns. Tyrell Blair is arrested.
June 20, 1993	Pasqualito kills Frankie Cuevas in the 34th precinct in **The Fat Frankie Homicide**. El Feo, Freddy Krueger, and Manny Crespo are in the getaway van.
July 27, 1993	Funi, accompanied by Rob Base and Frankie Robles, kills Rey Alejandro Rivera in the 46th precinct.
September 15, 1993	The takedown of 28 gang members; an indictment of a special narcotics grand jury is issued with 58 counts.
September 20, 1993	Jude Anne Bohan accuses Sarap Majid, a witness to the conspiracy, of snitching and threatens her with bodily harm in the 34th precinct.

February 4, 1994	Chocolate is killed in Santo Domingo by five military and police officers in the Dirección Nacional de Control de Drogas. Police suspect Morenito, of 166th Street and Amsterdam in the 34th precinct, of putting out the contract.
February 25, 1994	Jude Ann Bohan and Steven Bohan ascertain the location of Sarap Majid, and Pasqualito puts a $50,000 contract out on her life. Also issues threats against Corky Rios, another witness.
March 24, 1994	Pasqualito is arrested at Las Americas Airport in Santo Domingo.
March 29, 1994	Nelson is arrested in the Dominican Republic. Pasqualito is brought back to New York by Tebbens and Dugan.
April 4, 1994	Nelson is brought back to New York by Tebbens and Dugan.
Spring 1994	Police receive reports that Fat Danny threatens to have Tebbens killed, attempts to buy witnesses, especially those to The Quad, begins coercion of other co-defendants, particularly Platano, and warns others not to involve Victor, his half-brother, in The Double.
August 1994	Pasqualito beats up Platano in his cell; in retaliation, Nelson beats up Pasqualito.
September 7, 1994	The Wild Cowboys trial begins under Justice Leslie Crocker Snyder, New York State Supreme Court.
November 7, 1994	Fat Danny, Victor, Renny Harris, Stanley Tukes, and Shorty beat up Glen Stretching in the holding pens at The Tombs.

Fall 1994	Threats surface against Justice Snyder and her entire family, Teresa Matushaj (Justice Snyder's assistant), ADA Dan Brownell, and Detective Mark Tebbens. Contracts are said to be out to Freddy Krueger.
December 2, 1994	El Feo is arrested at the Hilton Hotel in Miami.
April 27, 1995	In **The Great Back Problem**, Fat Danny claims complete disability after a minor traffic accident.
May 15, 1995	Jury reaches a verdict in the Wild Cowboys case.
June 27, 1995	Justice Snyder sentences all nine trial defendants to lengthy terms.
August 1995	PO Patrick Regan is tried and convicted in federal court for perjury.
March 19, 1996	Judge Denny Chin sentences Patrick Regan to one year and a day in federal prison.
April 15, 1996	El Feo goes on trial in federal court before Federal District Judge Shira A. Scheindlin.
May 10, 1996	Raymond Polanco is indicted in federal court, Eastern District of New York, for narcotics and firearms trafficking, drug-related murders, and the murder of David Cargill.
July 10, 1996	Jury finds El Feo guilty of conspiracy to traffic narcotics and of conspiracy to commit seven murders.
January 29, 1997	Judge Scheindlin sentences El Feo to life imprisonment with no possibility of parole.

February 3, 1997	Raymond Polanco goes on trial in federal court before Federal District Judge Sterling Johnson, Jr.
March 5, 1997	Jury finds Raymond Polanco guilty of narcotics and firearms trafficking, two murders to further that enterprise, and the murder of David Cargill.
March 31, 1997	PO John Moynihan is ordered to departmental trial for illegal search and seizure and perjury; his trial is postponed until summer.
March–April 1997	Linwood Collins is retried for The Rooftop Murder; jury finds him guilty.
April 3, 1997	Freddy Krueger is apprehended in the Dominican Republic by DNCD officers.
April 18, 1997	Patrick Regan, his appeal to the U.S. Court of Appeals denied, enters federal prison.

abbreviations

ADA   Assistant District Attorney
ATF   Alcohol, Tobacco, and Firearms
AUSA   Assistant United States Attorney
CPoP   Community Policing Program
DA   District Attorney
DANY   District Attorney of New York
DEA   Drug Enforcement Administration
DNCD   Dominican Dirección Nacional de Control de Drogas
DR   Dominican Republic
EMS   Emergency Medical Service
ESU   Emergency Service Unit
FBI   Federal Bureau of Investigation
HIDTA   High Intensity Drug-Trafficking Area Task Force
HIU   Homicide Investigation Unit
IAB   Internal Affairs Bureau
INS   Immigration and Naturalization Service
JATLF   Joint Auto Larceny Task Force
MCC   Metropolitan Correctional Center
MNHS   Manhattan North Homicide Squad
NYPD   New York City Police Department
PO   Police Officer
RICO   Racketeer Influenced and Corrupt Organization
RIP   Robbery Identification Program
SRI   Senior Rackets Investigator
TNT   Tactical Narcotics Team

notes on sources

This book is based on years of talking and working with criminal investigators, both police detectives and prosecutors. My work with detectives came first. From January 1992 until September 1993 I spent nearly five tours every week with the 34th precinct detective squad, doing either day or night shifts, followed by two tours a week with that squad through June 1994.

My fieldwork in the 34th precinct was prefaced in fall 1991 with a month-long stint with the Midtown North squad and three months with the Central Robbery unit of the New York City Transit Police, whose members taught me basic police procedures. Before beginning this fieldwork, I was a full participant in training sessions in robbery investigation with the New York City Transit Police and in homicide investigation with the NYPD.

I engaged in every phase of detective work in the field and in the squad room. This included interviewing victims of fraud, burglary, robbery, and assault, among many other crimes; interviewing gunshot victims in the crash rooms of Columbia Presbyterian and Harlem hospitals; standing over corpses at murder crime scenes; informing family members of the violent death of one of their own; canvassing whole neighborhoods to glean information about crimes; escorting witnesses and attending lineups; sitting with witnesses while they pored over books of mug shots, or tried to make identifications with new photo-imaging technology, or worked with police artists to devise sketches of suspects, or, in one case, underwent hypnosis to recall the image from a fleeting glimpse of a possible child murderer; doing stakeouts in the subway and surveillances in the street; playing the role of a lucky winner of a free trip to Atlantic City in a police sting operation designed to apprehend warrant fugitives; banging on doors late at night to find an errant witness or to make an arrest; making gun arrests on the street in a near-riot; ducking bottles, refuse, and debris thrown from rooftops in the middle of an actual riot; observing autopsies of homicide victims at the morgue; engaging in endless conversations about the details of particular cases and the possible connections between them; poring over hundreds of investigative reports and case files; listening to the raucous storytelling that fills dead time in squad rooms; participating, both as butt and perpetrator, in the daily practical jokes common to every squad; and interviewing witnesses, suspects, and confessed felons, usually robbers. On the advice of district attorneys, I absented myself from interrogations of homicide suspects, relying for these data on statements taken from suspects or culprits by detectives. In addition, I participated, and continue to participate, in a great number of social events with detectives, including meals, parties, celebrations, weddings, memorial services, and funerals.

I began my involvement with prosecutors while working with the police. In summer 1992, in a prelude to later intensive study at the District Attorney of New York, I spent one full day a week with DANY's Trial Bureau 50 in the Early Case Assessment Bureau, sitting with ADAs as they interviewed police officers from every Manhattan precinct and frequently the officers' newly arrested prisoners in order to draw up the formal instruments accusing those arrested of crimes. I also attended several trials prosecuted mostly, but not exclusively, by ADAs from Trial Bureau 50 during 1992–93, focusing on trials for crimes committed in the 34th precinct; I participated in pre-trial and in-trial strategizing sessions with the prosecutors and detectives in two of those trials.

I observed large portions of the eight-month Wild Cowboys trial in 1994–95, sitting on the bench with Justice Leslie Crocker Snyder for several days a week for several months. After the trial concluded, I spent the entire summer of 1995 with the Homicide Investigation Unit of DANY. HIU prosecutors gave me access to key investigative reports leading to the prosecution of the Wild Cowboys, the case files of the individual crimes that were joined into the legal conspiracy case, and all the court exhibits outlining the case for jurors. HIU also gave me access to its copy of the trial's 30,000-page transcript [*People v. Daniel Rincon et al.*, New York State Supreme Court, Indictment 10614/93]; portions of this book rely heavily on the sworn testimony of various witnesses recorded at trial. ADA Dan Brownell allowed me to use his remarkably detailed handwritten index of the daily direct testimony, which served as an indispensable guide to the mammoth transcript. From mid-September 1995 until February 1997, I spent several days a month at HIU, finishing up my work. I also attended other trials connected to the Wild Cowboys case.

Throughout the course of this fieldwork, I repeatedly interviewed, both formally and informally, more than 200 detectives, scores of uniformed and plainclothes police officers, and more than 40 prosecutors, as well as several court personnel. Most important for this book were several interviews with Detectives Mark Tebbens and Garry Dugan; with ADA Dan M. Rather, whose investigation brought the Wild Cowboys case together; with ADA Dan Brownell, who led the prosecution team in court; with ADAs Don Hill, Lori Grifa, and Walter Arsenault; and with Justice Leslie Crocker Snyder and her two court attorneys, Alex Calabrese and Teresa Matushaj.

These interviews frame all the materials in this book, including a range of other primary and secondary data not already mentioned. I specify these by chapter below, drawing attention to still other interviews that help contextualize the work.

The rendering of Spanish names in this book reflects the widely varied usage of Spanish and "Spanglish" speakers in New York, as well as discrepancies in spelling of persons' real and street names in the records of police, prosecutors, and courts.

A Quad in the Bronx

This chapter is based on an analysis of the case files, all housed at HIU, on The Quad, The Double, and other murders in the 40th precinct, along with investigative and intelligence reports produced by the HIU staff as the unit began its inquiry into the Red Top crew. The case files include all witness statements cited in the text. I made several visits to the Beekman Avenue area with Detectives Mark Tebbens, Garry Dugan, and later Eddie Benitez to familiarize myself with the geography of the neighborhood.

A Death on the Highway

I base the chapter on an analysis of the case file on Homicide 22/91, The Cargill Homicide, housed at the 30th precinct, coupled with several interviews with Detectives Jerry Dimuro, who caught the case, and Garry Dugan, who assisted him. I also had helpful conversations with Detective Tommy McCabe and New Jersey State Trooper Brian Long.

I also attended part of the trial of Raymond Polanco in order to hear the direct testimony of Kevin Kryzeminski and Lenny Sepulveda on the Cargill homicide [*United States v. Raymond Polanco*, United States District Court, Eastern District of New York, 96CRZ29, Indictment 9601154, February 10, 1997]. Conversations with Special Agent Julian Blanco of ATF and George Slater of NYPD's Major Case Squad provided me with some additional information about Polanco.

Fort "Yo No Sé!"

I collected the material on drug-related homicides in the 34th precinct from July 1992 into the spring of 1994. In addition to obtaining first-hand knowledge of a great many cases in 1992 and 1993, I examined the files from every homicide case from 1987 through 1993 (638), except for the 11 files that are missing from the precinct. I assigned the 379 cases to the drug-related category only when there was clear and unmistakable evidence of such a connection. I talked to the detectives who caught and worked these drug-related cases in almost every instance. The figures provided for drug-related homicides are therefore conservative, although they do not differ greatly from official police statistics on the phenomenon. One must, however, always approach the latter statistics with caution. Police investigators and their supervisors usually make the classification of "drug-related" or "non drug-related" during the initial stages of an investigation and rarely change the designation once made. There are also considerable pressures on precinct commanders to avoid, whenever possible, categorizing murders as drug-related. Detectives with long experience in the precinct argue that the numbers of drug-related homicides in both police statistics and those presented in this book are low. I reviewed the materials once again with senior detectives in August 1996 to update the data. My understanding of the overall patterns and peculiar logic of drug-related violence is derived from hundreds of conversations over the years with Detectives Gennaro Giorgio, Joe Montuori, John Bourges, Tim Muldoon, Bobby Small, Tony Imperato, Pete Moro, and Joel Potter, as well as Garry Dugan and Mark Tebbens.

I read the entire Buczek homicide file housed at the 34th precinct and interviewed at length Detective John Hickey (ret.) of the Manhattan North Homicide Squad, one of the principal investigators on the case.

The good offices of William Bowden, Chief Counsel at the Office of Comptroller of the Currency and his Deputy Chief, Robert Serino, enabled me to learn some of the intricacies of international money laundering from several experts in the field, including Julie Stanton of Millbank, Tweed, Hadley, & McCloy, John Byrne of the American Bankers Association, and Harold Lippman of the United States Senate Permanent Subcommittee on Investigation.

For the material on Joseph Occhipinti, I drew on a synopsis of his federal trial transcript [*United States v. Joseph Occhipinti*, United States District Court, Southern District of New York, Indictment 91-1681] done by Gary Ford, a research assistant, my own analysis of both Occhipinti's and the government's appellate briefs, a systematic survey of a great number of journalistic articles written about the case, as well as the materials inserted into the *Congressional Record* noted in the text. Interviews with Ray Hagemann on January 14, 1994, and February 24, 1997, helped contextualize these materials; Hagemann provided me with the affidavits of Ramon Rodriguez, as well as with a copy of correspondence between Guy Molinari and Acting Attorney General William Barr protesting the FBI follow-up investigation to the Occhipinti affair. Finally, I conducted two lengthy interviews with Joseph Occhipinti in July 1996 and January 1997; I also had several shorter conversations with him in February 1997. Occhipinti provided me with: copies of his own investigative reports on Freddy Then; Ramon Rodriguez's affidavits; affidavits from the undercover agents who investigated bodega owners who brought charges against him; and the affidavit from Manuel de Dios Unanue mentioned in the text. In July 1996 I was also able to survey Occhipinti's remarkable and thoroughly well organized collection of materials on Dominican organized crime. Finally, I interviewed several senior detectives in the 34th precinct who worked with Occhipinti during Project Bodega.

I was already working in the 34th precinct when the string of murders and assaults described in the last part of this chapter occurred. I constantly engaged Detective John Bourges in conversations about them. Bourges drew up the first chart that linked the several incidents, as he tried to discern the social origins of the mayhem.

Uptown Murders

A lengthy interview with Detective Greg Modica of the Manhattan Robbery Squad provided much of the material on the garage robberies discussed in this chapter. For the analysis of uptown murders, I have drawn heavily on several interviews with ADA Dan Rather over the spring and summer of 1995 and from lectures on November 1 and 2, 1995, that Rather gave at Williams College to my "Crime in the Streets" class.

Cracking the Case

This chapter relies heavily on the reports of HIU investigators, coupled with interviews with them. I take the quotes from various gang members directly from the investigative reports. The description of the car chase of August 4, 1992, is based on detailed interviews with Johnny Moynihan and Paddy Regan, coupled with a review of the case record housed at HIU. I also used the transcript of Tezo's videotaped interview with ADA David Blaxill.

Lenny's Boys

The quotes from Freddy Sendra come from his direct testimony in the trial of *People of the State of New York v. Daniel Rincon et al.*, New York State Supreme Court, Indictment 10614/93, pp. 2342–2606, and also from his testimony before the Tenth May/June 1993 Special Narcotics Grand Jury *People of the State of New York v. Lenin Sepulveda et al.*, pp. 34–155 and 972–982. I interviewed Sendra at length on February 9, 1997, at the Kintock Group in Newark, New Jersey, and in several subsequent telephone conversations. I also drew on Nelson Sepulveda's testimony, both direct and cross, in *People of the State of New York v. Daniel Rincon, et al.*, New York State Supreme Court, Indictment 10614/93, pp. 13571–14365.

The Takedown

This chapter also relies on the records and reports of HIU investigators, coupled with interviews with them, as well as Nelson Sepulveda's testimony at trial.

Downtown Justice

This chapter draws on my own observations of the Wild Cowboys trial, as well as on the trial's lengthy transcript. I also relied on court exhibits of evidence produced by the three prosecutors. Justice Snyder's lengthy statement at sentencing is taken directly from the transcript, edited with her permission.

Urban Badlands

The material on Jose Reyes and Francisco Medina comes from verbal witness testimony and from summary statements of both prosecution and defense at Reyes's federal trial [*United States v. Jose Reyes,* United States District Court, Southern District of New York, Indictment S1 94 Cr. 872]. I also utilized HIU investigative reports on Medina. For the account of Medina's apprehension, I am indebted to interviews with Michael Stanton, Laurie Horne, Kevin O'Brien, and Joseph LoBue.

The account of the 1992 riots and their aftermath in Washington Heights is based on my own first-hand observation while I was with the 34th precinct detective squad. I have also drawn upon the Manhattan District Attorney's account of the events, that is, "Statement of Robert M. Morgenthau, District Attorney, New York County, September 10, 1992." The District Attorney's report is admirable for the conciseness and accuracy of its narrative; moreover, his investigation was independent from that of the police department and provides a useful check on my field materials.

I relied on some public reports analyzing different aspects of Mayor Dinkins's policies during his tenure in City Hall. On the Korean grocery store boycott, see "Report of the Mayor's Committee investigating the protest against two Korean-owned groceries on Church Avenue in Brooklyn," August 30, 1990. See also "An analysis of the report of the Mayor's committee investigating the protest against two Korean-owned groceries on Church Avenue in Brooklyn," November 1990, a report of the Committee on General Welfare, New York City Council. See also the legal proceedings "Boung Jae Jang t/a Family Red Apple Co. and Man Ho Park t/a Park Fruit and Vegetable Market against Lee Brown NYC Police Commissioner and the NYCPD, Respondents-Appellants, Case no. 90-02710." On the Crown Heights crisis, see *A Report to the Governor on the Disturbances in Crown Heights,* 2 vols. (Albany, New York: New York State Division of Criminal Justice Services, 1993).

Troubled Order

The Local Motion cases that later came under scrutiny all occurred during my time at the 34th precinct and were a subject for much discussion among detectives. I read the entire trial transcript, complete with all accompanying materials, of the Patrick Regan trial [*United States v. Patrick Regan*, United States District Court, Southern District of New York, 95 Cr. 29]. I also analyzed both Regan's and the government's appellate briefs. These were coupled with a series of intensive interviews with Paddy Regan and Johnny Moynihan. I also had several helpful conversations with David Greenfield, Regan's lawyer.

Epilogue

The epilogue draws on intensive interviews with Paddy Regan, and a review of his report of his March 18, 1992, arrest of Francisco Medina housed at HIU.

acknowledgments

This book was a long time in the making and owes a great deal to several institutions and many individuals. The Notes on Sources cite dozens of people by name who shared insights, documents, and information of every sort that directly contributed to the book. They are only a few of the hundreds of men and women who, over the last several years, took the time to teach me about the truth-is-stranger-than-fiction criminal justice system. I am extremely grateful to all of them.

The New York City Police Department and the former New York City Transit Police Department have my deep appreciation for giving me permission to do my work and for aiding me in innumerable ways as it progressed. Detective Al Marini of the Detectives' Endowment Association initiated me into the world of police detectives. Detectives Gennaro Giorgio, Joe Montuori, Tim Muldoon, John Bourges, Tommy Burke, and Detective Sergeants Tommy Burke and Ed Keitel, among a great many others, were my guides through it. Then-Detective Lieutenant, now Detective Captain Joseph Resnick allowed me to establish residence in his fabled Three-Four squad, a remarkable team of officers who accepted "The Professor" as one of their own.

The office of the District Attorney of New York permitted me to reconstruct the making of the Wild Cowboys case. In particular, ADA Warren Murray, Chief of DANY's Trial Bureau 50, introduced me to prosecutorial work and has aided all my efforts to understand it; and Walter Arsenault, Chief of DANY's Homicide Investigation Unit, has been highly supportive of my research from start to finish.

My deepest debt of gratitude to the "forces of order" goes to Detectives Mark Tebbens and Garry Dugan, ADAs Dan M. Rather and Dan Brownell, and Justice Leslie Crocker Snyder and her court attorney, Teresa Matushaj. *Wild Cowboys* could never have seen the light of day without the constant help of these extraordinarily generous, talented, and dedicated men and women.

357

A fellowship from the National Endowment for the Humanities, administered through the good offices of Leon Bramson, helped me at a critical moment. A research grant from the Harry Frank Guggenheim Foundation, administered by Joel Wallman and Karen Colvard, enabled me to collect data on drug-related violence in Washington Heights.

At my home base, Williams College, resources from the Willmott Family Professorship made possible my extended fieldwork with the police. The Oakley Center for the Humanities and Social Sciences aided my work by underwriting major conferences on the New York City criminal justice system in 1993 and 1996; my thanks to the Center's former directors, Professors Jean-Bernard Bucky and Charles B. Dew. President Emeritus Francis C. Oakley and President Harry C. Payne provided funds for speakers in my "Crime in the Streets" course, making it a lively and challenging forum. My students in that course over the last several years listened patiently and responded creatively as I grappled with my field materials.

A visiting professorship at John Jay College of Criminal Justice in 1996–97, thanks to T. Kenneth Moran, Chairman of the Law and Police Science Department, and President Gerald W. Lynch, helped me bring this book to conclusion.

Duffy Graham read an early draft of the manuscript with penetrating insight. At Harvard University Press, William Sisler and Michael Aronson supported the project from its beginnings; Heather Quay tempered it with judicious legal advice; Jill Breitbarth designed the book with great inventiveness; and Susan Wallace Boehmer immeasurably improved the text with her matchless editorial imagination and skills.

Janice Michiko Hirota and Yuriko Hirota Jackall read the manuscript with the greatest care. They also sustained me in every way throughout a long, tumultuous ride. I am delighted to dedicate this book to them.

May 1997
New York City

index